Rhetorica Rising

MOVEMENT RHETORIC/RHETORIC'S MOVEMENTS

Victoria J. Gallagher

MOVEMENT
RHETORIC
RHETORIC'S MOVEMENTS

Also of Interest

Activist Literacies: Transnational Feminisms and Social Media Rhetorics,
Jennifer Nish

*The Democratic Ethos: Authenticity and Instrumentalism in US Movement
Rhetoric after Occupy,* A. Freya Thimsen

Liturgy of Change: Rhetorics of the Civil Rights Meeting, Elizabeth Ellis
Miller

*Community and Critique: The Rhetorical Activism of Black American Women's
Memory Work,* Sara C. VanderHaagen

Peace by Peace: Risking Public Action, Creating Social Change, Lisa Ellen
Silvestri

*Your Daughters Will Prophesy: Religion and Rhetoric in the Nineteenth
Century Woman's Movement,* Lisa Marie Gring-Pemble and Martha
Watson

RHETORICA RISING

Feminist Rhetorical Methods for Social Change

EDITED BY

**EILEEN E. SCHELL, K.J. RAWSON,
CURTIS J. JEWELL, ABIGAIL H. LONG,
SIDNEY TURNER, AND GABRIELLA WILSON**

THE UNIVERSITY OF
SOUTH CAROLINA PRESS

© 2025 University of South Carolina

Published by the University of South Carolina Press
Columbia, South Carolina 29208

uscpress.com

Printed in the United States of America

Library of Congress Cataloging-in-Publication Data can be found at
http://catalog.loc.gov/.

ISBN: 978-1-64336-586-2 (hardcover)
ISBN: 978-1-64336-610-4 (paperback)
ISBN: 978-1-64336-611-1 (ebook)

CONTENTS

LIST OF ILLUSTRATIONS

Figures

Tables

SERIES EDITOR'S PREFACE

The University of South Carolina series "Movement Rhetoric/Rhetoric's Movements" builds on the Press's longstanding reputation in the field of rhetoric and communication and its cross-disciplinary commitment to studies of civil rights and civil justice. Books in the series address two central questions: In historical and contemporary eras characterized by political, social, and economic movements enacted through rhetorical means, how—and with what consequences—are individuals, collectives, and institutions changed and transformed? How and to what extent can analyses of rhetoric's movements in relation to circulation and uptake help point the way to a more equal and equitable world?

In this timely and accessible edited collection, the work of scholars and activists is put into conversation with the themes of the Movement Rhetoric/Rhetoric's Movements series, advancing the terrain of feminist rhetorical theory and methods while reckoning with the successes and failures of feminist rhetorical studies and social justice movements. In the introductory essay, the editors provide a fruitful overview of twenty-first-century social justice movements as well as the political and institutional efforts that have successfully reversed some of the gains of both these and earlier twentieth-century movements. Each of the ensuing chapters explores feminist rhetorical methods and methodologies in relation to past, present, and ongoing social justice movements while also addressing contemporary rhetorical contexts that are characterized by political polarization, the weaponization of (dis)information, attacks on a wide variety of rights, and unequal access to resources. *Rhetorica Rising* showcases how scholars and activists are illuminating new sites of inquiry by centering underrepresented ways of knowing and enacting responsive research ethics within communities.

Introduction

Eileen E. Schell and K.J. Rawson

We take our title *Rhetorica Rising* from the many activist movements that have arisen in the last decade and a half in response to the need for social transformation. Since 2010, when we published our first major scholarly work on feminist rhetorical methods and methodologies, *Rhetorica in Motion: Feminist Rhetorical Methods and Methodologies,* we have witnessed and, in many cases, taken part in multiple risings and uprisings, which have shaped the kairotic moment of this project. We begin this introduction with a brief overview of many of those movements because they serve as the backdrop for this volume, especially in relation to the ways that our research in feminist rhetorics needs to respond to social justice movements addressing economic exploitation, racial justice, LGBTQ+ rights, environmental justice, and reproductive justice. We spotlight a few of those movements here to lay the groundwork for what is to follow, noting that our overview is meant to highlight specific developments that have influenced many of the essays engaged in this volume, but it is not meant to be an exhaustive account. Taken together, the US-based progressive social movements of the past few decades that we summarize below form a striking and richly varied landscape of rhetorical activity that has shaped the growth of social justice struggles and feminist rhetorics within and beyond the academy.

The Landscape of Rhetorical Change

There are many points of entry for considering social movements in the United States of the twenty-first century against a backdrop of the Global War on Terror, an economic recession, tumultuous US election cycles, and uprisings against racism and police violence. We begin with the Occupy movement as its grassroots approach set the stage for many of the social movements that followed. In response to government aid for troubled banks and corporations in the wake of what was deemed the Great Recession of 2007–2009, the issue of a growing gap between working people and corporations along with mega-wealthy individuals (referred to as the 1%) sparked the Occupy movement. Occupy Wall Street began on September 17, 2011, sparked by Adbusters, a Canadian political publication that opposes capitalistic exploitation through art, counter-advertising, and direct action. Fueled by alliances across labor organizations and unions, protestors occupied Zuccotti Park in New York City and 900 other locations across the globe. Activists opposed the "prevailing political order of economic inequality and the unaccountable capitalists who had driven the world into recession only a few years prior."[1] While some have claimed that Occupy was a failed movement, others have pointed to several examples of its success: organizing for better wages for fast-food workers; improved minimum wages in 33 US cities; debt relief for college students; and better housing policy for low-income families.[2]

Two years later, in 2013, the Black Lives Matter (#BlackLivesMatter) movement was started by three Black women—Alicia Garza, Patrisse Cullors, and Opal Tometi—in response to the acquittal of vigilante George Zimmerman, who murdered Black teenager Trayvon Martin while he was walking from a store to his mother's home.[3] The Black Lives Matter movement, with over 40 chapters across the United States and internationally, works to stop violence against Black people by vigilantes and state actors such as police departments, drawing on the distinctive hashtag #BlackLivesMatter.[4] Following in the wake of Martin's murder by Zimmerman, Michael Brown, an unarmed 18-year-old Black teenager, was murdered in 2014 by a Saint Louis County police officer in Ferguson, Missouri. Uprisings took place in Ferguson and other cities to expose and fight state-sanctioned violence against Black people, evoking the names of those who had been murdered by the police: Tamir Rice, Tanisha Anderson, Mya Hall, Walter Scott, Sandra Bland, Michael Brown, George Floyd, and others. As the #BlackLivesMatter website indicates, the movement "is an ideological and political intervention in a world where Black lives are systematically and intentionally targeted for demise," and it serves as an "affirmation of Black folks' humanity, our contributions to this society, and our resilience in the face of deadly oppression."[5] The leadership of #BlackLivesMatter is diverse–led by women, trans, and queer people–upending the patriarchal, heteronormative dynamics of so many other social movements. Moreover, #BlackLivesMatter has inspired racial justice movements in Brazil, India, and Japan.[6] #BlackLivesMatter has also issued a statement in support of

Palestinian rights, standing in solidarity with Palestinians and their allies who "have demanded an end to Israeli occupation, settler colonialism and violence" in the occupied territories.[7] As coeditors, we have been inspired by the leadership, activism, and transnational solidarity of #BlackLivesMatter.

Parallel to uprisings around police violence among Black communities, Indigenous communities have continued longstanding resistance to environmental harms caused by oil and gas companies encroaching on tribal lands and threatening the contamination of water and land. In 2016, the Standing Rock Sioux tribe, in solidarity with other tribes and a range of environmental action groups, waged a battle against the proposed siting of the Dakota Access Pipeline on tribal land. This resistance became an international movement to stop the pipeline and preserve the water and land of the Standing Rock Sioux in accordance with an existing US government treaty.[8] The No Dakota Access Pipeline (#NODAPL) movement's actions included encampments on the land, "marches, letter-writing campaigns, divestment campaigns, bank shutdowns, elaborate banner drops, blockades, and sabotage of ETP [Energy Transfer Partnership] property and pipeline construction equipment."[9] Water protectors from a range of Indigenous nations confronted armed police and the National Guard and they were beaten, arrested, and tear gassed, but persisted and built solidarity with direct action, cross-organization solidarity, legal action, and via social media using the hashtag #NoDAPL. While direct and legal action did not halt the pipeline, #NoDAPL sparked an intergenerational movement to defend tribal sovereignty and protect the water and earth from harm that spread across national borders.[10] Furthermore, this movement intersected with struggles in Flint, Michigan to address the Flint lead crisis in the water system. African American youth activist Mari Copeny, also known as Little Miss Flint, wrote a letter to President Obama protesting the Flint lead crisis in the water system, which sparked the President's visit to Flint and his approving $100 million to address the crisis. Copeny has since joined with other climate activists to address climate justice through the National Climate March and the Women's March.[11] A reckoning regarding environmental racism and climate justice continues with many organizations and activists speaking out for effective climate policy and sustainable change.

Parallel to climate justice movements are ongoing movements to address gendered abuses of power and sexual violence. The #MeToo movement, founded by Tarana Burke back in 2006, centered around the program Jendayi Aza, which supported young women of color and eventually became Burke's nonprofit JustBe, Inc., which was adopted in the Selma, Alabama public school district. This organization created space for "young women of color to share their stories," [and] "Burke began using the phrase 'me too' to promote the idea of "empowerment through empathy."[12] In 2017, actress Alyssa Milano encouraged women to draw on Burke's iconic phrase as the hashtag #MeToo to call out sexual misconduct on Twitter. The hashtag was subsequently used over 19 million times on Twitter to expose sexual violence and share stories of survivors, inspiring legal action and public callouts by survivors as well as encouraging legislation to improve workplace policies and practices.[13] According to law professors Jamillah Bowman Williams and Elizabeth Tippet, "between 2017 and 2021, states introduced 2,324 #MeToo-related bills and passed 286. In late 2017 and early 2018, many of the laws focused specifically on sexual harassment, including topics like antiharassment training, NDAs [Non-Disclosure Agreements], and accountability for government officials."[14] While there is much more work to be done, especially for low-wage workers who lack specific workplace protections, the #MeToo movement continues to draw attention to sexual assault, workplace harassment, gender discrimination, and the gender pay gap that persists in corporate America, Hollywood, higher education, and other places. The #MeToo movement has sparked activism globally: in China at "universities and factories, in newsrooms and on film sets, and within the NGO community and activist groups"; in India in Bollywood and in the news media; in Japan in journalism, fashion, and within the government; and in France, as the country enacted legislation around cat-calling and street harassment.[15]

When Donald Trump was elected in 2016, his unapologetic misogyny combined with Hillary Clinton's defeat as the first woman Presidential candidate to be nominated by a major political party led to vigorous protests from women's organizations (even as many white women voted for him). According to the Pew Research Center, exit poll data indicated that 47% of white women voted for Trump in comparison with the 45% of white women who voted for Democratic candidate Hillary Clinton.[16] In contrast, Black women voted in massive numbers for Clinton (98%) and Hispanic women as well (67%).[17] This discrepancy sparked Black feminist Mikki Kendall to call out the ways that white women and mainstream white feminists have oppressed women of color by ignoring everyday issues such as "[f]ood insecurity and access to quality education, safe neighborhoods, a living wage, and medical care."[18] Kendall called for a "hood feminism" that will support the everyday lives of those who identify as women, especially those most marginalized.[19]

Resistance to the Trump administration's attitudes toward women crystallized with the Women's March, which began on Facebook the day after the election, when retired lawyer Teresa Shook called for a pro-woman march in response to Trump's election.[20] After thousands signed up to march, veteran activists and organizers began planning a protest for January 21, 2017, centered on Washington, DC, with ancillary protests in other cities within the United States and worldwide. Hundreds of thousands of people protested, many wearing distinctive pink cat's ear hand-knitted hats (dubbed "pussy hats" in protest of Trump's "grab them by the pussy" comment and later critiqued as racist and transphobic as they conflated women and pink vaginas). Protestors marched in opposition to the threats represented to reproductive rights, human rights, and civil rights. Annual Women's Marches and organizing have continued beyond the 2017 protest, with events and organizing taking place locally, nationally, and internationally. At the same time, the Women's March has been rightfully criticized for lacking diversity and being focused primarily on white, cisgender women and issues that pertain to them. Organizers of future marches and actions have worked to remedy that gap and continue to be held accountable by journalists and activists for creating a more inclusive resistance movement.[21]

Many who attended the 2017 Women's Marches showed up at airports to protest Trump's 2017 Muslim ban when he signed an Executive Order preventing "foreign nationals from seven predominantly Muslim countries from visiting the country for 90 days, suspended entry to the country of all Syrian refugees indefinitely, and prohibited any other refugees from coming into the country for 120 days."[22] Women's Marchers also attended "marches and demonstrations for immigrants, science, the environment, health care, fair taxation, LGBT rights, and for Truth (about the Trump campaign's Russia connections). . . . Each protest recruited some new activists, most of whom did not return home and give up on politics."[23] In other words, these movements began to build on one another, and activist energies and strategies moved across and among a range of social justice issues.

Within this same timeframe, youth activist movements arose in response to climate change and rampant gun violence. Youth climate activist Greta Thunberg of Sweden gained the world's attention when, at age 15, she sat outside the Swedish Parliament with a sign proclaiming a climate strike every school day, a protest that continued for 251 weeks.[24] Thunberg and the students who eventually joined her founded #FridaysforFuture (#FFF). In September of 2018, #FFF's call for action, plus Thunberg's public rhetoric and speaking appearances online and across the globe, sparked youth and other groups to pursue social action to end fossil-fuel reliance, reduce warming to 1.5 C globally, and work toward climate justice.[25] A focus on Thunberg's climate activism, though, should not obscure or elide all the work by youth of color who have been advocating for action on climate change across the US and the globe, including Colombian American Jamie Margolin, founder of the Zero hour climate movement and Ethiopian American Elsa Mengistu, who organized fellow students at Howard University to combat climate change, among others.[26]

Youth activists have also been instrumental in social protest against the epidemic of gun violence in the United States. Some of the survivors of the mass shooting that killed 17 students and staff at Parkland, Florida's Marjory Stoneman Douglas High School formed March for Our Lives as a way of promoting an end to gun violence through gun-control legislation, lobbying legislators, canvassing young voters to support gun control progressive candidates, and holding mass demonstrations. The first march was held in February 2018, and marches have continued with over 400 nationally and globally in response to the ongoing gun violence epidemic that has not been met with much meaningful legislative action.[27] The work to curb an epidemic of gun violence and create common-sense gun-control continues, despite a powerful gun lobby and a lack of political will among legislators to address the crisis.

Even as a vigorous reproductive justice movement has historically fought battles to ensure continued provisions of reproductive rights, a watershed moment came on June 24, 2022, when the Supreme Court overturned Roe v. Wade via Dobbs v. Jackson Women's Health Organization. Overturning Roe vs. Wade was the result of decades of organizing by anti-choice organizations, politicians, and special interest groups. The overturning has had disastrous consequences for all facing reproductive healthcare decisions in states with partial or full abortion bans. In spite of decades of organizing by reproductive rights organizations, we are at a critical juncture in securing reproductive justice, a term coined by the SisterSong Women of Color Reproductive Justice Collective, meaning "the human right to maintain personal bodily autonomy, have children, not have children, and parent the children we have in safe and sustainable communities."[28] The way forward will be to defend wide scale access to reproductive health care, not just individual choice. Abortion and contraception have been accessible for wealthy or middle-class women, many of whom are white, who dominate the women's rights movement, but reproductive justice centers the needs of women of color and other marginalized women and trans people.[29] As

SisterSong points out, "Even when abortion is legal, many women of color cannot afford it, or cannot travel hundreds of miles to the nearest clinic. There is no choice where there is no access."[30] While abortion access is undeniably important, other aspects of reproductive healthcare are also important: "contraception, comprehensive sex education, STI prevention and care, alternative birth options, adequate prenatal and pregnancy care, domestic violence assistance, adequate wages to support our families, safe homes, and so much more."[31] There is much more work to be done in a dynamic and hostile environment toward reproductive justice. Moving beyond individual choice frameworks to include all affected by the denial of access and care will be crucial.

In the wake of the overturning of Roe vs. Wade, conservative politicians in the US have now turned their attention towards attacking LGBTQ+ rights, particularly the rights of transgender people. Record numbers of anti-LGBTQ+ bills target a wide range of human rights—including freedom of speech and expression, protection from discrimination, access to healthcare and public facilities, ability to participate in sports and clubs, education that includes sexuality and gender expression, and many other areas—with some conservatives such as *Daily Wire* host Michael Knowles openly stating that, "for the good of society . . . transgenderism must be eradicated from public life entirely."[32] These legislative efforts are happening within the broader context of rising hate crimes against LGBTQ+ people, including the 2016 mass shooting at the Pulse nightclub in Orlando, Florida, and the sharp increase in anti-LGBTQ hate crimes in 2022.[33] In response to these attacks on LGBTQ+ people and rights, a groundswell of pro-LGBTQ+ advocacy has mobilized from within and outside the community and activist responses have surfaced in legislatures, courtrooms, and on the streets.

While this overview of social justice movements is partial and incomplete and does not encompass all the ways these movements have been taken up at the grassroots, community level, what this overview demonstrates is the way that individuals and groups in their communities are speaking back to power and fighting for survival through rhetorical action. It is within this dynamic and energized landscape of multiple uprisings that we are revisiting inquiry into feminist methods and methodologies in the field of rhetoric and composition. *Rhetorica Rising* explores feminist rhetorical methods and methodologies in relation to past, present, and ongoing social justice movements and within our contemporary contexts, inflected as they are by political polarization, the weaponization of (dis)information, attacks on reproductive and transgender rights, unequal access to resources, and injustices based on race, sex and gender, ability, and class. Contributors to the volume speak to the various ways the field has evolved over the last few decades as we have taken up the challenge of creating intersectional feminist scholarship that engages with Black, Indigenous, and People of Color (BIPOC) histories and rhetorics, decolonial rhetorics, digital studies, disability studies, LGBTQ+ studies, transnational studies, and reproductive justice.

Revisiting Feminist Rhetorical Methods and Methodologies

In 2010, we coedited the volume *Rhetorica in Motion: Feminist Rhetorical Methods and Methodologies* (University of Pittsburgh Press), which explored the ongoing development and debates over what constitutes feminist research methods and methodologies in feminist rhetorics. Following Sandra Harding's lead in the classic volume *Feminism and Methodology*, we defined research methods as a "technique for (or way of proceeding in) gathering evidence" and methodology as a "theory and analysis of how research does or should proceed."[34] We noted that Harding also introduces the term epistemology to describe "a theory of knowledge," or how we come to know what we know and who is qualified to be a "knower."[35] In *Rhetorica in Motion,* we examined what it would look like to combine rhetorical research methods with qualitative, quantitative, and digital methods. Chapter contributors also examined ways to connect feminist rhetorical studies to rising interdisciplinary fields of study, including Latinx studies (Callafel), digital studies (McKee and Porter), disability studies (Dolmage and Lewiecki-Wilson), queer and transgender studies (Rawson), transnational feminisms (Hesford, Crawford), aging studies (Ranney) and writing pedagogy (Micciche), among others. With the first volume, we hoped to spark conversations about feminist rhetorical methods and methodologies and provide resources and guidelines that graduate students and faculty could use as they undertook specific research projects, cleared IRB (Institutional Review Board) processes, wrote grant proposals, and made the case for their research to be valued in tenure and promotion processes.

As our scholarship and careers continued after the publication of *Rhetorica in Motion,* we realized how foundational feminist methods were for both of us as scholars and activists, even as we worked on projects where feminism was not the sole focus. For example, K.J. went on to create the Digital Transgender Archive (www.digitaltransgenderarchive.net), which not only highlights feminism as one of its six core values ("We recognize the harmful effects of gender-based inequity and discrimination, and we are committed to challenging sexism and gender inequity"), but it also has feminist frameworks built into the site's architecture, such as prompting users for their consent to opt into seeing explicit content.[36] Eileen had begun writing about the rhetoric of the crisis in family farm agriculture in the United States and across the globe, finding transnational solidarity with the food democracy movement built by feminist activists such as Dr. Vandana Shiva and the movement Navdanya, which advocates for food and seed sovereignty, championing small farmers and producers across the globe in the face of growing domination of agribusiness conglomerates like Monsanto and Archer Daniels Midland.[37] The work on food democracy also sparked Eileen to consider how environmental justice and climate activism movements were being spearheaded by feminist activists such as Nobel Prize winner Dr. Wangari Maathai of Kenya, whose organizing of the Greenbelt Movement taught rural Kenyan women to use tree planting to fight deforestation and climate change.

In the years following *Rhetorica in Motion*'s publication, we were often approached by graduate students and faculty at conferences who told us they relied on the book's guidance on feminist rhetorical methods and methodologies, and we were regularly asked if there would be a second volume. In 2018, Rebecca Dingo contacted us about composing a second volume, possibly basing it on a symposium that she was planning to run at the University of Massachusetts, Amherst on feminist rhetorical methods and methodologies. Unfortunately, the symposium was canceled due to the COVID-19 pandemic. Still, the idea of a new volume had sticking power. Eileen had already been talking to graduate students at Syracuse University about the project, and she taught a graduate class in Fall 2021 on Feminist Rhetorics in which four graduate students–Curtis Jewell, Abby Long, Sidney Turner, and Gabriella Wilson–expressed interest in working on a new collection.

Teaming up again for a second collaboration, we were thrilled to be able to work with a larger editorial collective that spans three generations of scholars, including Eileen as a longstanding leader in the field, K.J. as a mid-career scholar, and four early career scholars who are in various stages of their graduate education. As feminist scholars, we wanted to thoughtfully navigate our positions of relative power to shape conversations in the field, and we wanted to work with a new generation of feminist graduate students to explore how they were using and reworking feminist rhetorical methods and methodologies. We wanted to be sure this volume represented the needs and concerns of those entering the field of feminist rhetorical studies instead of mainly highlighting the work of established scholars or being framed solely by the concerns we had as senior and mid-career scholars. More than a decade has passed since the publication of *Rhetorica in Motion,* and this collection is a well-timed continuation of that work, foregrounding new developments and growth in feminist methods in light of recent and ongoing movements for social justice.

Expanding the Horizons of Feminist Rhetorics

Feminist rhetorical studies over the past three decades have become an increasingly important part of the field of rhetoric and composition, with many doctoral students pursuing dissertations on feminist rhetorics, faculty publishing books focused on feminist research, editing anthologies of women's/feminist rhetorics, and scholars across all ranks taking part in the biannual Feminisms and Rhetorics Conference, which started in 1997. The book series Feminisms and Rhetorics–originally at Southern Illinois University Press, now at Parlor Press–publishes innovative feminist rhetoric scholarship that has inspired multiple generations of scholars in the field. Feminist scholars in rhetoric and communication studies have also intertwined their scholarship with activism and community-engaged work, as contributors in this volume demonstrate.

As we consider the feminist conversations and social movements that have transpired since publishing *Rhetorica in Motion* in 2010, we have seen an expanded focus on several key areas of feminist scholarship and activism in the field, which we will briefly highlight in relation to chapters that readers will encounter in this collection. From the outset, we find ourselves reflecting on what Jacqueline Jones Royster and Gesa E. Kirsch refer to as the "major shifts in recent decades in rhetorical inquiry" and a "new and changed landscape for narratives in the history of rhetoric."[38] As Royster and Kirsch argue, feminist rhetorical studies has gone beyond "rescue, recovery, or (re)inscription" to "stretching the boundaries of our work to reach beyond the basics (i.e., re-forming the master narratives in the history of rhetoric simply to include women) toward the development of new paradigms for how our work itself might be shaped."[39] They specify four critical terms of engagement for feminist rhetoricians: "critical imagination, strategic contemplation, social circulation, and globalization."[40] Critical imagination becomes "a mechanism for seeing the noticed and the unnoticed, rethinking what is there and not there."[41] Strategic contemplation goes hand-in-hand with the processes of critical imagination by allowing scholars to take "the time, space, and resources to think about, through, and around our work as an important meditative dimension of scholarly productivity," allowing scholars to better engage in a dialogue with "our rhetorical subjects, even if only imaginatively, to understand their words, their visions, their priorities whether and perhaps especially when they differ from our own."[42] To understand our rhetorical subjects, though, we must also understand how they are represented through processes of "social circulation," the ways in which their rhetorical performances "ebb, flow, travel, gain substance and integrity, acquire traction," and how specific rhetors have "participated actively in setting, shaping, and deploying rhetorical trends and practices writ large."[43] In understanding the ways feminist rhetors have shaped and deployed specific rhetorics, we must also consider the ways that rhetoric is located and engaged across geographic boundaries, "recast[ing] perspectives of rhetoric as a transnational, global phenomenon rather than a Western one."[44] In keeping with Kirsch and Royster's strategies for engagement, we consider how they give us ways to imagine the feminist rhetorical methods and methodologies needed across geopolitical locations and in ways that foster social justice, not just academic publications and careers.

One specific way that feminist rhetoric scholars have revamped thinking about feminist methods is by continuing to challenge our geopolitical mappings of rhetorics and feminisms, going beyond the confines of the nation-state to think transnationally about flows of bodies, goods, economics, power, and discourse as they move across borders. Hesford and Schell argue in their special issue of *College English* on transnational feminist rhetorics that a transnational feminist rhetorical perspective "strives to address how rhetorical concepts are shaped by cultural, social, and economic interconnectivities and interrelations and cross-border and cross-cultural mobilizations of power, language resources, and people."[45] In the same vein, Rebecca Dingo urges rhetoricians to consider how "rhetorics travel—how rhetorics might be picked up, how rhetorics might become networked with new and different arguments, and then how rhetorical meaning might shift and change as a result of these movements."[46] She further offers a "transnational feminist rhetorical methodology that seeks to identify how arguments are networked, how and why rhetorics travel and circulate and then how (due to rhetorical occasions such as the rise of neoliberal economics) they shift and change as they move across geopolitical boundaries to reflect different ideas about production, labor, and global citizenship."[47] These initial mappings of transnational feminist rhetorics and their methodologies have set the stage for a steady stream of feminist scholars who are expanding and going beyond Euro-Western notions of who is doing and practicing rhetorics and to what ends.[48] In this volume, Nelesi Rodrigues draws on transnational feminist and diasporic frameworks to examine social justice choreography and movement as practiced by the Ananya Dance Theatre (ADT).

As feminist rhetoric scholars have reframed the conversation about geopolitics and the nation-state, feminist scholars across disciplines and communities have further shifted from a focus on Euro-Western contexts to embracing a focus on intersectionality and a more complex understanding of what the Combahee River Collective referred to as "interlocking oppressions," the idea of "struggling against racial, sexual, heterosexual, and class oppression" and "developing an integrated analysis and practice based upon the fact that the major systems of oppression are interlocking."[49] The idea of interlocking oppressions challenges the single-axis framework of either race or gender and instead considers the multidimensionality of oppression, specifically centering the experiences of Black women, as Black feminist legal scholar Kimberlé Crenshaw has argued.[50] Crenshaw's groundbreaking work on intersectionality has shaped the thinking of many feminist scholars in women's and gender studies and across multiple disciplines, including feminist rhetorical studies. The development of intersectional feminist rhetorical methodologies, as Karma Chávez and Cindy Griffin argue, is vital for addressing the "rich and complex facets of identity and subjectivity and to explore the overt and covert uses and manifestations of power and privilege."[51] They further argue that drawing on intersectional theories of rhetoric allows feminist rhetoricians to "lay a foundation for productive conversations around power, identities, and subjectivities that have been erased, ignored, and under-and inappropriately theorized."[52] In this volume, Andrea Riley Mukavetz, Christina V. Cedillo, Tarez Graban and Michael Healy, sarah madoka currie and Ada Hubrig, and Stephanie Jones take up that charge to address subjectivities that have been "erased, ignored, and under-and-inappropriately theorized."[53]

The idea of embodied, corporeal rhetorics are often circulated in feminist rhetorical studies and the field of rhetoric and composition broadly, but the origins of those theories of the body and materiality are less well acknowledged and credited to women of color feminists Cherríe Moraga and Gloria Anzaldúa, who argued in *This Bridge Called My Back* for a "theory of the flesh," built on what they refer to as "the physical realities of our lives–our skin color, the land or concrete we grew up on, our sexual longings all fuse to create a politic born of necessity."[54] This framing of a theory of the flesh has allowed women of color feminists, in the words of Bernadette Cal-lafell, to "theorize about our experiences when we have been denied access to traditional forms of knowledge production."[55] We can see aspects of this discussion in the focus in rhetorical studies in work to claim a "rhetorics of the flesh" that draws on women of color feminisms and cultural rhetorics to address a "poetic and embodied way of knowing and being."[56] Alejandra I. Ramírez and Ruben Zecena draw on this framework along with queer theory and cultural rhetorics to challenge "normative discourses about migrant mothers and disrupt anti-immigrant rhetoric that renders migrant mothers as always already criminal and abject."[57]

Just as theories and practices of intersectionality and theories of the flesh have dramatically shifted how we talk about and engage feminist rhetorics, transgender studies has similarly challenged how gender is defined and by whom and who can practice feminist rhetorics. In *Rhetorica in Motion*, K.J. Rawson questioned how feminist recovery work and gendered analysis "relied upon normative notions of gender to identify and categorize what counts as feminist rhetoric."[58] Rawson pointed out the ways that many feminist rhetoricians drew on "fixed identity categories, typically 'woman' or 'female,'" and how feminist recovery work had "mostly recovered a gender-normative body of texts—those produced by biologically born, self-identified, or historically identified women."[59] Courses and anthologies on "women's rhetorics" continue that practice even while including authors who engage queer and transgender theories that challenge gender normativity.

A growing focus on queer and transgender studies within rhetoric and composition has sparked an ongoing interrogation of the ways in which feminist rhetorical studies must challenge its normative assumptions about gender. Rawson argues for drawing on transgender critique to do so, as this approach "queers feminist rhetorical studies by pushing for an engagement with broader, more expansive definitions of gender that more closely mirror the complexities of lived gender."[60] Scholars across the field have begun to open space for scholarship on feminist rhetorics that is inclusive and representative of "gendered people of all varieties [who] are invested and engaged in feminist rhetoric."[61] The recent special issue in *Peitho* on Transgender Feminisms coedited by GPat Patterson and Rawson calls for an approach to feminist rhetorical studies that acknowledges the important role that transgender theory can play in challenging the biases and limitations of feminist thought when it relies on "cis-centric gender binaries" and also on "reductive narratives about trans people." As Patterson points out, these very "cis-centric gender binaries" then become the vehicles for the violence done to trans people in relation to "access to housing, employment, medical care, legal documents, bathroom access—along with a host of other indignities."[62] A critique of gender normativity will be vital to creating intersectional, embodied feminisms that challenge anti-trans legislation and discrimination and also to challenging ableist assumptions about the body as well. Rachel Lewis in this volume picks up some of the threads of queer and transgender critique to consider feminist abolitionism and the agency of incarcerated people by focusing on a case study of letters written by LGBTQ+ incarcerated authors.

Another challenge to our field's normative assumptions about people and presumed identities has come from feminist disability studies, which has become a vital site for challenging ableist assumptions about the body in feminist rhetorical histories, making space for understandings of rhetoric that challenge notions of ability and rhetorical fitness.[63] As Simi Linton argues in the seminal piece "What is Disability Studies?," the conversation about disability studies is evolving and shifting while complicating and critiquing binary categories of disabled/non-disabled and the idea of physical and sensory impairment versus other kinds of embodied differences.[64] Scholars such as Margaret Price have further complicated disability studies frameworks to consider not only "physical and sensory impairments" but also "persons with disabilities of the mind."[65] As disability studies have been taken up in rhetorical studies, so have calls to consider the ways in which white bodies have been centered in so many accounts of disability rhetorics. Christina V. Cedillo, drawing on the hashtag #DisabilityTooWhite created by Black disability activist Vilissa Thompson, reminds us that disability studies frameworks and advocacy often reinforce whiteness, rhetorically and spatially, erasing race in relation to disability. She argues that "we must approach race and disability as 'interlocking forms of oppressions' that are 'interconnected and collusive.'"[66] sarah madoka currie and Ada Hubrig in this volume further complicate disability studies frameworks and challenge readers to center the rhetorical agency and material situations and knowledges of crip-mad people (see madoka currie and Hubrig, this volume).

Engaging technologies from a feminist lens is also a vital and growing area of work. For decades, interdisciplinary feminist scholars, ranging from Moya Bailey,[67] Donna Haraway,[68] and Catherine Knight Steele,[69] to scholars in rhetoric and writing studies such as Cindy Selfe and Gail Hawisher,[70] Samantha Blackmon,[71] TreaAndrea M. Russworm and Blackmon,[72] Kishonna Gray,[73] and others, have engaged and examined the radical possibilities, power relations, and often undertheorized materialities of digital worlds challenging digital pasts, presents and imagined futures that are exclusionary, that erase, harm, or ignore users while allowing others to hijack digital realms to threaten and enact gendered and racialized violence (see Jones, this volume).

At the same time, digital technologies make possible much of our daily workplace and teaching lives, providing scholarly research tools for uncovering and recovering the stories and experiences of those who have been ignored or omitted in the dominant version of the historical record (see Graban and Healy, this volume). In a compelling special issue of *Peitho* focused on internet research ethics, cluster editors Kristi McDuffie and Melissa Ames and their contributors explore questions about how to highlight and complicate ethical standards and practices for feminist internet research. The coeditors argue that "although online research data sets are more and more often being treated as 'big data,' defined in innumerable ways, feminist Internet researchers demand that online information be treated as human subjects research rather than textual research."[74] They also address the need for researchers to challenge and complicate the idea of what is public with interrogations of access, privacy, and accuracy in the age of bots, trolls, misinformation, and Artificial Intelligence (AI).[75] Furthermore, they provide advice about how feminist internet researchers can address their research positionalities and hold themselves accountable to their participants, their privacy, their rights, and the shifting dynamics of online spaces.[76]

Within the past few years, as artificial intelligence has rapidly expanded into widespread public use, its seismic impacts are only minimally understood, but feminist theorization has started to emerge that proposes more ethically sound AI approaches. JoAnne E. Gray and Alice Witt argue for an approach to AI ethics that privileges a *feminist data ethics of care for machine learning,* which foregrounds the ways that machine learning, and other kinds of AI, are not value neutral, but are "situated and positional" and that "representational and allocative harm" can be done in the "machine learning pipeline."[77] They propose five key principles that will address these inequities:

1. ensuring diverse representation and participation in the machine learning economy;
2. critically evaluating positionality;
3. centering human subjects at every stage of the machine learning pipeline;

4. implementing transparency and accountability measures; and
5. equitably distributing the responsibility for operationalising a feminist
   data ethics of care praxis.[78]

Many of these principles echo longstanding best practices in feminist methods, which demonstrates the enduring value of feminist ethics, particularly as we navigate new cultural terrain with the continuing emergence of AI.

Inspired by Royster and Kirsch's framing of feminist rhetorical practices of critical imagination, strategic contemplation, social circulation, and globalization, this volume seeks to move the conversation about feminist rhetorical methods and methodologies to consider transnational feminist rhetorical methodologies, intersectional theories of feminist rhetorics, contestations of gender influenced by transgender critique, disability studies frameworks, and feminist engagements with technologies across the varied chapters of this book. We also seek to understand, too, how we can revisit our field's work on the recovery of feminist rhetorical history with new lenses and a fresh understanding of the materialities of history-making and monumentalizing (see Enoch and Woods, this volume). Building on recent scholarship in feminist rhetorical studies, *Rhetorica Rising* furthers the shared feminist rhetorical project of inclusion, recovery work, and pursuit of emancipatory futures by considering embodied, material, and digital work as sites of inquiry and taking up pressing feminist methodological concerns regarding ethics, trauma, care, and relationality. Megan Schoettler's thoughtful chapter on creating a trauma-informed approach to feminist rhetorical work provides guidelines we all desperately need as researchers.

Collection Overview

Rhetorica Rising assembles a chorus of feminist perspectives to showcase how both emerging and established scholars can illuminate new sites of inquiry, center underrepresented ways of knowing, and enact responsive research ethics within communities. As contributors address the specific subjects and sites of their research, they also examine and reflect on their ethical choices and positionalities as feminist researchers who draw upon specific methods and methodologies while navigating material contexts and their embodied locations. As coeditors of this volume along with the graduate student coeditors, we encouraged collaboration and self-reflexive writing as key feminist practices in this volume. Collaboration was and is integral to not only the work of the editorial team but is also a guiding force for many of the contributing authors who have co-authored chapters or who have collaborated with stakeholders on their data design, collection, and/or interpretation.

While this is the type of collection that could be organized into a dozen different configurations (and we entertained many!), we ultimately organized the book into three parts. In the first part, titled "Reclaiming Space and Centering the Body," the four chapters offer feminist methods that explore constructions of the self within larger communities, particularly by (re)centering the body in relation to spaces and sites of power. Andrea Riley Mukavetz opens this section with a grippingly honest reflection on navigating institutions of higher education, tribal politics, and the profession of rhetoric and composition. In "An Affinity for Spiky Things: Kwe as Method for Navigating Academic Spaces," she considers her role in Indigenizing and decolonizing academic spaces, and she explores survivance "within the context of a social climate where many forces are seeking to exterminate Indigenous land and life." Having left the academy and now working as a Community Engagement Manager for the City of Grand Rapids, Michigan, Riley Mukavetz's insights are urgent as she unpacks the "complexity of belonging and the shared work of creating space while respecting boundaries and invitations."

How to forge community is a theme that Nelesi Rodrigues also explores in "Movement as Method: Deciphering the Spells of Ananya Dance Theatre." Rodrigues offers an extended reflection on her participant-observation with the Ananya Dance Theatre (ADT), a "BIPOC organization doing social justice choreography grounded in a transnational feminist and diasporic framework." Taking up "movement as a subject and method," Rodrigues includes beautiful descriptions of dance as she argues that movement technique functions as an embodied composing practice. Rodrigues considers ADT's pedagogies of movement and pays particular attention to the company's invention practices and how they might help to reframe understandings of invention in our field.

In "'Nosotros no somos mitos del pasado ni del presente': The Problem of Ethos and Exigence in Latin American Indigenous Women's Rhetorics," Christina V. Cedillo similarly offers compelling retheorizations of key rhetorical concepts—in their case, ethos and exigence—to "show how coloniality uses language to sustain its authority and obscure the material and physical damage it inflicts on colonized people." Focusing on Indigenous women in particular, Cedillo considers two cases from Guatemala's

Civil War that "highlight how Eurowestern notions of ethos and exigence fail to account for the material and temporal aspects of ongoing colonial oppression and why, as a result, Indigenous rhetorics must always account for rhetorical erasure and genocide." This chapter both demonstrates and advocates for an intersectional feminist methodology that centers "Indigenous peoples' perspectives, goals, and rhetorical sovereignty" and challenges unexamined norms in our field that ultimately uphold colonial values.

The final chapter in the first part, sarah madoka currie and Ada Hubrig's "Against the Asylum: a re-rhetorica of madness," reclaims madness as a site of rhetorical possibility and powerfully advocates for the rhetorical agency of Mad people. Framed as an intervention, this chapter "refigure(s) feminist rhetorics as a methodology to resist the stigmatization and vilification of madness that has been a staple of asylum rhetorics permeating Western culture." madoka currie and Hubrig offer three feminist methodological approaches—embracing reality, disavowing hierarchical logics, and practicing radical consent. As with the chapters that precede it, this chapter both enacts and advocates for feminist rhetorics that challenge major tenets of the rhetorical tradition while centering those who are multiply marginalized.

This careful attention to rhetorical power is a theme that comes into even sharper relief in the second part of this collection, "Enacting Care in Ethical Research Relationships." While all of the contributors to this book are attuned to ethical research, the authors in this section foreground practices of care as they construct, approach, and reflect on their research relationships at all stages of the research process. These chapters engage community sites while asking readers to critically reflect on whose stories are privileged through our research methods and methodologies. Readers are also encouraged to reflect on how feminist methodologies can inform how we care for our communities and for individuals when vulnerability, trauma, and precarity are central to our work.

Relying on feminist and trauma methodologies, Megan Schoettler's "Lessons from Advocacy: A Feminist and Trauma-Informed Methodology" draws on both her own activist research and her experiences as a sexual assault survivor advocate. Woven into short vignettes from her community research partnership with the Midwest Rape Crisis Organization (MRCO), Schoettler examines the limitations and affordances of trauma-informed methodology and explores the varying roles she occupies in her research. Schoettler ultimately offers five principles of feminist trauma-informed methodology that can help "feminist researchers avoid retraumatizing participants, honor the stories and resilience of survivors, and foster productive engagement with our social and material worlds."

Reflecting a similar level of care but approaching research relationships from a different perspective, Jessica Restaino and Timothy Oleksiak take an innovative approach in their chapter, "Desiring Consent: A Reflexive Methodology for Feminist Research," by revisiting Restaino's award-winning book, *Surrender*. They are particularly interested in reconsidering Restaino's research relationship with Susan Lundy Maute, a central figure in the book, as they examine the interplay between desire, pursuit, and consent. Drawing on queer rhetorics, Restaino and Oleksiak offer an extended consideration of the complexities of desire in research encounters. As they unpack various moments of communication between Restaino and Maute, they ultimately make a case for the importance of consent and the need for more transparent and intentional approaches to it in feminist research.

One of the most challenging sites to explore ethical research relationships—prisons—is the focus of Rachel Lewis's chapter, "Collective Identity in Feminist Rhetorical Research." Lewis demonstrates how feminist rhetoric is well-suited for abolitionist work by focusing on a case study of letters written by LGBTQ+ incarcerated authors. Noting that "incarcerated subjects constitute a major sector of voices that are consciously removed from public spheres and deliberately destabilized," Lewis applies feminist methods to this large corpus of letters and identifies several key themes and rhetorical strategies that the letter writers use to negotiate their disempowered positions.

In "Caring for *Cuentos* of Reproductive (In)Justice: Feminist Methods for Confianza, Curation, and Care-ful Digital Design," Rachel Bloom-Pojar and Danielle Koepke introduce the "confianza" methodology that they developed as part of a community-engaged digital storytelling project in collaboration with promotores de salud (community health care workers) affiliated with Planned Parenthood of Wisconsin. Contributing to the field's attention to stories and storytelling as a feminist method, the authors explore how storytelling is used to advance reproductive justice initiatives and how those stories should be handled with care and trust, particularly when they are published in digital spaces.

The third and final part of this collection, "Navigating Materiality, Memory, and Futurity," makes connections across a range of sites for knowledge-making and knowledge preservation. The chapters in this section consider how researchers come to terms with their own embodied ways of knowing and how those ways of knowing interact with our physical and digital worlds. As a whole, these chapters offer incisive explorations of how our methods and methodologies are entangled with and emerge from material, digital, and rhetorical sites.

Focusing on the worlds in and around gaming, Stephanie Jones engages Black digital rhetoric to advocate for increased inclusion for Black women gamers in her article, "Dangerous Moves: On Reclaiming Video Gaming through Black Feminist Rhetoric & Remix." Jones draws on her gaming experiences and scholarship at the intersection of game studies, digital rhetorics, feminist studies, and Afrofuturism to "methodologically explicate rhetorical theories that disrupt coded biases in digital texts and performances." She ultimately develops a method of Afrodigitized critical questioning to disrupt "normalized narratives of exclusion" and offers hopeful possibilities for Black women to successfully navigate and transform exclusionary gaming environments.

"The Promise(s) and Peril(s) of Big Data: Historiography, Data Feminism, and Tracing Women of Color," by Tarez Samra Graban and Michael Healy, reveals the "intricacies of how digital histories get reconstructed using linked-data tools." Arguing for the critical and contextual incorporation of data feminism into digital recovery projects, particularly for addressing women of color in our field, Graban and Healy enact a digital trace of the institutional and disciplinary legacies of three lesser-known administrators of college literacy programs: Mary Edna Brown, Leonea Barbour Dudley, and Sarah Nevelle Meriwether. Not content to analyze and critique without offering solutions, the authors offer "incremental searching methods in order to help readers envision the complex im/material entanglements that require care and curation when engaging with data-bound subjects."

Advancing our field's attention to memory and recovery practices, Jessica Enoch and Carly S. Woods bring our attention to sites of public memory and memorialization. In their chapter, "What Should We Ask? Feminist Methodological Inquiries into Commemoration," Enoch and Woods analyze Sharon Hayes's 2017 *If They Should Ask* sculpture, which calls attention to the near complete absence of women among Philadelphia's hundreds of monuments/sculptures. As they help readers "identify and think through the various feminist approaches scholars could employ to inspect this memory artifact," the pair draws on interdisciplinary scholarship across museum studies, memory studies, and art history. They offer questions that feminist scholars can apply when approaching sites of public memory that centralize gender.

The book concludes with an afterword, "Looking Forward," from the four graduate student coeditors: Curtis J. Jewell, Abigail H. Long, Sidney

Turner, and Gabriella Wilson. The authors discuss their experience coediting the collection, working to honor the perspectives of all editorial members, and finding consensus while simultaneously developing their own approaches to research ethics and practices. Through an interrogation of the collaborative editing process and their own positionalities, they consider how a feminist method of response provides them with a way to attend to the power relations, differences, and labor in their collective work. The chapter concludes by positing the need for emerging scholars and their mentors to explore how feminist rhetorical methods and methodologies shape their work.

Ending the volume with the vision and voice of emerging scholars is a fitting way to wrap up a collection that is so thoroughly invested in feminist mentorship practices and in collaboratively working toward our shared futures. As our academic work continues within and alongside the activist movements of the past 15 years, our field's engagement with feminist methods and methodologies has become all the more pressing. Our hope is that this collection furthers this ongoing work of feminist rhetorical scholarship, inspires the next generations of feminist scholars, and helps advance the critical social justice uprisings of the early twenty-first century. In her 2000 *Rhetoric Society Quarterly* article, Patricia Bizzell praised feminist researchers for adopting feminist "methods which violate some of the most cherished conventions of academic research, most particularly in bringing the person of the researcher, her body, her emotions, and dare one say, her soul, into the work."[79] She argued that those methods "have made all the difference" in the field.[80] We hope this volume will also continue to make a difference in seeing the ways that feminist rhetorical research methods and methodologies are vital and much needed as we engage research that will be transformative.

NOTES

1. Akin Olla, "Occupy Wall Street Swept the World and Achieved A Lot Even If It May Not Feel Like It," *The Guardian,* October 6, 2021. https://www.theguardian .com/.
2. Mat Hanson, "The Fight for $15," *The Forge,* April 15, 2021, https://forgeorganizing .org/article/fight-15.
3. Black Lives Matter, "About: Black Lives Matter," https://blacklivesmatter.com/ about/.
4. Black Lives Matter, "Herstory: Black Lives Matter," https://blacklivesmatter.com/ herstory/.
5. Black Lives Matter, "Herstory."
6. Shahin, Nakahara, and Sánchez, "Black Lives Matter," https://doi.org/10.1177/ 1461444821105.

7. The Movement for Black Lives, "End U.S. Complicity in Israel's Abuses of Palestinians," https://m4bl.org/statements/end-us-complicity-in-israels-abuses-of-palestinians/.
8. Native Knowledge 360°, "Treaties Still Matter: The Dakota Access Pipeline," https://americanindian.si.edu/nk360/plains-treaties/dapl.
9. "The #NoDAPL Movement Was Powerful, Factual, and Indigenous-Led," *The Daily Outrage: The CCR Blog,* last modified February 21, 2018, https://ccrjustice.org/home/blog/2018/02/21/.
10. Wes Enzinna, "'I Didn't Come Here to Lose': How a Movement Was Born at Standing Rock," *Mother Jones,* December 2016, https://www.motherjones.com/.
11. Mari Copeny, "About Mari," https://www.maricopeny.com/about.
12. Kerri Lee Alexander, "Tarana Burke," National Women's History Museum, last modified 2020, https://www.womenshistory.org/education-resources/biographies/tarana-burke, par. 3.
13. Kerri Lee Alexander, "Tarana Burke," par. 4.
14. Jamillah Bowman Williams and Elizabeth Tippett, "Five Years On, Here's What #MeToo Has Changed," *Politico,* October 14, 2022, https://www.politico.com/, par. 5.
15. Sarah Wildman, "#MeToo Goes Global," *Foreign Policy,* 2019, https://foreignpolicy.com/, par. 2.
16. Pew Research Center, "An Examination of the 2016 Electorate, Based on Validated Voters," last modified August 9, 2018, https://www.pewresearch.org/.
17. Pew Research Center, "An Examination."
18. Kendall, *Hood Feminism,* xiii.
19. Kendall, *Hood Feminism,* xiii.
20. History.com, "2017: Women's March," https://www.history.com/this-day-in-history/womens-march.
21. Dorothee Benz, "The Women's March: Protest and Resistance," *Learning for Justice,* March 20, 2023, https://www.learningforjustice.org/.
22. ACLU: Washington, "Timeline of the Muslim Ban," last modified February 21, 2018, https://www.aclu-wa.org/pages/timeline-muslim-ban.
23. Peace Women: Women's International League for Peace and Freedom, "Does the Women's March Still Matter? Does It Still?," http://peacewomen.org/, par. 7.
24. Remy Tumin, "Greta Thunberg Ends Her School Strikes After 251 Weeks," *New York Times,* June 10, 2023, https://www.nytimes.com/.
25. Fridays for Future, Who We Are: Fridays for Future," https://fridaysforfuture.org/what-we-do/who-we-are/.
26. Nylah Burton, "Meet the Young Activists of Color Who Are Leading the Charge Against Climate Disaster," *Vox,* October 11, 2019, https://www.vox.com/identities/2019/10/11/20904791/young-climate-activists-of-color.
27. March For Our Lives, "We Marched for Our Lives, Again," last modified 2024, https://marchforourlives.org/march22/.
28. SisterSong: Women of Color Reproductive Justice Collection, "What is Reproductive Justice?" https://www.sistersong.net/reproductive-justice.
29. SisterSong: Women of Color Reproductive Justice Collection, "About Us," https://www.sistersong.net/about-x2.
30. SisterSong, "What is Reproductive Justice?"
31. SisterSong, "What is Reproductive Justice?"
32. ACLU, "Mapping Attacks on LGBTQ Rights in U.S. State Legislatures," https://www.aclu.org/legislative-attacks-on-lgbtq-rights; Matthew Rodriguez, "CPAC

Speaker Michael Knowles Says 'Transgenderism Must Be Eradicated,'" *Them*, March 6, 2023. https://www.them.us/.

33. Brooke Migdon, "FBI Crime Statistics Show Anti-LGBTQ Hate Crimes on the Rise," *The Hill*, October 16, 2023, https://thehill.com/.

34. Harding, *Feminism and Methodology*, Introduction, 2, 3.

35. Harding, *Feminism and Methodology*, Introduction, 3.

36. Digital Transgender Archive, "Policies," https://www.digitaltransgenderarchive.net/about/policies.

37. Schell, "Framing the Megarhetorics."

38. Royster and Kirsch, *Feminist Rhetorical Practices*, 13.

39. Royster and Kirsch, *Feminist Rhetorical Practices*, 14.

40. Royster and Kirsch, *Feminist Rhetorical Practices*, 19.

41. Royster and Kirsch, *Feminist Rhetorical Practices*, 20.

42. Royster and Kirsch, *Feminist Rhetorical Practices*, 21.

43. Royster and Kirsch, *Feminist Rhetorical Practices*, 23.

44. Royster and Kirsch, *Feminist Rhetorical Practices*, 25.

45. Hesford and Schell, "Introduction," 465.

46. Dingo, *Networking Arguments,* 2.

47. Dingo, *Networking Arguments*, 7.

48. Baniya, "Managing Environmental Risks"; Dingo, *Networking Arguments*; Hesford and Schell, "Introduction"; Nish, *Activist Literacies*; Richards, *Transnational Feminist Rhetorics*; Riedner, *Writing Neoliberal Values*; Wang, "Comparative Rhetoric"; Wingard, *Branded Bodies*.

49. The Combahee River Collective, "A Black Feminist Statement," 271.

50. Crenshaw, "Demarginalizing the Intersection," 139–40.

51. Chávez and Griffin, Introduction, 2.

52. Chávez and Griffin, Introduction, 2.

53. Chávez and Griffin, Introduction, 2.

54. Moraga and Anzaldúa, *This Bridge*, 23.

55. Calafell, "Rhetorics," 105.

56. Ramírez and Zecena, "The Dirt," https://constell8cr.com/issue-2/the-dirt-under-my-moms-fingernails-queer-retellings-and-migrant-sensualities/.

57. Ramírez and Zecena, "The Dirt."

58. Rawson, "Queering," 40.

59. Rawson, "Queering," 40.

60. Rawson, "Queering," 42.

61. Rawson, "Queering," 52.

62. Patterson, "Because Trans People," https://cfshrc.org/article/because-trans-people-are-speaking-notes-on-our-fields-first-special-issue-on-transgender-rhetorics/.

63. Dolmage and Lewiecki-Wilson, "Refiguring Rhetorica," 24–27.

64. Linton, "What is Disability," 519–20.

65. Price, *Mad at School*, 5.

66. Annamma, Connor, and Ferri, "Dis/Ability," 47; Cedillo, "#DisabilityTooWhite," par. 18, https://sparkactivism.com/disabilitytoowhite/.

67. Bailey, *Misogynoir Transformed*.

68. Haraway, "A Cyborg Manifesto."

69. Steele, *Digital Black Feminism*.

70. Hawisher and Selfe, *Passions*; Selfe and Hawisher, *Gaming Lives*.

71. Blackmon, "'Be Real Black.'"

72. Russworm and Blackmon, "Replaying Video."

73. Gray, *Race, Gender, and Deviance.*

74. McDuffie and Ames, "Cluster," 97.

75. McDuffie and Ames, "Cluster," 98–99.

76. McDuffie and Ames, "Cluster," 99–100.

77. Gray and Witt, "A Feminist Data," https://doi.org/10.5210/fm.v26i12.11833. For more on a feminist data ethics of care framework see also D'Ignazio and Klein, *Data Feminism,*

78. Gray and Witt, "A Feminist Data," https://doi.org/10.5210/fm.v26i12.11833.

79. Bizzell, "Feminist Methods," 16.

80. Bizzell, "Feminist Methods,"16.

WORKS CITED

ACLU. "Mapping Attacks on LGBTQ Rights in U.S. State Legislatures." https://www.aclu.org/legislative-attacks-on-lgbtq-rights

ACLU: Washington. "Timeline of the Muslim Ban." Last modified February 21, 2018. https://www.aclu-wa.org/pages/timeline-muslim-ban.

Annamma, Subini Ancy, David Connor, and Beth Ferri. "Dis/ability Critical Race Studies (DisCrit): Theorizing at the Intersections of Race and Dis/Ability." *Race Ethnicity and Education* 16, no. 1 (2013): 1–31. https://doi.org/10.1080/13613324.2012.730511.

Bailey, Moya. *Misogynoir Transformed: Black Women's Digital Resistance.* New York: New York University Press, 2021.

Baniya, Sweta. "Managing Environmental Risks: Rhetorical Agency and Ecological Literacies of Women During the Nepal Earthquake." *Enculturation* 32 (2020). http://enculturation.net/managing_environmental.

Bizzell, Patricia. "Feminist Methods of Research in the History of Rhetoric: What Difference Do They Make?" *Rhetoric Society Quarterly* 30, vol. 4 (2000): 5–17.

Blackmon, Samantha. "'Be Real Black For Me': Lincoln Clay and Luke Cage as the Heroes We Need." *CEA Critic* 79, no. 1 (2017): 97–109. https://doi.org/10.1353/cea.2017.0006.

Calafell, Bernadette M. "Rhetorics of Possibility: Challenging the Textual Bias of Rhetoric through the Theory of the Flesh." In *Rhetorica in Motion: Feminist Rhetorical Methods and Methodologies,* edited by Eileen E. Schell and K.J. Rawson, 104–17. Pittsburgh, PA: University of Pittsburgh Press, 2010.

Cedillo, Christina. "#DisabilityTooWhite: On Erasure's Material and Physical Dimensions." *Spark: A 4C4Equality Journal* 4 (2022). https://sparkactivism.com/disabilitytoowhite/.

Chávez, Karma R., and Cindy L. Griffin. Introduction to *Standing in the Intersection: Feminist Voices, Feminist Practices in Communication Studies,* edited by Karma R. Chávez and Cindy L. Griffin, 1–32. Albany, NY: SUNY Press, 2012.

The Combahee River Collective. "A Black Feminist Statement." *Women's Studies Quarterly* 42, no. 3/4 (2014): 271–80.

Crenshaw, Kimberlé. "Demarginalizing the Intersection of Race and Sex: A Black Feminist Critique of Antidiscrimination Doctrine, Feminist Theory, and Antiracist Politics." *University of Chicago Legal Forum* 1989, no. 1 (1989): 139–69.

Digital Transgender Archive. "Policies." https://www.digitaltransgenderarchive.net/about/policies.

D'Ignazio, Catherine, and Lauren F. Klein. *Data Feminism.* Cambridge, MA: MIT Press, 2020.

Dingo, Rebecca Ann. *Networking Arguments: Rhetoric, Transnational Feminism, and Public Policy Writing.* Pittsburgh, PA: University of Pittsburgh Press, 2012.

Dolmage, Jay, and Cynthia Lewiecki-Wilson. "Refiguring Rhetorica: Linking Feminist Rhetoric with Disability Studies." In *Rhetorica in Motion: Feminist Rhetorical Methods and Methodologies,* edited by Eileen E. Schell and K.J. Rawson, 23–38. Pittsburgh, PA: University of Pittsburgh Press, 2010.

Gray, Joanne E., and Alice Witt. "A Feminist Data Ethics of Care Framework for Machine Learning: The What, Why, Who and How." *First Monday* 26, no. 12 (December 2021). https://doi.org/10.5210/fm.v26i12.11833.

Gray, Kishonna L. *Race, Gender, and Deviance in Xbox Live: Theoretical Perspectives from the Virtual Margins.* Waltham, MA: Anderson Publishing, 2014.

Haraway, Donna. "A Cyborg Manifesto: Science, Technology, and Socialist-Feminism in the Late Twentieth Century." In *Simians, Cyborgs, and Women: The Reinvention of Nature,* 149–81. New York: Routledge, 1991.

Harding, Sandra. Introduction to *Feminism and Methodology: Social Science Issues,* edited by Sandra Harding, 1–15. Bloomington, IN: Indiana University Press, 2013.

Hawisher, Gail E., and Cynthia L. Selfe, eds. *Passions, Pedagogies, and 21st Century Technologies.* Champaign, IL: National Council of Teachers of English, 1999.

Hesford, Wendy S., and Eileen E. Schell. "Introduction: Configurations of Transnationality: Locating Feminist Rhetorics." *College English* 70, no. 5 (May 2008): 461–70.

Kendall, Mikki. *Hood Feminism: Notes from the Women that a Movement Forgot.* New York: Viking, 2020.

Linton, Simi. "What is Disability Studies?" *PMLA: Publications of the Modern Language Association of America* 120, no. 2 (2005): 518–22. https://doi.org/10.1632/S0030812900167823.

McDuffie, Kristi, and Melissa Ames. "Cluster Editor's Introduction: Defining a Feminist Approach to Internet Research and Ethics (Again)." *Peitho* 25, no. 3 (Spring 2023): 94–103.

Moraga, Cherríe, and Gloria Anzaldúa, eds. *This Bridge Called My Back: Writings by Radical Women of Color.* Albany: SUNY Press, 2015.

Nish, Jennifer. *Activist Literacies: Transnational Feminisms and Social Media Rhetorics.* Columbia: University of South Carolina Press, 2022.

Patterson, GPat. "Because Trans People Are Speaking: Notes on Our Field's First Special Issue on Transgender Rhetorics." *Peitho* 22, no. 4 (Summer 2020). https://cfshrc.org/article/because-trans-people-are-speaking-notes-on-our-fields-first-special-issue-on-transgender-rhetorics/.

Price, Margaret. *Mad at School: Rhetorics of Mental Disability and Academic Life.* Ann Arbor, MI: University of Michigan Press, 2011.

Ramírez, Alejandra I., and Ruben Zecena. "'The Dirt Under My Mom's Fingernails': Queer Retellings and Migrant Sensualities." *Constellations* 2, no. 9 (October 2010). https://constell8cr.com/issue-2/the-dirt-under-my-moms-fingernails-queer-retellings-and-migrant-sensualities/.

Rawson, K.J. "Queering Feminist Rhetorical Canonization." In *Rhetorica in Motion: Feminist Rhetorical Methods and Methodologies,* edited by Eileen E. Schell and K.J. Rawson, 39–52. Pittsburgh, PA: University of Pittsburgh Press, 2010.

Richards, Rebecca. *Transnational Feminist Rhetorics and Gendered Leadership in Global Politics: From Daughters of Destiny to Iron Ladies.* Lanham, MD: Lexington Books, 2017.

Riedner, Rachel. *Writing Neoliberal Values: Rhetorical Connectivities and Globalized Capitalism.* New York: Palgrave MacMillan, 2015.

Royster, Jacqueline Jones, and Gesa E. Kirsch. *Feminist Rhetorical Practices: New Horizons for Rhetoric, Composition, and Literacy Studies.* Carbondale, IL: Southern Illinois University Press, 2012.

Russworm, TreaAndrea M., and Samantha Blackmon. "Replaying Video Game History as a Mixtape of Black Feminist Thought." *Feminist Media Histories* 6, no. 1 (2020): 93–118. https://doi.org/10.1525/fmh.2020.6.1.93.

Schell, Eileen E. "Framing the Megarhetorics of Agricultural Development: Industrialized Agriculture and Sustainable Agriculture." In *Megarhetorics of Globalized Development,* edited by J. Blake Scot and Rebecca Dingo. Pittsburgh, PA: University of Pittsburgh Press, 2012.

Selfe, Cynthia L., and Gail E. Hawisher. *Gaming Lives in the Twenty-First Century Literate Connections.* New York: Palgrave, 2007.

Shahin, Saif, Junki Nakahara, and Mariana Sánchez. "Black Lives Matter Goes Global: Connective Action Meets Cultural Hybridity in Brazil, India, and Japan." *New Media & Society* (2021). https://doi.org/10.1177/14614448211105.

SisterSong: Women of Color Reproductive Justice Collection. "About Us." https://www.sistersong.net/about-x2.

SisterSong: Women of Color Reproductive Justice Collection. "What is Reproductive Justice?" https://www.sistersong.net/reproductive-justice.

Steele, Catherine Knight. *Digital Black Feminism.* New York: New York University Press, 2021.

Wang, Bo. "Comparative Rhetoric, Postcolonial Studies, and Transnational Feminisms: A Geopolitical Approach." *Rhetoric Society Quarterly* 43, no. 3 (2013): 226–42.

Wingard, Jennifer. *Branded Bodies, Rhetoric, and the Neoliberal Nation-State.* Lanham, MD: Lexington Books, 2013.

PART I

Reclaiming Space and Centering the Body

The chapters in this first part, "Reclaiming Space and Centering the Body," examine how feminist rhetorical methods and methodologies can be used to dismantle structures of normalcy that have limited who can claim rhetorical agency. Contributors theorize and enact feminist rhetorical methods that center the body and reclaim space while reflecting on what feminist rhetorical methods and methodologies are needed to navigate spaces that may be colonizing, hostile, indifferent, and that threaten erasure. They meditate on how survivance in the face of threatened erasure is key to negotiating institutions in settler colonial spaces (Riley Mukavetz) and how to counteract rhetorical norms in disciplinary discourses by centering Indigenous perspectives (Cedillo). They argue that movement is also key to initiating change—not only through social protest movements—but the movement of BIPOC performers seeking to enact social justice in the artistic medium of dance (Rodrigues). Finally, the contributors in this part reframe what it means to address stigmatization and vilification of bodies that are considered to be mad and to challenge major tenets of the rhetorical tradition while centering the perspectives and experiences of crip-mad activists (madoka currie and Hubrig). Taken together, these chapters offer strategies for transforming spaces to be more conducive to equitable and just rhetorical participation, allowing for resistance, negotiation, and the reshaping of existing power structures.

ONE

An Affinity for Spiky Things

Kwe as Method for Navigating Academic Spaces

Andrea Riley Mukavetz

This Is a Story about Ribbon Skirts

In 2017, I began my second tenure-track job. Making a lateral shift from a position that was supposed to be my ideal, dream job to another institution. Already exquisite at compartmentalizing the trauma and violence that comes with navigating the academic industrial complex, I am honest that this shift will not release me but it is merely an approach to survival. A year into this new position, I begin dreaming about ribbon skirts.

A ribbon skirt is an article of clothing worn by tribal nations women and sometimes two-spirit people. Every tribal nation has their own philosophy to making a ribbon skirt and tribally specific teachings. For the Anishinaabek, our skirts tell a story about women's connection to the land and our roles and responsibilities to our communities as caregivers, providers, and protectors. I dreamed of the real traditional ones with the elastic waist, the calico cotton prints, and just a few ribbons inches above the hem of a skirt.

For the most part, I know that my gifts are as a storyteller and writer. I've tried to make other things but I've never really taken to it. I am not thinking so much about being good at something as these beliefs of success and value are often reflective of capitalism—that our products are made for others to be consumed or purchased. Instead, I am thinking about how one listens to the materials for a teaching. While learning quillwork, my aunty Boni taught me that materials are relatives and they find ways to communicate with us.

I can't stop thinking about ribbon skirts. What stories the colors say, how to lay the ribbons flat and evenly. I dream of butterflies, sturgeon, and canoes for applique. When I sew, I hold needles in my mouth. Boni once cautioned me from holding quills in my mouth. She does it and it's something that has taken her a long time to learn that relationship with the materials. Only those who want to get poked should put sharp things in their mouths, she said to me, once while looking over her glasses. I can't help myself—that's where those needles belong. They are telling me stories. Sometimes, I put a Swisher Sweets cigar in my mouth, unlit, inhaling the sweet tobacco as I sing and sew. This is something I learned from my uncles who used to hold a cigar and a clean lure in their mouths as they fished. I am a part of a long tradition of tribal nations people making knowledge with, from, and alongside the land—our bodies are deeply interconnected with that tradition. I am a part of a legacy of people who just can't seem to take pointy things out of their mouths even though they know they might get poked.

When I arrive at my institution, I learn that I am the only academic Indigenous faculty member on campus. Later, I'll learn that there are two more of us, but I am the only one who is out as Indigenous. Now, we have two full-time Anishinaabekwe staff on campus and one we had to fight like hell to get.

Together, we are three generations of Nish women finding ourselves at every table and poking at every silo at the university. It's after being invited to these tables, often thinking I am around people who are way above my pay grade, that my ribbon skirt dreams come to me. I am told that these dreams come to me because it marks a moment of growth—a change in my role in the community. In 2017, things are not great for Indigenous people at my institution. Indigenous students have little access to community members and do not know of any Indigenous faculty or staff. Because of how data is collected and stored, it's difficult to even know who our students are unless they tell us.

At 40, I've finally had to admit that I am no longer a youngster. Being an in-betweener, I've had to shift my role in my community. Where I still take the time to observe and listen, more and more, I am asked to speak, facilitate, and intervene. *You're the right person to do this, Andrea*—the elders and aunties tell me. The ribbon skirt teaches me how to take up space in academia even when it is exhausting. The ribbon skirt reminds me that I am accountable to every Indigenous student on campus, their families, our communities, the next generation, and always the land.

I am making another ribbon skirt. A gift to an elder who has exited academia. She isn't the first or the last. Lately, I am bearing witness to generations of Indigenous women who exit their chosen professions. Experts in their fields who have changed their institutions but refuse to experience any more harm, are fired, or put on a pathway to retirement. What's common to these stories is how allies, coworkers, and friends who've benefited from the expertise and contributions of these professionals have chosen to not defend these aunties in fear of retaliation, losing popularity, or directing questioning toward themselves.

Bearing witness to this exit—to the harm inflicted onto older generations of women holding ground, using the wisdom gained from their successes and failures to educate the next generation reminds me of how settlers used narrative to contribute to the harm of older Indigenous women. In "The Pocahontas Perplex," Rayna Green provides an ethnographic study of the word "squaw." It connotes images of ugliness in that traditional euro-centric way, like exaggerated facial features. Green explains that we need to consider another perspective to the "squaw:" she serves as an intervention—a disruption of anticipated violence between settlers and young Indigenous women[1] or The Pocahontas, the Tiger Lily. In *Life Stages and Native Women,* Kim Anderson describes how older Indigenous women have always protected younger generations especially children.[2] Parents would literally leave their children in the care of aunties and elders. They watched us as we slept, fed us, and served as our educators, our teachers. Before we felt the impact of settler colonialism, the community made sure aunties and elders were rich with resources, protected even when they provided important critiques regarding diplomacy and peacekeeping, resource sharing, or inappropriate sexual relationships. This additional layer of history which is tied to crucial roles of tribal nations communities were strategically rewritten and visually revised to mock and undermine the role of aunties and elders.

This ribbon skirt is purple tie-dye. It's a working skirt—long and extra flowy so she can harvest medicines. As I make it, I hum. Praying healing into the skirt, re-telling every teaching ever given, thinking about every time she taught me through observation, through bearing witness to her figuring out her own survival tactics. Embedded in each stitch is a promise that she can leave when she's ready—that what she built will remain. One reason why it's so difficult to leave an institutional space and shift roles is the fear of who will step up to tend to the next generation.

It takes me two years to tell her that I was attacked by a coworker and about the retaliation I experienced for demanding accountability. For two years, I listened to her stories—to my friends' stories of pain, trauma, and healing. I said nothing of my own. I cannot. Instead, I made a red ribbon skirt. Red and black for murdered and missing Indigenous women—as a reminder for every time we were treated like squaws: disposable and objectified. I sew flying cranes to remind me that I am free to leave when ready and that I come from a long line of hereditary chiefs—of strong facilitators.

In 2019, a new university president was hired. To welcome her, all leaders from historically underrepresented groups come together for a luncheon. We brought gifts that represent our identity or work on campus. I brought a tobacco pouch (asemaawazh) and a lecture. This was a difficult moment for the Indigenous women on campus because we were beginning a new academic year weary from years of tension, harm, exploitation, and feelings of failure for not advocating for visibility and resources. This is what I said to her:

> There are three Indigenous women running the university to ensure that Indigenous students are recruited and retained, that faculty are held accountable and guided regarding Indigenous content. We are showing up in meetings across institutional silos to share our input and expertise. We are not just staff and faculty but we are the aunties of the community and institution. If the university messes up, she nor GVSU [Grand Valley State University] people will hear about it—we will. The community will approach us and we will be asked to address it and to fix it. We will be held accountable by a set of rules and practices external to the institution but reflective of Anishinaabek governance.

She nods her head. I provide her with the asemaa and tell her I am looking forward to working with her. I sit down next to my Anishinaabekwe coworker who rubs my shoulders and says, "You go, my girl."

We are the aunties that no one likes because we form deliberate positions to enact critique, form strategic relationships, and demand accountability to imagine better futures for the next generation. We make our failures, successes, and mistakes visible as teachings for the next generation so we can show them how to do the work once we are gone. It is the responsibility of our accomplices, relatives, coworkers, and community to shield us and provide resources to educate and nurture the next generation.

Responding to the Call

Relatives,

I was drawn to this call because the editors asked about productive engagement. The editors posed, "How can feminist rhetorical methods and methodologies foster productive engagement with our social and material worlds?" After years of being in the academy, I have rarely experienced or felt productive engagement. I couldn't stop grappling with this question because I so rarely experience what feels like productive engagement. Instead, it felt like contentious relationships and non-consensual interactions. Too often, I have been in meetings with settlers both well-meaning and not who cite their feminist positionalities or their commitment to social justice work. They use this language to ignore the strategic boundaries of women of color and Indigenous women in the name of serving the institution.

In this essay, I want to dwell on the cultural implications of productive engagement. To aid my approach, I draw upon both AnaLouise Keating and Patricia Roberts-Miller who have written about what happens when our subject position guides our approach to communication and decision making. When leaning on Keating, Roberts-Miller, and the wisdom of Anishinaabekwe (Anishinaabe) women for guidance on creating spaces for productive engagement, I can make visible the stuckness that I felt when trying to process the call by editors.

In *Transformation Now!*, Keating examines how one responds to oppression. As Keating notes, we react oppositionally as in if you do not share my worldview or subject position then you are against me. This rhetorical strategy reflects a century of activism and coalition work to challenge systematic oppression and social injustices. Yet, Keating argues that this approach is no longer useful because it creates an oppositional consciousness that "represents a binary either/or epistemology and a praxis that structures our perceptions, politics, and actions through a resistant energy—a reaction against that which we seek to transform."[3] Admittedly, Keating deeply challenges the stories I tell about my lived experiences in academia—in the world. Where I am someone who always strives for compromise—for consensus, I am damn tired. This fatigue can allow for a comfortable and reliable argumentation but not one that leads to productive relationships or strategic thinking. Too often, I fantasize about burning everything to the ground and Keating has yet to fully convince me that fraught spaces like academia shouldn't burn. Yet, as Anishinaabekwe, I understand the importance of pausing before judgment, of observation, and a willingness to listen to aunties. In the narrative approach that Keating discourages, it is familiar to cast me as the victor, the expert, the hero, or the badass auntie. It's easier to frame the people in these stories as The Racist, The Sexist, or the arms of the Evil Administration. I am not interested in easy stories and relationships. I'm interested in the stories and relationships that cause pain, anger, joy, laughter, and grief. By making the spiky, painful stories visible and interrogating them—teachings for action, empathy, understanding, and relational accountability become present.

From studying and experiencing the narrative approaches of settler colonialism, I understand the political, social, and cultural profit of oppositional narratives. To further explain this, I lean on Patricia Roberts-Miller's analysis of demagoguery. Roberts-Miller explains that the Us vs. Them framework is a central component of demagoguery. Demagoguery, according to Roberts-Miller, breaks the rules of public discourse.[4] It relies on identity to reject or listen to arguments. Where Roberts-Miller examines demagoguery within politics and public discourse, I believe that academics can learn a lot about this framework especially as our communities grow smaller, our access to each other is easier, and more of us become invested in challenging social injustices and systematic oppression. Keating acknowledges this challenge to academics directly by focusing on argumentation. She writes, "I attribute these limitations to the underlying binary systems on which our oppositional framework defines reality—and, by extension, knowledge, ethics, and truth—in limited, mutually exclusive terms. In this either/or system, we have only two options: Either *I'm* right and I win, or *you're* right and you win."[5] Whether we identify as feminist rhetoricians, cultural rhetoricians, or critical race theorists, our identities as scholars and activists are entrenched in righting wrongs, making space for new possibilities for rhetorical knowledge, and challenging the social injustices that occur within our discipline, home institutions, and the world. Where I am all for disagreements, productive critiques, and extending rhetorical knowledge especially for the most resilient and systematically ignored communities, I want us to consider how we use our identities and subject positions—the ones we often consider to be on the right side of justice—and perhaps, how those rhetorical strategies reflect settler colonialism and white supremacy. I invoke this consideration to you all, dear relatives, as well as to myself.

One solution to demagoguery, according to Roberts-Miller, is to enact democratic deliberation, which includes having capacity to admit one is wrong. She emphasizes that good disagreements are important and necessary to democracy. Like Keating, she encourages readers to admit when we are wrong and when we make mistakes. When I put Keating and Roberts-Miller in conversation with each other, I come to understand that for us to have productive engagement is a part of radically transforming society—of transforming academia (or, at least being able to thrive and not simply survive in the toxic academic industrial complex). This, relatives, is where I want to dwell. To listen to the advice of these scholars as I share teachings from my own lived experience navigating academic spaces and provide them as an offering to understanding why I still pause when prompted to engage—productively with you all—with my colleagues, friends, family. For me, as someone who is often the only person like myself in the room, who writes to affirm Anishinaabek and educate non-Native people, I am often stuck in feeling like I am in tension or opposition to others. Often when explaining the making of Indigenous space, there is an assumption that I am attempting an exclusionary politic. Instead of my using this exclusionary politic, I invite you to think about the complexity of belonging and the shared work of creating space while respecting boundaries and invitations. To make Indigenous space is a collaborative effort across communities and institutional spaces. No matter how much we wish it could be just us, it cannot. We live in this paracolonial occupied land. We need to choose each other as relatives and kin to imagine liberatory futures. But to do this, we have to establish some boundaries around how we understand belonging and access. There are three turns in this story that make up the practices of taking up space—survivance, resurgence, and cultural continuance. I choose to tell this in this order. But, make no mistake, these are cyclical and interconnected.

This Is a Story about Survivance

I am a cultural rhetorician. A sub-field of engagement that I have been told repeatedly is a trendy and niche topic. I have spent my entire educational life deeply struggling in higher education. I have never been smart enough, a good writer, or a proper theorist. My scholarship is easy. It's pandering. It's tokenizing. It's profiting off of my niche identity. At least, this is what some people say. But, I do not need their approval. I do not write for them. It took coming to cultural and Indigenous rhetorics to write just that. Before, I struggled to understand what it meant to contribute and participate in a profession. I didn't know how to belong. For me, cultural and Indigenous rhetorics as a form of knowledge making is a story about survivance. After all, survivance is a key practice and embodied state of being for Indigenous people navigating the ongoing impacts of colonialism. To enact survivance is to simultaneously make decisions that ensure survival for oneself or the next generation as well as resisting current colonial practices. It is a decision to seek culturally affirming ways of being while also resisting the kinds of stories and frameworks that create hostility and fragility.

In a previous position, I was hired to teach non-western and decolonial ways of thinking in a doctoral program. I thought it was my dream job. I entered into a program where feminist frameworks and methodologies were reinforced and centered. We all thought that our orientations to rhetoric would be complementary. Instead, my presence made visible the absence of Indigenous visibility—the presence of the settler fragility. The graduate students hated me. My evaluations were terrible—at times, students lied. Other times, they would write really anti-Indigenous responses like "(they) felt they were missionaries and were being invaded by Indigenous ideas in the classroom." Most of the time, they simply checked out and during the seminar would work on other materials. They would go to the faculty and say I yelled at them, pounded the table, or was not organized. Those evaluations—those teaching experiences haunted me. But what made it even worse was that I would go to my colleagues asking for help—expressing feelings of discrimination. Yet, my coworkers were unwilling to believe my experience through that framework. After all, they had excellent experiences with the same students. The problem was me. Admittedly, I had a lot to learn about facilitating graduate seminars. Yet, there wasn't a space for me to grow as a teacher while receiving the necessary support to address this climate. Instead, I was advised to develop a following of graduate students. I needed to simply be a better teacher—more nurturing, more organized, more transparent.

Throughout all of this, my coworkers and I did the best we could. They planned baby showers for me. I celebrated their scholarship and awards. We laughed together and commiserated. Yet, the harm I experienced continued. As I did not receive the support I needed—things became tense and worse. These relationships ceased to exist. I had to leave—find a way out because this dream job turned out to be far from it. To survive is to know when to leave—to end things. It is this kind of experience that leads me to parse through a description of productive engagement that makes visible the challenges that come with it.

My presence as a cultural and Indigenous rhetorician—as someone from mixed, non-European ancestry serves as critique, as reminder of settler colonialism and how it operates even through well-meaning, social justice minded scholars. The knowledge I create—the knowledge I carry forth is culturally contested. It asks a lot of people outside of my social group. To bring this into academia and seek to form relationships with others— critique and tension needs to be negotiated. I ask, "what do we do when well-meaning folks determine your experience isn't an act of settler hostility?" I share this story because our profession can be divisive when it comes to "alternative rhetorics." We've all heard scholars describe these traditions as a game of identity politics. How can there be productive engagement when there cannot be consensus on one's reality—on one's approach to knowledge? When there is not a shared framework for lived experiences—for what knowledge and realities are believed—then the engagement falters. It creates more tension.

This Is a Story about Cultural Continuance

My current university does not have a Native Studies program. Most likely, we will never have one. It's just me walking the halls in my ribbon skirts writing bibliographies of Indigenous scholarship to share with faculty and students. I have made a few requests for collaboration and after these discussions, I am unwilling to sacrifice my body/mind to create it. There are typical classes in History and Anthropology *on* Indigenous people. These are complicated for all the reasons I just said and didn't. In the beginning of this story, there is not one course centering Indigenous worldviews and histories taught by an Indigenous person. The messaging we get from the academic community—from students is that there is a particular kind of pain to take a course about Indigenous content taught by a settler. There's a particular pain due to having to admit authority to a settler about your ancestors' histories and lived experiences. To be evaluated, to be graded, to be expected to teach and collaborate when navigating the loneliness of being the only Native person in a classroom space. This is not how we learn. We learn on the land guided by elders, cousins, niblings, and aunties. We learn through observation. Like that important scene in *Reservation Dogs,* "just get out there and learn, fucker."[6] In "Land as pedagogy," this is what Leanne Simpson offers as she tells a story about Kwezens who learns to tap sugar: "The process of coming to know is learner-led and profoundly spiritual in nature. Coming to know is the pursuit of whole-body intelligence practiced in the context of freedom, and, when realized collectively, it generates generations of loving, creative, innovative, self-determining, inter-dependent and self-regulating community minded individuals. It creates communities of individuals with the capacity to uphold and move forward our political traditions and systems of governance."[7] As I continue to tell this story, I hope you hold on to these keywords of freedom, governance, and the description of generations. Anishinaabeg pedagogy–Anishinaabekwe worldviews promises a different future—a different methodology that is counterintuitive to the academic industrial complex.

For the next generation, for myself, for the community, I create a course called Anishinaabek Lifeways. This course tells the story of Anishinaabek through the nation-state created boundaries of Michigan. It tells the story of Anishinaabek past, present, and future without being solely a story about the interplay of Anishinaabek and settlers. This course values Anishinaabeg pedagogy that is land-based and consensual. I want to teach them what Simpson describes about learning. Since this pedagogy is consensual, I ask "do you want to do some foraging and harvesting? I want to show you the ravines and the paw paw trees."

They all say yes. During the planning, we discuss accommodations and mobility. It's a two-mile walk down ravines with no accessible path. Before this, I've walked these ravines dozens of times with friends, coworkers, and my husband and our children. The ravines are technically campus land and also connect to a county park and a training area for the crew team. It's also the sacred, ancestral land of the Odawas. This part of Grand River tells a story of their migration, where they set their camps up, and how they practiced agriculture and diplomacy. Like a good Michigan September, it's wet so we wait. It rains for weeks with loud booming thunder. So, I assign some reading instead. I assign Matthew Fletcher's *The Eagle Returns: The Legal History of the Grand Traverse Band of Ottawa and Chippewa Indians*. We dedicate two classes to understanding the Treaty of Washington and examine the complexity of Anishinaabek governance. It's a significant treaty because it ceded 1/3 of what is Anishinaabek land to Michigan and led to Michigan becoming a state. We talk about gender roles, consensus, and Indian Agents in the process of treaty making. We read Andrew Blackbird, William Warren and George Copway who wrote during the nineteenth century and cover the history of Anishinaabe peoples. I ask everyone, *do you see your ancestors here? I can see mine.*

What does it mean to read a book on the history of a place—a story where everyone knows how it ends except the author? They find their ancestors in these texts. All of them: settlers and Indigenous students. They identify the beliefs, the practices, and the survivance strategies that have allowed them all to be on what remains Indigenous land even if that land base is no longer the same. There's a lot of grieving in this process but also joy. For example, a Grand Traverse student learns that a fishing practice his relatives taught him is not just a weird thing his family does but a documented strategy for fishing in the deepest parts of Lake Michigan. We learn why Torch Lake is called Torch Lake.

It's a beautiful day for paw paw harvesting. It's the end of September— warm and sunny. I grab my harvesting knife, asemaa, and a bag. I go first to set a pace. In the five weeks we've spent together, I've learned that this group of students includes experienced foragers, food sovereignty activists, and water protectors. I ask them to help me tell the story of these ravines through what they experience. We establish that no one can eat anything that is not approved by the designated experts first. I show them how to identify poison ivy because I promised my dean that no one would get poison ivy or cut themselves on this trip.

We stop to admire the black walnuts and talk about how to process them. Students gather the walnuts laughing at the stain on their fingers. We stop to admire the autumn olives. I tell them to taste them and then tell a story about the Department of Natural Resources attempting to manage deer and birds through the autumn olive, hoping that will detract from the agriculture in the area during the 1970s. I laugh and tell them that the deer and birds hate autumn olive, but it makes good fruit leather. This story was gifted to me by my foraging instructor who also loves autumn olive.

The students are anxious to find fruit. I show them how to shake the trees. *Step over the poison ivy,* I remind them. Some students shake the trees while others have the responsibility to see where the food drops and retrieve it. We shake a few trees, hold our breath while waiting to listen for the drop of fruit. We shake the trees instead of picking because this is one way to determine if the fruit is ripe. If we pick the paw paws when they are not ready, there is a small chance they will ripen on their own. No sounds except black walnuts falling and squirrels yelling at us. Immediately, I worry that this activity will bear no fruit. I cannot tell you the pleasure of hearing groups of students draw their breath in anticipation and then cheer and clap when fruit drops. Listening and watching them work together to identify and find fruit. They bring me what they find and I cut slices to share. Fingers sticky and sweet from overripe fruit. We discuss if it tastes more like a pear or a banana. One Native student, a Cherokee, shrugs his shoulders and says "it's alright" and walks away as 10 Nish students throw him death glares and cackle. We get to the end of the trail where the trees begin to thin, where the black walnut trees are replaced by hazelnut, and it opens to a drop off site for the crew team. We stand at the docks and I ask them to imagine what this space would be like before the university. I ask them to try to block out the sounds of cars and trucks and the smell of diesel from Lake Michigan Road and imagine dozens of fires set up.

I pull out my tobacco and the Native students gather around. I tell the class, we're going to provide our offering, and explain that they can watch or give us space. For a few Native students, this is their first opportunity to learn this teaching or they are so far away from their ancestral land they haven't been near this kind of practice in at least two years. Even as Anishinaabekwe, I still am choked up at the idea of watching this generation of Anishinaabek stand at the river offering prayers and inviting them. I don't know if they realize that this is exactly what Blackbird, Copway, and Warren hoped would happen.

I struggle agreeing that the Treaty of Washington ceded Anishinaabek land because to cede something implies willingness and consent. There cannot be consent to a decision, a policy, a practice, a relationship if one feels threatened—if every decision they make is intended to support the next seven generations. Drawing from Powell, Konkle, and Brooks, nineteenth century Indigenous intellectuals teach us something about the complicated decisions they had to make to survive during a time frame when they were literally writing for their survival. As I have learned from Fletcher's analysis of the Treaty of Washington, many Anishinaabek did not want to sign that treaty which resulted in a rift in our own confederacy. For those who signed, they did so because of what they feared if they didn't. They wanted a permanent land base, excluded the possibility of removal to the west, and hunting and fishing rights. As Fletcher writes, "No treaty is valid under American law until the Senate ratifies it, and so the Senate rewrote Articles 2 and 3 to limit the reservations to five years, and to provide the optional removal of Indian communities. . . ."[8]

As Fletcher observes, Article 13, which had no time limit and therefore was considered permanent, on tribal hunting, fishing, gathering, and other rights "until the land was required for settlement" is what brought about acquiescence to these changes.[9] In other words, the chosen leaders, ogemuk went to the table again and again to ensure good faith in the treaty. They objected. They compromised but ultimately didn't get what they fought for because they were not present for the changes made by the Senate. This is not a story of consensual cession but of reluctantly agreeing to something due to fear, threat, exhaustion, and the inability to come to consensus. In many ways, this is what it feels like to make Indigenous space in higher education. Few times does a win feel like a win if we're met with ongoing resistance, reluctance, lack of transparency, skepticism, or proving that we're worthy enough of resources.

I tell this story because I am coming to terms with the fact that I will most likely never be able to start a Native Studies program at my university. Instead, there will just be this course that will run once a year. Hopefully, it will fill. The rest of the courses related to Indigenous content will be taught by non-experts. Hopefully, I will stay. In this scenario, we make the space we can when we are left with few options, when well-meaning allies are only willing to do so much. I cannot convince my colleagues—the leadership to invest in something they do not think is deserving of resources. I have learned—the hard way—that consent goes both ways. No matter how deserving I think the community is—or how ethically right it is, an appeal can only go so far. So, I take pleasure in these moments of land-based relationships, of showing students the paw paw trees, and remembering the way it felt when a student told me I was the first person to teach her how to offer asemaa. We will continue on, for us, regardless.

This Is a Story on Resurgence

There is a prophecy of the seven generations. Many tribal nations have a version of it. The Anishinaabeg as well. There are two parts to it. The first part relates to governance and the cyclical understanding of time and relationships. Every decision we make, we consider the seven generations who came before us: we consider the actions, histories, experiences, and struggles of those who came before us—what they sacrificed, what they left unfinished. We make decisions considering the seven generations after us—to make sure that what we decide is sustainable. The next part, I will not say too much about because there are aspects of sacred knowledge I do not want to share. But, to summarize, there's a prophecy related to the impact of colonialism. Of these seven generations each has a different experience with colonialism. The seventh generation is the generation who will rise up and begin a new journey. Some believe we are in the 8th fire. Others believe we are not quite in the 7th. Either or any way, the point of this knowledge share is context. It's to explain how resurgence is central to taking up Indigenous space. And, it's not pretty. As Simpson writes on the relationship between Kwe and resurgence, she explains, "At its core, kwe as method is about refusal. It is about refusing colonial domination, refusing heteropatriarchy, and refusing to be tamed by whiteness or the academy."[10] As Anishinaabekwe, as someone in my aunty years, I think a lot about what it means to participate in refusal as resurgence—how refusal does not always mean walking away or an unwillingness to collaborate but a reorientation to what and who is being centered. Within refusal, within resurgence, I believe there to be a teaching on productive engagement with, for, and alongside Indigenous people.

I am asked to teach a service-learning course called "Wicked Problems of Sustainability." I have told part of this story before in my interview on *Pedagogue:* I collaborated with an environmental organization who wanted me to consult for them on their strategic mission related to decoloniality. We agree that we will do that work, together, in this course. I will consult and they will attend class and work with Environmental Studies majors offering them professional pathways. As a class, we examine settler colonialism and environmental racism as a "wicked problem" and seek guidance from systematically oppressed communities who engage in justice and advocacy work. I emphasize, again and again, the cycle of benevolence that comes with service-learning and how we are choosing another path.

Spending the semester listening to this organization's work, their relationships, their challenges, the students look to me and say, "Dr. RM, we can't advise them to do decolonial work. They aren't ready and we are not sure they have the commitment or connections." In their presentation, they address this and offer narrative writing strategies and actions to enact settler harm reduction. I share this because the students drew from Simpson to affirm their strategy of refusal as reorientation: from decolonial to settler harm reduction.

Months later, students from the class drop by my office to say, "we have an idea about land repatriation, will you help us?" Like requests from elders, I can't say no to a group of students invested in changing an institution. All Environmental Studies majors who belong to student groups like the Farm Club or the Student Environmental Coalition realized the relationship between settler colonialism and environmental conservation in our class. They want to do something around sugar bush and maple syrup but the community members and Indigenous students decline and tell them that they really want an agricultural space for their own use and ceremonies.

We imagine a teaching lodge for Native American Student Affairs (NASA) to use, to receive community teachings, and be able to smudge without enduring remarks about how a classroom smells like dank weed or having a fire marshal knocking on the door. They want gardens so they can grow their own medicine and foods. It's a beautiful dream reflective of both the loneliness of what it means to be so far away from community while knowing that there is community near them invested in their successes and educational journeys. I could never, ever imagine making a request like this to my own institution especially at the age of 20. This is something I've come to realize in my aunty years: the appreciation, the joy, the challenge of bearing witness to a younger generation stronger, braver, and more tactical than the one before. Again, a group of young people teaching older generations how to re-establish boundaries by expressing needs through relationships and observations.

It takes almost two years of planning including supervising internships, requesting community feedback, securing funding, and writing a formal proposal with 12 students. We receive approval from the Advisory Council and our dean. We have our lodge builders scheduled for summer but are told we cannot build yet. What we didn't anticipate was how this proposal would be received by Facilities Service and General Council. We literally did not include them in our intended audience. Legal council is concerned that this project will violate the Michigan affirmative action law that states public institutions cannot show preference for one race over another. Facilities Service doesn't understand that Anishinaabek have our own technologies and engineering practices. They say things in meetings like "how do you know it won't blow over and hurt a student during a high wind alert?"

The Nish women and I do our aunty thing and through education. We ask pointed questions like "do you have the same concern with pop up tents for graduation?" We explain the technology of saplings and how, like all cultures, we adapt and use contemporary technologies. Our dean, aware—even through Zoom—of the offensiveness of this question remarks that wigwams and lodges are ancient technologies that have been used successfully over time. This doesn't satisfy Facilities. They will only approve of this project by refusing responsibility or a role in the project.

We meet with a local lawyer who specializes in tribal law and Indigenous rights about the affirmative action situation. For free, she confirms that there is no violation because Indigenous people are not a race but sovereign nations. At the same time, the university is investing millions of dollars into special programs and spaces for veterans.

My dean advises me to rewrite components of the proposal. He knows I am not thrilled by this request. We also know that if I do not agree the proposal will not be approved. He assigns a staff person to support my case by researching models of Indigenous space at peer institutions. I request written feedback from both Facilities and Council on the actual areas of the proposal that do not meet their policies. It's easy changes but changes that hurt, like taking out language around land repatriation or that the internship we designed is specifically for an Indigenous student. I'm a good enough rhetorician to say what needs to be said while still getting what I want. What feels especially poignant is that the settler students who initiated this project never expected to be a part of the product. They wanted to help create space and use their privilege and connections without benefiting from it. This is a rare and exceptional belief that few hold when collaborating with Indigenous people. For the most part, the aunties keep the Indigenous students out of this part of the conversation. It's already too painful for us to participate in. This is often the complexity of Anishinaabeg teaching: when is the pain too much for the younger generation to bear? When can they learn from our pain to learn the necessary strategies to keep fighting?

Before the meeting, there have been multiple exchanges between leadership and council. We have our meeting and the lead council who expressed concerns is not present. We learn that the Legal is already aware that we are not in violation of policy but they want to be extra cautious. I dwell on this idea of the costs of caution, of rejecting one group's needs for empowerment, growth, and education for the sake of not showing preference.

We are unsurprised. As I press on this, my dean gently pulls me back and asks me if I am willing to go through with the suggestions. I've already written revisions to the language and sent them to the aunties and lodge builders requesting their permission and input. We shift. We anticipate. We prepare.

We get our approval but by the time that this occurs the lodge team needs to move on. There are other communities waiting on them. We find another lodge team, but we won't be able to build for another year. I take one of the builders to the farm and we walk the land. My daughters are running around poking their faces through plants and letting me know there aren't any snakes. The farm manager welcomes us and gives the girls a bucket to pick beans. The builder and I talk for a long time. As we walk through the land, he picks raspberries and pops them in his mouth remarking on the sweetness. I pull sour cherries from the trees and suck the flesh from the pit.

How does one navigate an institution that has a centuries-old repertoire of colonial rhetorical practices to rely on? What makes these practices so troubling and dangerous is how easy it is to identify both the long-term success of these practices AND how they have changed and adapted as settler colonialism, white supremacy, transphobia, ableism continues to adapt.

I can identify every practice, every tactic that has been used to justify external and internal colonization that has been used against me as I try to make Indigenous space—I feel my own disempowerment through every time I settle the settlers. It feels so similar—too similar to those nineteenth century survivance practices around land and education. I make a treaty knowing that there will be concessions later on.

In June, we build. It's incredible. There are about thirty of us from all over the institution, from across the state of Michigan. Grandmas come. There are infants nursing. My job is to organize, to facilitate, and to make sure everyone is fed. The soil is difficult to manage. We make jokes about how our ancestors would never pick this land to build a lodge. Of course, we would get the plat with the most difficult soil to dig. We have a ceremony. We sing songs. We thank the water. We receive so many teachings. During this time, the institution leaves us alone. The farm manager stops by to help for a bit. The director stops by to mow the lawn for us. We exchange gifts. They let us be. It takes two days and over 20 hours of nonstop labor to build this lodge. My children are laughing and climbing the lodge. I pause because I know in some spaces this would not be allowed. The builder says to me, "Let them. We can't let the next generation be afraid of our practices or they will not continue them." I tuck that teaching away and hold on to it.

I recall another conversation that the builder and I had when we walked the land together. I had asked if he was willing to include the non-Indigenous students and staff in parts of the construction of the lodge. He told me that at the end of the day, we welcome the people who show up to do the work and have a commitment to the community or nothing will ever get done. He says to me, this is an Anishinaabeg practice. Making Indigenous space, no matter how much we might want it to be just us, includes everyone. Returning to Keating, she writes that in oppositional politics, "There's no room for contradiction (*we're both right, even though our views seems strikingly differently*); for overlapping perspectives and friendly disagreements (*we're both partially right and partially wrong*); for the building of new truths (*let's take your perspective, my perspective, and at least one more perspective and develop several synergistic alternatives—new perspectives!*). . . ."[11] For me, this last story helps me re-build an understanding of productive engagement that addresses the stickiness and pain I parsed through prior. Productive engagement is culturally situated, relational, and an ongoing navigating of boundaries and consent *and* when adding additional layers of settler colonialism and white supremacy, it can hurt—really hurt throughout the process depending on who one seeks engagement with. For me, it took a long time to both remember that pain as a teaching while also letting it go. Instead, I focus on the way the saplings felt while trying to not so gently bend them, the laughter of children running around the lodge, and the way everyone consumed the wild rice soup I made for lunch.

As I end this story share, I am worried that this last story about resurgence and refusal doesn't appear to be as much refusal as it felt. I am worried that you, dear readers, might be like "Andrea, girl, I expected a refusal to colonial domination." Remember, dear relatives, in this story, I am not the hero or the badass auntie. They are not the arms of the evil institution. I cannot refuse colonial domination because we all live in an ongoing colonial nightmare. I could have refused to agree to the administration's terms. I could have had another foresight and refused the request from the students. From an Anishinaabekwe framework, that didn't feel right. It didn't reflect the teachings and communities I serve. Instead, refusal felt more like refusing to give up while learning about my boundaries. It was a refusal to carry that pain and instead, I transformed it to something else: cultural continuance, survivance, and joy for making the space I crave—the community desires. It was a refusal to allow a few difficult meetings to shadow the beauty of productive engagement. Refusal can be a strong no. It can also be a reorientation, a compromise, or a willingness to admit differences while moving forward. It can also be a space to navigate contradiction hoping for a collaboration that feels nuanced, relational, and a willingness to learn and grow together.

NOTES

1. Green, "The Pocahontas Perplex."
2. Anderson, *Life Stages*.
3. Keating, *Transformation*, 2.
4. Roberts-Miller, *Demagoguery*.
5. Keating, *Transformation*, 5–6.
6. Harjo, Sterlin, Chad Charlie, and Taika Waititi, writers. *Reservation Dogs*. Season 2, episode 3, "Roofing." Directed by Erica Tremblay, featuring Devery Jacobs, D'Pharaoh Woon-A-Tai, and Lane Factor. Aired August 10, 2022. https://www.hulu.com/watch/6ce54e07-c474-4512-8499-794890bbbea4.
7. Simpson, "Land," 7.
8. Fletcher, *The Eagle*, 27.
9. Fletcher, *The Eagle*, 27.
10. Simpson, "Land," 34.
11. Keating, *Transformation*, 6.

WORKS CITED

Anderson, Kim. *Life Stages and Native Women: Memory, Teachings, and Story Medicine.* Winnipeg: University of Manitoba Press, 2011.

Fletcher, Matthew. *The Eagle Returns: The Legal History of the Grand Traverse Band of Ottawa and Chippewa Indians.* East Lansing: Michigan State University Press, 2012.

Green, Rayna. "The Pocahontas Perplex: The Image of Indian Women in American Culture." *Massachusetts Review* 16, no. 4 (Autumn 1975): 698–714.

Keating, AnaLouise. *Transformation Now! Toward a Post-Oppositional Politics of Change.* Champaign, IL: University of Illinois Press, 2012.

Roberts-Miller, Patricia. *Demagoguery and Democracy.* New York: The Experiment, 2017.

Simpson, Leanne Betasamosake. "Land as Pedagogy: Nishnaabeg Intelligence and Rebellious Transformation." *Decolonization: Indigeneity, Education & Society* 3, no. 3 (2014). 1–25.

TWO

Movement as Method

Deciphering the Spells of Ananya Dance Theatre

Nelesi Rodrigues

In 2021, as part of my dissertation research, I travelled to the Twin Cities to attend one of Ananya Dance Theatre's (ADT) Summer Dance Intensives. One of those days, ADT dancers invited me to join them for a community event outside the Intensive's programming: the inauguration of Midway Peace Park, a public space in St. Paul, Minnesota near the Shawngram Institute for Performance and Social Justice, ADT's physical home.[1] The opening of that park was a result of community-organizing efforts in the area. ADT contributed to the Midway Peace Park celebration with a choreopoem by Ananya Chatterjea (ADT's founder and director) that doubled as a blessing for the space and the people who had brought and continue to bring it to life.[2] When the time came, ADT dancers and I walked to the center of the park and began a demonstration of the choreopoem as we invited everyone present to join us with their movements, their words, their intentions. We performed the choreopoem three times:

Here

we honor life-force/
connect ancestral lines/ the history in this soil

We hold space / for tears and joy/
Weave our people together

We invite in/ our braided futures/
Reach towards the light

In solidarity and shared breath
we invoke
renewal/
justice/
healing/
joy

may it be so.

A series of moves landed these words in our bodies and invited our full presence then and there: Walking around in a circle to take in the place where we stood. Feeling our feet on the ground and our bodies' full weight as we stood still, then lowered our centers of gravity. Materializing threads and roots as we moved our arms, stretching them up and out to one side, then down and out to the other. Making room in our bodies for that moment by opening our torsos to each side, letting the sunshine come in through our ribs. Manifesting renewal, justice, healing, and joy by bringing our bodies down and up, as if digging to plant seeds that then grew towards the sun.

Each iteration of the choreopoem performance gathered more attention from people scattered around the park. I could feel each word and gesture gain power from our collective holding of them through focused witnessing, through collective movement, through shared emotion. Knowing that *it may be so*—if we keep moving like this.

Between 2020 and 2023, I conducted interviews and participant observation with ADT, a BIPOC organization doing social justice choreography grounded in a transnational feminist and diasporic framework—the meanings of which I discuss in this piece. Yorchhā is the name of ADT's unique movement technique developed by Ananya Chatterjea. The vignette above illustrates something that interested me since my initial conversations with members of the ADT community: The company's approach to movement and the dance pedagogy resulting from it play a key role in how artists rely on physical movement for invention in dance and in life. During interviews, ADT dance practitioners often shared stories where Yorchhā lessons overflowed the dance floor into everyday life. They spoke about this movement technique in relation to gender identity and expression, navigating difficult relationships, and personal journeys to decolonize one's ways of living.

Increasingly, I wanted to know: (1) How might a transnational feminist and diasporic framework shape creative movement and its meaning?

(2) How might creative movement facilitate transnational feminist theorizing? And (3) What could scholars in rhetoric and composition learn from ADT's ways of moving?[3] To answer these questions, I situate my work in the context of BIPOC feminist rhetoricians who have attended to the role of embodiment in rhetoric, and amid discussions about the disciplinary location(s) of invention. Then, I share three mo(ve)ments from my time with ADT that animate how creative movement and transnational feminisms inform each other in ADT's pedagogy, and how this pedagogy in turn shapes dancers' inventions. Throughout, I place ADT movements in conversation with contemporary theories on rhetorical invention. These mo(ve)ments, I contend, illuminate how embodiment and movement can support a way of inventing that is intentional, political, and deeply relational. I close the chapter with reflections on movement as method.

Invention in the Diaspora and "at Home"

In a 2002 essay titled "Rhetorical Invention: The Diaspora," Janice Lauer declared invention's disciplinary exodus. After being the motor behind a significant corpus of scholarship in composition and rhetoric between the 1960s and the 1990s, she stated, "invention today can be found in a diaspora of composition areas rather than in discussions labeled 'invention.'"[4] In the introduction to the edited collection that contains Lauer's essay, Janet Atwill provokes readers with a series of related questions: "Why does the metaphor of migration seem such an apt description of invention? Is there something in the character of invention that makes it prone to migrate? Or is there something in the institution that makes invention ill at ease?"[5] When I read Atwill's questions, I wonder: How do diasporic theories of invention depart from "more institutional" (read white, male) ones?

Lauer's choice of the word "diaspora" resounds with implications. Diasporas are forced migrations; they are prompted by hardship. Among invention's diasporic locations, Lauer included writing across disciplines/curriculum; public contexts and cultural studies; studies of gender, race, and cultural difference; and theories of technologies. It is no coincidence that some of these locations were founded by Black feminists and other marginalized scholars. Lauer suggested that theories of invention in the diaspora could make the field "sensitive to cultural, gender, and racial differences."[6] However, at the time she lamented that these "diasporic advances" in rhetorical invention had not resulted in more pedagogical tools and guides.

When I read "Rhetorical Invention: The Diaspora" more than twenty years after its original publication, I recognize in Lauer's overview some pedagogical tools and guides that feminist rhetoricians (and BIPOC feminist rhetoricians in particular) have increasingly (re)claimed and cultivated as part of their research and teaching praxes. For instance, commenting on Judith Langer's research on Writing Across the Curriculum (WAC), she mentions that teachers in biology, history, and literature "were increasingly focusing on the tentative nature of 'truth' and emphasizing active questioning and interpretation."[7] And in her overview of research in cultural, gender, and race studies, she identifies attention to intersectionality, relationality, collaboration, dialogue, use of storytelling and the personal, nonlinearity, viscerality, and embodiment as distinctive contributions to invention. Some of these have made their way back to rhetoric and composition, as the work of Aja Martinez, Karma Chávez, Jo Hsu, and Louis Maraj—just to give a few examples—illustrate. Like other diasporas, once people and ideas leave, it does not mean they never return. It does mean that "home" is forever changed.

Recent works from rhetoric and composition establish connections between movement and invention. Cory Holding examines the work of John Bulwer's manuals about rhetorical gestures that consider expressions of the hand as "rhetoric-in-formation."[8] In his discussion of the role that environments play on invention, Thomas Rickert foregrounds the connection that Indra McEwen makes between "*chōra*" and the Greek words for dance (*choron*) and dance floor (*choros*)—movement and/in place.[9] Jennifer LeMesurier finds invention at the hinge of language and movement in formal dance education settings. Krista Ratcliffe's notion of "interpretive invention" introduces listening as an embodied and relational practice central to discussions on invention. And Karma Chávez doubles down on the link between invention and relations in her discussion of how coalitional subjectivities expand inventional possibilities. This chapter argues that the geographic, political, and creative layers of movement often get enmeshed, and that understanding and attending to these entanglements is key to contemporary ways of inventing.

From Theory of the Flesh to Movement as Method

During the nine years that I lived as an international graduate student and a "non-resident alien" in the United States, I became acutely aware of how my movements were in many ways restricted. To keep my legal status, I needed to carefully comply with migratory regulations about how long and under what conditions I could remain within or outside certain national borders.

Having a passport from Venezuela, a country with virtually non-existent diplomatic relations with the United States, made it always hard and sometimes impossible for me to travel abroad. A complex humanitarian crisis in the country where I grew up made it increasingly difficult for me to return "home," to the point that I can only conceive of this word within air quotes. But let me be clear—I was able to plan my migration, and my experience of movement is still privileged relative to the millions of migrants and refugees who leave their countries suddenly because they have no other choice, even when their destinations are uncertain and their journeys unsafe.

During my first years as a migrant, I also learned that moving my body in intentional ways alongside others in dance workshops, on the street, in my bedroom, even in writing classrooms, empowered me and kept me grounded. Eventually, I made these movement(s)—creative, geographical, political—the focus of my research. I understand movement (a spectrum that includes stasis as much as dynamism) as a generative lens to recognize the synergies and productive tensions between seemingly different lines of inquiry, and as a method for decolonizing my research and teaching.

My engagement with movement as method extends work by other feminist writers and rhetoricians, particularly Third World feminists preoccupied with the meaning-making capacities of embodiment and movement: Cherríe Moraga's Theory in the Flesh urges us attend to the "physical realities of our lives" to resist "easy explanations" about us.[10] As a method, Bernadette M. Calafell writes, Theory in the Flesh has "commitments to experience as theory building."[11] Jaqueline Jones Royster and Gesa Kirsch (drawing on Malea Powell's reflections on her archival work) have underscored the potency of this method in their discussion of strategic contemplation as an embodied practice.[12]

More specifically on movement, Laura Micciche draws connections between feminist writing practices and political action. She argues that feminist ways of writing—intentional, inquisitive, imaginative—have the capacity to *mobilize* (more recently, this connection between writing and movement has been further explored by scholars such as Karma Chávez and Jo Hsu).[13] Micciche asks: "What would it mean to read feminists as rhetorical theorists of writing, rather than predominately as social theorists?"[14] In this chapter, I study ADT's transnational feminist ways of moving (and their entanglements with the written and spoken word) as rhetorical. In attending to ADT's dance pedagogy, I gain a deeper understanding of the rhetorical and pedagogical possibilities of movement as method.

Mo(ve)ment No. 1. Invention Comes from Intention

Over the course of four years, between 2020 and 2023, I attended weekly online Yorchhā technique classes (ADT's movement technique), three two-week-long ADT summer dance intensives, participated in community events in person and online, and conducted in-depth interviews with company dancers, collaborators, and community students. In this context, fieldwork was, by choice and by force, "a practice of apprenticeship rather than a form of expertise."[15] In becoming a Yorchhā apprentice, I started to understand ADT's movement pedagogy as rhetorical in the way that Jo Hsu defines rhetoric: "a technology of attention."[16] For ADT professional and community dancers, creative movement is not just an occupation or a hobby; it is a way of being in the world and engaging with the parts of experience that overwhelm many of us. To ADT, dancing is a way of remaining alive in the struggle.

During my fieldwork, I learned that understanding Yorchhā as a tool for inquiry has been part of this dance technique from its inception. Yorchhā combines elements from three traditional Indian forms, some of which are known as gendered dances: Odissi, Chhau (a martial art), and Vinyasa yoga. Yorchhā is a response to feeling that, in their orthodox versions, none of these forms engaged with the complex lived realities of ADT dancers and the communities of which they are a part. It is also a push back against assumptions that dances of difference (often grouped under the label of "world dances") cannot be contemporary. During one of our conversations, Ananya Chatterjea explained her reasons for de/reconstructing traditional Indian forms: "I wanted to talk about contemporary realities! I don't wanna dance about, you know, heroines in love or goddesses. So, what is the language for that?"[17] As a dance form, Yorchhā is intentional and specific in its articulation from fluid softness to warrior strength. It celebrates the feminine and masculine energies present in all of us, and it empowers us to summon those energies as needed. This is the range that is necessary to delve into stories of displacement, dispossession, solidarity, and resistance.

ADT's Yorchhā is porous in the sense that it is never taught as an abstract technique that exists outside a specific context and experiences. During one warmup session in the 2021 ADT Summer Intensive, Ananya taught us a sequence focused on opening our sternums, one of the principles of Yorchhā. While demonstrating how to protect our bodies from injury while engaging in this type of movement, she explained it this way: "When we open our chest to the sun, the movement has to come from our core." As we rehearsed the sequence a few times, she continued offering statements to frame and direct our movements, to infuse mechanics with intention: "The sun shines on everyone, not on just a few!" "Open chest should be part of all liberation dances." In moments like these, ADT students not only learn the mechanics of movement, but they are also prompted to connect life and dance (e.g.: ribcage expansion and the question of who gets to take up space). Intention, in this case, qualifies and directs movement.

What do we dance for? What can this move offer in this moment? These are questions that undergird Yorchhā practice and that dancers are prompted to revisit once and again. E.K., a non-binary artist, explained in conversation how Yorchhā classes had become a space for self-exploration and self-expression that they could carry over to everyday life:

> My inward understanding [of my gender identity] and altering how I relate to my body, Yorchhā provided such a big foundation for that. 'Cause it is a transnational feminist dance, right? A lot of it—it's all hip, all curve, all give us all this juicy [their hand gestures drawing curves in the air] (. . .) Oh! It was so good! and I had never given myself permission to explore these things before. (. . .) And so, yeah, Yorchhā was very much like, "here are these shapes, here are these rhythms, here are these ways of being brown and queer and femme as hell," and I took to it, and it felt really, really, really good. So, for me, it just gave me that foundation of expression, and being, and way of holding myself.[18]

ADT's transnational feminist and diasporic framework is multilayered: It recognizes a world characterized by marginalization, unequal distribution of labor, resource exploitation, forced and voluntary human flows, all conditions that disproportionally affect BIPOC women and femmes. At the same time, it insists on the power of community-based practices to resist oppression. In the specific context of the arts, ADT expands access (i.e., who gets to become a professional dancer? who gets to enjoy dance performances?) and challenges the unequal valuation and circulation of dance forms (i.e., the implication that "world dance" and contemporary dance are mutually exclusive). The company uses creative movement to facilitate engagement with social justice issues including access to clean water, gender violence, and labor rights. While they regularly reach communities via stage productions and participatory performances, community workshops and Yorchhā classes offer participants unique opportunities to engage with big questions via movement in a sustained and intimate way. In one of her books about South-South choreographies, Ananya Chatterjea asks: "Can formalized technique resist hardening into a transactional unit and remain a vital epistemological modality?"[19] In other words, can it remain a responsive/adaptive way of knowing? In my study of ADT and Yorchhā, opportunities to tease out the intention behind our movements seem a key part of the answer.

Mo(ve)ment No. 2. Relational Metaphors for Meaning-full Movement

During an ADT remote lesson, this time led by dancer and artistic associate kealoha ferreira, she teaches a movement phrase reminiscent of water—abundant torso flexions, big and fluid arms, circular motion. After introducing the phrase, she offers additional guidance:

> The whole time, the navel is super engaged. This [points at her navel] never lets go. And because this [the navel] never lets go, we have the ability to move front, side, down, up; front, side, down, up [she simultaneously moves in these directions]; all the time. We have the ability to shift and be fluid like water because we have some type of central connection, yeah? Actually, in a lot of cultures—I mean, this is *mula bandha* in yoga, but also in Hawaiian culture this is your *na'au,* this is your *piko,* and so, this is your source of connection to ancestral memory, to wisdom . . .[20]

In this moment, the Indian *mula bandha* and the Hawaiian *piko* and *na'au* coexist and reveal the navel as a grounding source across cultures. Another practice often modeled by ADT instructors during classes involves situating Yorchhā in place and bringing it in conversation with different cultural backgrounds—*this* is transnational feminist dance. In another session, Ananya encourages us to find energized softness in our movement: "We can find the softness of the Mississippi river. In spite of what we humans do to the river, it insists in beauty. Embody that lotus flower that grows in the mud!" In doing so, she directs dancers' attention to their relationship with place. It is not a general prompt to "flow like a river;" it is more specifically "find the softness of the Mississippi" that flows through Mni Sota Makoce, home of ADT. Furthermore, she qualifies the movements of the Mississippi: its softness and beauty exist as resistance, in spite humans' careless actions. In offering the image of the Mississippi, Ananya brings a specific river to our shared imaginary and invites us to dive deeper, to meditate on relation as we search for our own modulations of "energized softness." I summon other rivers in my life: the Mississippi, the Orinoco, and the Ohio rivers—geographically apart—flow through my body as I dance.

Rhetorician Jennifer LeMesurier uses the term "somatic metaphors" to write about the connections between language, image and movement: "[linguistic images that dance teachers use] to evoke these remembered embodiments in their students for specific movement purposes."[21] In this case, however, ADT instructors summon metaphors to do something more than appealing to memory or general cultural topoi (e.g., the clouds, a vase, etc.). Through deliberate specificity, instructors prompt dancers to interrogate the context of their movement and put themselves in relation to the land and to others. In this process and the conversations that tend to follow these exercises, dancers learn to acknowledge the range of experiences gathered on the dance floor at any given time. Because of their explicit goal of grounding movement in place and in community, "relational metaphors" might be more fitting to refer to ADT's way of using language and images to prompt movement. Ananya Chatterjea refers to this connection between political imagination and creative movement as "deep embodiment"; a way to stimulate dancers' abilities to put themselves in relation. She explains: "the same movement with different contextual information and imaginative wings will be completely different depending on where you take it, you know?"[22] In ADT pedagogies, relational metaphors are central to teaching students to engage with movement with attention to specificity and plurality.

Mo(ve)ment No. 3. Embodied Listening and Emerging Relations

The original ADT company cohort came out of a call that Ananya Chatterjea put out in 2004 searching for women of color with or without previous dance training and interested in exploring politics through dance. For Hui Wilcox, answering that call was the beginning of a decades-long journey with ADT. She recalls how it felt to walk into that first meeting: "We had an African American storyteller in her sixties, an Asian American singer, an adopted biracial writer. [. . .] Most people were not trained dancers [. . .] I think people were just really amazed that there was a space for people like us to even come together, you know? in the Twin Cities."[23]

ADT members learned early on that it was necessary for their movement to grapple with the frictions that come with multiplicity. As long-time members of ADT articulate in their collaborative essay for the edited collection *Critical Transnational Feminist Praxis*: "The term that qualifies us for this company—women of color—means different things for different members, and allowing for these divergent meanings is politically indispensable and sometimes personally painful."[24] For ADT members, "women of color," "transnational feminisms" and "diaspora" remain touchstones that are none-theless open to contestation. This openness is connected to Chatterjea's goal of ensuring that ADT's way of moving remains "a vital epistemic modality." Over the years, ADT's terms have expanded to account for different experiences in their ensemble. For instance, as LGBTQI+ dancers have joined community classes and professional training, the company has developed more nuanced understandings of home and belonging.

Invention and listening are intimately related, as Krista Ratcliffe has previously noted in her work. Rhetorical listening, she explains, offers a way to understand rhetorical practices as more than "mastering arguments." Rhetorical listening "proceeds via different body organs, different disciplinary and cultural assumptions, different figures of speech, and most importantly different stances."[25] ADT pedagogies underscore the embodied nature of rhetorical listening and demonstrate how a certain kind of creative movement can support its practice. In an autobiographical essay, dancer and sociology scholar Hui Wilcox writes about a time when, during an early ADT workshop, participants' responses to the idea of borders were in deep tension with each other: migrant women of color saw national borders as a State mechanism of oppression and wanted to abolish them, while Indigenous women in the room associated borders with their demands for land sovereignty and insisted in the importance of protecting them.[26] How could they hold these different experiences and desires simultaneously? She remembers this impasse as a transformative moment for ADT: "We needed to learn each other's stories."[27] ADT uses embodied practices to foster curiosity, support negotiation, hold tensions, tease out differences, and build solidarity among dancers. In this context, dance supports rhetorical listening. This commitment to listen and to hold each other's truths makes possible works such as *Pipaashaa, Extreme Thirst* (2007), where dancers engage with "the dumping of toxic waste in Cote d'Ivoire and the ensuing protests in Abidjan, and the soil contamination in Minneapolis's "Arsenic Triangle" area and the continued efforts of organizers to get this addressed."[28]

Karma Chávez writes about the inventional possibilities of coalitions: "We coalesce to increase access, to alter our ability to make arguments, to broaden the resources for rhetorical invention within our reach in order to challenge imaginaries and make people's lives, our own and others, more livable."[29] Because coalition insists on preserving multiplicity while sharing a purpose or direction, there are challenges to remaining (in) it. But it is this very tension between togetherness and difference that makes it so powerful. Paraphrasing Carrillo Rowe, Karma Chávez explains that "one achieves a coalitional subjectivity when she sees her oppression and privilege as inextricably bound to others and when she cannot envision her existence and politics as separate from others' existence and politics."[30] When ADT members choose to move in a certain direction together—whether it is creative, spatial, or otherwise—the aspiration is that their movement is informed by their enmeshments. Learning to listen and to move with others is a transnational feminist lesson that becomes animated in ADT's creative movement.

Spellcasting, Movement, and the Middle

On the morning of June 24, 2022, I was riding a train on my way to my third Ananya Dance Theatre's Summer Intensive when my phone buzzed with a long-feared news notification: "Supreme Court overturns Roe v. Wade; states can ban abortion." My ears rang. I started sinking in my seat. Feelings and thoughts felt jumbled inside me until a movement phrase that I had learned a few days before pulled me back up: a percussive warrior walk, defiant gaze, imaginary shield and sword in hand, an arm reaching over my head to pounce, sharp as my fearless gaze—Take de, take de, take de, take take![31] My body became energized and my thoughts sharper as I imagined/felt myself performing this movement phrase once again, all of it amplified by the knowledge that I would not be/was not alone. To meet this moment with movement felt like the beginning of an answer.

One artist I interviewed for this project referred to this capacity of ADT's dance to "put other things in motion," to mobilize (in the political sense of the word) those who practice it in various ways, as "spell making." This idea of "spells" gets to the knowledges and positioning required for what Debra Hawhee calls "to invent in the middle." The middle implicates us. To occupy it is to be in relation; the middle is a location that emerges when we acknowledge our surroundings and our interconnectedness. Hawhee explains that "in the middle": "'I invent and am invented by others' (in each encounter). The middle, then, at once combines and exceeds the forces of active and passive."[32] To invent in the middle is to proceed with awareness of both our power and our limits. It is recognizing that how we show up counts, that our presence and sense of direction alters the whole. And it is also recognizing that we are not all that counts, that "our spells" having their intended effect is not solely up to us. Inventing in the middle is another piece of movement as method.

When it comes to conducting research in rhetoric and composition, movement as method involves understanding that the different scales in which we occupy and traverse the world are often entangled, and that these ways of moving (or staying still) are rhetorical and political. Movement as method affirms the value of embodied research, whether this means conducting participant observation or attending to how our bodies respond when we engage in research tasks considered "less experiential."

Movement as method can also support the teaching of writing. Using embodiment and creative movement prompts to initiate class discussions can encourage students to bring multiple ways of knowing into writing classrooms. As it was shown in the case of relational metaphors, deliberately bringing together language and embodiment to center lived experience, positionality, and relationality can infuse meaning and direction into the work that students and instructors do in classrooms. Embodiment and movement can also facilitate storytelling and community-building moments with and among students.

As writers, using movement as method involves understanding that "fleshing out" our ideas is difficult work that activates our bodies, and that rather than understanding that activation as an interference, we must approach it as a way into, a way through, and a way towards. Attending to embodiment and movement in our writing practice can help us express ourselves with honesty, vulnerability, and accountability. It can prompt us to formulate different questions and articulate the context and purpose of our work. Movement as method, in the way I have discussed in this chapter, helps us be present in the middle.

NOTES

1. "Shawngram" means "resistance" in Bengali. With the inauguration of the Shawngram Institute in 2018, ADT strengthened its commitment to community-building in St. Paul, Minnesota.
2. The choreopoem is an expressive form that combines elements of poetry, dance, and music. The term was coined by Black feminist artist Ntozake Shange in 1974 with the piece, *For Colored Girls Who Have Considered Suicide / When the Rainbow is Enuf.*
3. Several dance studies scholars, including Dr. Ananya Chatterjea, have written insightful articles about ADT's choreographic process and stage work. The edited collection *Dancing Transnational Feminisms: Ananya Dance Theatre and the Art of Social Justice* gathers perspectives from company members and collaborators about different aspects of the company's work. One aspect of the company that remains less written about so far is their community-accountable pedagogies.
4. Lauer, "Rhetorical Invention," 2.
5. Atwill, Introduction, xi.
6. Lauer, "Rhetorical Invention," 12.
7. Lauer, "Rhetorical Invention," 3.
8. Holding, "The Rhetoric," 415.
9. Rickert, *Ambient Rhetoric*, 47.

10. Moraga, "Entering the Lives," 19.
11. Calafell, "Rhetorics of Possibility," 113.
12. Royster and Kirsch, *Feminist Rhetorical Practices*, 88.
13. Chávez, *Queer Migration*; Hsu, *Constellating Home*.
14. Micciche, "Writing," 173.
15. Puri, "Finding the Field," 41.
16. Hsu, "A New Plot," https://digitalstories.vjohsu.com/CW2022/.
17. Ananya Chatterjea, unpublished interview with Nelesi Rodrigues.
18. E.K., unpublished interview with Nelesi Rodrigues.
19. Chatterjea, *Heat and Alterity*, 113.
20. Yorchhā Foundations class, personal communication with Nelesi Rodrigues.
21. LeMesurier, "Somatic Metaphors," 365.
22. Ananya Chatterjea, unpublished interview with Nelesi Rodrigues.
23. Hui Wilcox, unpublished interview with Nelesi Rodrigues.
24. Tinsley et al., "So Much Reminds Us," 162.
25. Ratcliffe, *Rhetorical Listening*, 24.
26. Wilcox, "Dance," 65.
27. Hui Wilcox, unpublished interview with Nelesi Rodrigues.
28. Ananya Dance Theatre, "Pipaashaa: Extreme Thirst," https://www.ananyadance theatre.org/dance/pipaashaa/.
29. Chávez, *Queer Migration Politics*, 149.
30. Chávez, *Queer Migration Politics*, 11.
31. This is an example of a "Bol," polysyllabic phrases used in several traditional Indian forms to mark rhythm.
32. Hawhee, "Kairotic Encounters," 17.

WORKS CITED

Ananya Dance Theatre. "Pipaashaa: Extreme Thirst," https://www.ananyadancetheatre .org/dance/pipaashaa/.

Atwill, Janet M. Introduction to *Perspectives on Rhetorical Invention*, edited by Janet M. Atwill and Janice M. Lauer, xi–xxi. Knoxville, TN: University of Tennessee Press, 2002.

Calafell, Bernadette M. "Rhetorics of Possibility: Challenging the Textual Bias of Rhetoric through the Theory of the Flesh." In *Rhetorica in Motion: Feminist Rhetorical Methods and Methodologies*, edited by Eileen E. Schell and K.J. Rawson, 104–17. Pittsburgh, PA: University of Pittsburgh Press, 2010.

Chatterjea, Ananya. *Heat and Alterity in Contemporary Dance: South-South Choreographies*. New York: Palgrave Macmillan, 2020.

Chatterjea, Ananya, Hui Wilcox, and Alexandra Lebea Williams, eds. *Dancing Transnational Feminisms: Ananya Dance Theatre and the Art of Social Justice*. Seattle, WA: University of Washington Press, 2022.

Chávez, Karma R. *Queer Migration Politics: Activist Rhetoric and Coalitional Possibilities*. Urbana, IL: University of Illinois Press, 2013.

Hawhee, Debra. "Kairotic Encounters." In *Perspectives on Rhetorical Invention*, edited by Janet M. Atwill and Janice M. Lauer, 16–35. Knoxville, TN: University of Tennessee Press, 2002.

Holding, Cory. "The Rhetoric of the Open Fist." *Rhetoric Society Quarterly* 45, no. 5 (2015): 399–419.

Hsu, V. Jo. *Constellating Home: Trans and Queer Asian American Rhetorics*. Columbus, OH: Ohio State University, 2022.

Hsu, V. Jo. "A New Plot for Living: Storytelling as Collective Action and Homemaking." Paper presented at the Computers and Writing Conference, Greenville, NC, May 19–21, 2022. https://digitalstories.vjohsu.com/CW2022/.

Lauer, Janice M. "Rhetorical Invention: The Diaspora." In *Perspectives on Rhetorical Invention*, edited by Janet M. Atwill and Janice M. Lauer, 1–15. Knoxville, TN: University of Tennessee Press, 2002.

LeMesurier, Jennifer Lin. "Somatic Metaphors: Embodied Recognition of Rhetorical Opportunities." *Rhetoric Review* 33, no. 4. (2014): 362–80.

Madison, D. Soyini. *Critical Ethnography: Method, Ethics, and Performance*. Los Angeles: SAGE, 2020.

Micciche, Laura R. "Writing as Feminist Rhetorical Theory." In *Rhetorica in Motion: Feminist Rhetorical Methods and Methodologies*, edited by Eileen E. Schell and K.J. Rawson, 173–88. Pittsburgh, PA: University of Pittsburgh Press, 2010.

Moraga, Cherríe. "Entering the Lives of Others: Theory in the Flesh." In *This Bridge Called My Back: Writings by Radical Women of Color*, edited by Cherríe Moraga and Gloria Anzaldúa, 17–19. Albany, NY: SUNY Press, 2015.

Puri, Shalini. "Finding the Field: Notes on Caribbean Cultural Criticism, Area Studies, and the Forms of Engagement." In *Theorizing Fieldwork in the Humanities: Methods, Reflections, and Approaches to the Global South*, edited by Shalini Puri and Debra A. Castillo, 29–49. New York: Palgrave Macmillan, 2016.

Ratcliffe, Krista. *Rhetorical Listening: Identification, Gender, Whiteness*. Carbondale, IL: Southern Illinois University Press, 2005.

Rickert, Thomas J. *Ambient Rhetoric: The Attunements of Rhetorical Being*. Pittsburgh, PA: University of Pittsburgh Press, 2013.

Royster, Jacqueline Jones, and Gesa E. Kirsch. *Feminist Rhetorical Practices: New Horizons for Rhetoric, Composition, and Literacy Studies*. Carbondale, IL: Southern Illinois University Press, 2012.

Shange, Ntozake. *For Colored Girls Who Have Considered Suicide / When the Rainbow Is Enuf: A Choreopoem*. New York: Scribner, 2010.

Tinsley, Omise'eke Natasha, Ananya Chatterjea, Hui Niu Wilcox, and Shannon Gibney. "So Much to Remind Us that We Are Dancing on Other People's Blood: Moving toward Artistic Excellence, Moving from Silence to Speech, Moving in Water, with Ananya Dance Theatre." In *Critical Transnational Feminist Praxis*, edited by Richa Nagar and Amanda Lock Swarr, 147–65. Albany, NY: SUNY Press, 2010.

Wilcox, X. "Dance of the Spiraling Generations: On Love and Healing with Ananya Dance Theatre." In *Dancing Transnational Feminisms: Ananya Dance Theatre and the Art of Social Justice*, edited by Ananya Chatterjea, Hui Niu Wilcox, and Allesandra Lebea Williams, 56–70. Seattle, WA: University of Washington Press, 2022.

THREE

The Problem of Ethos and Exigence in Latin American Indigenous Women's Rhetorics

Christina V. Cedillo

It is not my intention to dissect the traditional rhetorics of Maya communities or to expose cultural elements that are not mine to reveal. Instead, here I aim to show how Latin American Indigenous women's rhetorics must account for the colonialism that sustains itself at their expense. In so doing, I illustrate how the imposition of even basic Eurocentric rhetorical terms can enact erasure. Researchers have long exploited Indigenous communities, observing and writing about them using Eurowestern lenses, leading to erroneous conclusions and stereotyped representation. These outcomes enable rhetorical erasure that frames Indigenous peoples as regressive or as having existed only in the past. Academic research contributes to this process by employing whitestream frameworks that do not account for the material and sociopolitical realities of colonized communities, finding them lacking when these communities' practices do not fit such frameworks. These reading practices have long authorized white supremacy's expropriative claims over Indigenous people, cultures, resources, and lands.

Therefore, in this chapter I argue for the deconstructive interrogation of established whitestream concepts as an intersectional feminist rhetorical methodology. Intersectional analysis postulates that "race, class, gender, sexuality, ethnicity, nation, ability, and age operate not as unitary, mutually exclusive entities, but rather as reciprocally constructing phenomena."[1] Rhetoricians must be attuned to the intersecting forces that constrain rhetors since traditional frameworks that frame speech as a given right and isolated from material, corporeal, and epistemic conditions can obscure any violence or threat encountered by a rhetor in speaking. Traditional Eurowestern terms and frameworks constructed around a speaker presumed to be white, cis, male, and ablebodied can enable erasure and deprecation when rhetors are judged as falling short of the rhetorical ideal due to the constraints they face. For example, concepts like ethos and exigence are predicated on individualism and privilege—on a single person being perceived as credible and having the power to determine when a matter is urgent or not. Communal modes of speaking or people constantly struggling to be recognized may be regarded as ineffective rather than deliberately disregarded. Nevertheless, concepts like ethos or exigence can still serve as a useful pivot if we use them to expose how terms themselves can be exclusive when understood through this narrow lens.

Below, I deploy these two fundamental terms, ethos and exigence, to show how coloniality uses language to sustain its authority and obscure the material and physical damage it inflicts on colonized people. I share two brief examples involving Guatemala's Civil War that highlight how Eurowestern notions of ethos and exigence fail to account for the material and temporal aspects of ongoing colonial oppression and why, as a result, Indigenous rhetorics must always account for rhetorical erasure and genocide. First, I discuss how activist Rigoberta Menchú (K'iche' Maya) employs testimonio, or collective witnessing, to relate the violence targeting Maya peoples during Guatemala's Civil War. Then, I show how the collectively memorialized figure of Claudia Patricia Gómez González (Mam Maya) attests to the violence still facing Indigenous migrants due to that same war. These examples illustrate the communal rather than individualistic quality of Indigenous voices and how exigence proves a constant rather than ephemeral state due to the ongoing subjugation and genocide of Indigenous peoples. Finally, I argue that taking up concepts like ethos and exigence uncritically without accounting for people's physical, material, and political circumstances can enable and sustain the erasure of colonized populations. However, these terms can be redeployed as tools of an intersectional deconstructive approach.

Ethos and Exigence

Intersectional feminist researchers must often claim, reframe, or invent research methods and methodologies to counter traditional whitestream rhetoric's marking of non-Western rhetorics as deficient forms of communication.[2] These approaches underscore why rhetorical concepts cannot be universalized. They also expose the inequitable power dynamics that distinguish Eurowestern rhetorics as the defining tradition against Othered traditions, many of which are much older and still inform our practices today even in the Eurowest. Thus, in this chapter I take up the notions of ethos and exigence to show how these central concepts may not adequately account for the unique dimensions of certain Indigenous rhetorical practices. Traditional views of ethos and exigence can contribute to the denigration of colonized peoples' practices and lives due to their inability to account for communally based praxes like testimonio and memorialization. Consequently, I argue that feminist methodologies must necessarily include deconstructing Eurowestern rhetorical concepts—rather than taking them as a given—so as to counter universalizing and denigrating attitudes. Feminist rhetoricians must critically and constantly interrogate even the most fundamental terms we use in our work to show that "methodological rigor does not lead to claims of objective truth but to claims about truth as seen from a given perspective,"[3] often from the colonial center of power.

Ethos determines the effectiveness of communication via a presumed sense of connection between rhetor and audience. A rhetor's words should adhere to the "conventional rather than the idiosyncratic"[4] to exemplify the sanctioned spirit of a group; at the same time, the rhetor must distinguish themselves from the group to further their goal. This view of ethos suggests a contrast between public and private life that has, historically, seldom been afforded to women and marginalized peoples whose lives have been highly circumscribed by social and legal strictures.[5] The notion of a public/private life divide also informs and is informed by Eurowestern modernity, with scholars arguing that members of "modern" societies have vivid private lives that foster introspection while those from societies "stuck in the past" have little to no sense of the individual.[6] Thus, a traditional view of ethos may render communally-based practices like testimonio and memorialization as negligible forms of communication and frame members of marginalized groups who engage these practices as quaint or regressive. Instead, ethos must be understood as a social, analytical, epistemological and political concept that informs what is possible or impossible for the speaker in a given moment based on their identity.[7]

Sociopolitical norms establish whether a person qualifies to be in the position to speak, assigning value that determines one's safety and access to a platform based on embodied identity. This obligates members of marginalized groups to use modesty or humility tropes and survivance rhetorics that adapt oppressor speech to be heard, and bolsters the impression that speakers are incompetent if their rhetorics don't align with dominant practices.[8] For example, Ersula Ore writes about the then-Senator Barack

Obama's 2004 Democratic National Convention keynote address, explaining that "the DNC podium was envisioned as a *certain kind of space intended for a certain kind of body*."[9] Ore notes that Obama even marked his presence on stage as "unlikely," demonstrating an "acute awareness of the rhetorical burden of being a phenotypically black rhetor in a white racialized space" and reminding us that our "post-racial" nation still has racism and inequity determine what rhetor can speak and where, even at the very centers of power.

Writing about the struggles of Afrocolombians in South America, Santiago Arboleda Quiñonez explains that marginalized groups must "dignify their existence" and that of their culture even in locations that claim to endorse "diversity, recognition and multiculturalism."[10] He discusses how anti-Black and anti-Indigenous economic and physical violence, *blanquea-miento* (whitening) practices, and disregard by the state function to erase Afrocolombian identity, not only discursively silencing the population but effectively serving as mechanisms of genocide that target other Indigenous groups. In response, they must establish rhetorical presence before their concerns will be heard.

As these critics show, a traditional view of ethos and exigence that frames these concepts as matters of speech in a fixed context ignores how even attempting to inhabit "the location or position from which [a] person speaks or writes"[11] proves a crucial aspect of the exigence motivating marginalized rhetors. With these scholars' works in mind, I thus aim here to contribute to the extant research that collectively examines how traditional Eurowestern frameworks disregard the needs and praxes of marginalized rhetors. As Ore, Arboleda Quiñonez, and many others remind us, we cannot overlook the body's ability to provide embodied "arguments" and determine reception.[12] Bodies play a crucial role in the construction of credibility, connecting identity and space(s); showing who one is in the flesh determines who one is rhetorically. Feminist rhetoricians must contend with the myriad ways that "ethos and/as exigence" proves a vital concern for members of marginalized groups, who must constantly combat erasure and assert the right to speak. We must also understand ethos and/as exigence not as a phenomenon made in words and space but as a composite nexus of meaning-making based in material and corporeal factors. Below, I use the notion of ethos and/as exigence to analyze the cases of Rigoberta Menchú and Claudia Patricia Gómez González, two Mayan women targeted by colonial violence. As a result, I hope to demonstrate the need for more methodologies based in material-corporeal conditions that deconstruct standard concepts.

The Problems of Ethos and Exigence in Testimonio

In 1992, on the 500th anniversary of Columbus's invasion, K'iche' Maya activist Rigoberta Menchú was awarded the Nobel Peace Prize for her work on Indigenous rights and for bringing global attention to the atrocities committed by the government during Guatemala's Civil War. Between 1960 and 1996, approximately 200,000 civilians were killed, many of them Maya. Guatemalan officials criticized the win, citing her involvement with Marxist guerillas. Detractors accused her of "damaging Guatemala's international image."[13] A majority of Guatemala's citizens are Indigenous, whose abuses by military and paramilitaries she recounts in her 1983 autobiography, *I, Rigoberta Menchú: An Indian Woman in Guatemala.* In the book, she describes the everyday lives of her community and provides insight into revolutionary organizing, arguing that leaders need not be intellectuals but must have "practical experience [because] you can only have real consciousness if you've really lived this life."[14] In 1998, US anthropologist David Stoll published a book titled *Rigoberta Menchú and the Story of All Poor Guatemalans,* in which he alleged that Menchú borrowed or changed events. Ostensibly, he did not wish to detract from her work yet wrote that he was obliged to show that a "valuable symbol can also be misleading."[15] Reporters sensationalized Stoll's claims that Menchú was less poor and better educated than she alleged and that the land battle she depicted was actually an acrimonious family feud. In subsequent years, Menchú defended her work, stating she was given the Nobel Peace Prize for her role in the peace process rather than a Nobel Prize in Literature.[16] She was also compelled to explain supposed inconsistencies in her narration of events for writing as if she were present, stating that she did so to protect members of her family who were.[17]

Many have deliberated whether details in Menchú's book are fabricated or flawed recollection. I am not interested in this question. Instead, as have others, I situate her book in the genre of *testimonio,* which relates a community's stories in one voice; the speaker "performs an act of identity-formation which is simultaneously personal and collective."[18] Testimonio is a Latin American rhetorical genre that empowers the speaker, typically a member of an oppressed group, by providing "crucial means of bearing witness and inscribing into history those lived realities that would otherwise succumb to . . . erasure."[19] Activists and researchers have taken up testimonio as a powerful feminist method, methodology, and praxis, due to its similarities to memoir and CRT counterstory. Yet testimonio can be perceived as rhetorical fraud or plagiarism when we regard speech as though it occurs vis-à-vis individualistic ethos rather than communally embodied experience. Audiences' own rejection or ignorance of a speaker's cultural norms can exacerbate these attitudes.

Menchú's detractors called her work intentionally misleading political propaganda, but testimonio *should* be "intentional and political."[20] Stoll and others ignored Menchú's purpose in writing the book, to convey the realities of state violence against all Indigenous communities targeted by the war rather than to center herself. Through testimonio, survivors provide flesh-and-blood proof of the community's collective trauma to remind audiences of their humanity. Yet testimonio is not mere ventriloquizing. Eurowestern readers like Stoll assumed Menchú had simply appropriated parts of her narrative, overlooking how oppressed groups use first-person narratives like testimonio to create "a discourse of solidarity" based in lived experience rather than in Eurowestern standards regarding what is "empirically, scientifically, or legally true."[21] Stoll did not consider that he did not have access to Menchú's corporeal connection *to her community* by virtue of having lived similar circumstances as a member *of her community*. Nor did he consider that embodied knowledge might have compelled her to change aspects of the story to spare others from retribution or pain, or to ensure that enough people and experiences were represented. Instead, he dislocated her story from its material and corporeal grounding based on a self-centering understanding of credibility.

Stoll also disregarded the endorsement of the community whose story was being told. A *New York Times* article reported that a municipal government worker who claimed to have read Menchú's book deemed it all lies; however, when members of her community were contacted by the media, even those who had not read the book were sympathetic. One neighbor stated, "The truth may be distinct from how she has told it, but that does not mean Rigoberta did not suffer greatly in those years."[22] Whether deliberately or due to cultural ignorance, Stoll framed Menchú's testimonio as a questionable autobiography, the value of which he himself established using a "facts-driven" rubric. Yet, as others have noted, Stoll did not bother to do the same with official records that the United Nations Commission for Historical Clarification had flagged for concealing "inconsistencies, denials, and abuses of the government and military forces" that had perpetrated genocide against Guatemala's Maya population.[23] Instead, he assumed that the exigence of Menchú's testimonio's centered around her own experiences rather than extended across her community's losses over the nearly-forty-year war.

Ultimately, when asked if his book would ruin Menchú's reputation, he said no, because Guatemala needed her to serve as a symbol that ensured that the Civil War's violent history was not repeated.[24] According to Stoll, then, Menchú proved credible only so far as she could embody her community's experiences as a passive national(ist) symbol but not as an actual human witness. He and others attempted to circumscribe the embodied knowledge that only she could provide and ignored how exigent circumstances may continue for those directly affected long after the danger has officially "passed" and outsider attention is withdrawn. As members of the dominant culture, they sought to lay claim to an "objective" reality, one where Menchú was either untruthful and more whitestream in terms of class and education than she led on, or else she was altogether illegible through Eurowestern frameworks. They created the controversy, adding a layer to the coloniality Menchú's book sought to expose for its continued effects on Guatemala's Indigenous peoples even after the war ostensibly ended. Writing about slavery's enduring effects on Black lives in the United States, Saidiya Hartman refers to this ongoing process as an "afterlife," explaining that Black people are "still imperiled by a racial calculus and a political arithmetic that were entrenched centuries ago."[25] Similarly, the structures that create a deadly colonial nexus around Indigenous migration have roots in five centuries of Indigenous oppression, and the genocidal apparatus set in place by Guatemala and the United States to destroy Maya communities and cultures continues to do its work as intended. The war must be understood less as an event and more as a process that, like the genocide it enacted/enacts, categorizes, segregates, and dehumanizes populations and sets them up for annihilation in the name of order.[26]

As academics, our research has the power to authorize ways of reading. If we are not to bolster colonial attitudes like those perpetuated by Stoll and others, we must be careful not to read texts like Menchú's through a simplistic, untrained comparative lens. As intersectional feminist researchers, we must analyze the kairos of a communicative context within the long chronos of colonization, account for a speaker's cultural and communal practices, and center the perspective of the audiences whose reception they highlight and prioritize. Moreover, we cannot ignore those real material and corporeal conditions that constrain a speaker's praxis especially when they differ radically from our own relatively privileged position.

Subverting Ethos and Exigence in Memorialization

Via a lens of Eurowestern exigence, based on teleological linearity and progress, Guatemala's Civil War ended once peace agreements were signed and the Commission for Historical Clarification (CEH) began its reconciliation work.[27] However, long before migrants ever encounter US Customs and Border Protection (CBP) or detention, they have already been targets of the US government through our nation's interventionism and "border wars." Documents declassified in 1999 reveal that in the late 1960s, the US State Department created a "safe house" for Guatemalan security agents who targeted Indigenous people, students, and activists, providing their military with $33 million dollars despite an appalling record of human rights violations.[28] Moreover, economic adversity and government corruption continue to motivate migration out of Guatemala, with money sent home by migrants constituting 10% of the nation's Gross Domestic Product.[29] One tragic case that illustrates the enduring afterlife of the war involves Claudia Patricia Gómez González, a Mam Maya migrant woman murdered by a Border Patrol agent in Rio Bravo, a colonia just south of Laredo, Texas.

In May 2018, Claudia traveled 1,500 miles in two weeks, borrowing money from her family to pay a *coyote* for passage to the United States. According to news reports, she either came to the US to work for money for college, or she had an accounting degree but could not find a job at home. Claudia had entered the United States with several companions, but the group split up when they encountered the agent in an overgrown lot. She and one of her companions remained while the others ran for safety. At first, CBP issued an official report accusing Claudia and her companion of assailing the agent with "blunt objects."[30] Then, over the next few days, CBP changed their narrative when a video recording the aftermath of the killing filmed by a Rio Bravo resident went viral. In 2019, the American Civil Liberties Union of Texas filed a $100 million claim against the United States, Border Patrol agent Romualdo Barrera, and 20 other "Agent Does" on behalf of her parents, Gilberto Gomez Vicente and Lidia Gonzalez Vasquez.[31] Yet as of this writing, no decision has been rendered.

On social media, artists depicted Claudia with flowers or a halo crowning her head resembling a folk saint, a person recognized as holy by their community though not the church. Muralists painted her image, her vibrant Maya clothing contrasted by images of the desert that claims many migrants' lives. Poets wrote verses celebrating her life and denouncing those who stole it. At protests across Latin America and the United States, people held up signs that read "*Somos Claudia*," "Defund ICE," and "Indigenous, Not Illegal," or that featured large images of Claudia rendered from family photographs. Like that of Menchú, Claudia's communally constructed figure shows up how the terms by which we typically define ethos and exigence fail to account for the brutal conditions used to target Indigenous communities. Claudia was a victim of the very same war narrated by Menchú, a war that did not end in 1996, but has continued to unfold through its deliberately activated effects.

Claudia's collective memorialization disavows processes of dehumanization by uniting people affectively, their shared anger, hope, and resistance superseding individualist logocentricity. Instead, commemorative iconography foregrounds a communally oriented empathic connection that stresses the shared humanity of people facing the same violence at different times and through different mechanisms. Collectively constructed subjects prove powerful counterstorying agents that allow people to "make sense of their experiences of oppression and trauma" together rather than alone.[32] They also disrupt the "oppressive and restrictive character of Western construction of identity" to provide a measure of protection for those who need to remain unknown.[33] Paradoxically, when they cohere through Claudia's image, her rhetorical figure simultaneously de-anonymizes survivors by "speaking" alongside rather than for other people whose dreams for a better life she shared.

This irony is underscored by the visual and aural transpositional rhetorics of Claudia's memorialization. Murals that depict her against a desert background do not associate Claudia with the verdant and populated site of her death—Laredo and Rio Bravo are popular migrant crossing sites located right on the Rio Grande and combined, they represent a population of approximately 260,600 people—but instead consciously draw public attention to Arizona's Sonoran Desert, whose desolate terrain claims countless migrants' lives every year. The point is clear: whether at risk due to hostile terrain or government agents, migrants hazard the dangerous crossing because the ongoing violence and hardship fostered by foreign intervention continue to make life back home intolerable. When protestors shout "*Somos Claudia*" and "Indigenous, Not Illegal," they remind the public that their own neighbors and loved ones may also be undocumented and that their lives are not worth any less because of it; they also counter colonization's attempts to rhetorically and procedurally render Indigenous people like Claudia "illegal" on their own continent by erasing the timeless migration routes that joined the Americas long before settlers' arrival. These rhetorics are not based on a faulty logic or crass appropriation of Claudia's voice suggested by an individualistic ethos; her memorializers know Claudia was murdered rather than claimed by the desert, and they know documented status grants many of them the privilege of speaking out publicly. These practices are intended to deliberately compose a communal ethos that counters the colonial forces that have tried to erase Indigenous peoples and histories; we are *all* called to bear witness and maintain Claudia's memory and that of every migrant preyed upon by the same colonial nexus.

For members of vulnerable Maya communities, land grabbing, violence, and erasure can be prevalent everyday threats. Mingled with the dangers attending the journey north and our own government's systematic abuse of migrants and asylum seekers, these factors are genocidal mechanisms that only become real to members of the dominant culture if and when they are covered by the media. One month after the Department of Health and Human Services reported that the US had "lost" 1,475 migrant children due to its family separation and detention policy,[34] Claudia's aunt, Dominga Vicente, spoke in Guatemala City. Vicente linked her niece's killing to the ongoing crisis of migrant deaths once people have been detained in the United States. Only two weeks earlier, 19-month-old Mariee Juárez had died of a lung infection after being released from an ICE facility where women and children were kept in overcrowded concrete-floored cages and received cursory to no medical assistance.[35] Later that same year, in December, Jakelin Amei Rosmery Caal Maquin, age seven, and Felipe Gómez Alonzo, age eight, died in US custody due to delayed medical attention.[36] Jakelin and Felipe were also from Maya communities, and they and Mariee were all from Guatemala. Their memories, too, and those of others killed or lost during the journey north were honored during subsequent protests and artistic displays honoring Claudia.

Collective memorialization can be understood as an intersectional feminist rhetorical practice because it counteracts a hegemonic cultural memory that intentionally works to "forget" gendered and raced violence that maintains colonialism and empire.[37] Unlike other forms of commemoration, it seeks not to let the past rest, allowing it to therefore be erased, but to keep a traumatic event at the forefront of public awareness. Collective memorialization refutes the exigence of a nightly news cycle to continuously extend urgency until justice for all has been served and coloniality ceases to claim more victims. Like testimonio, collective memorialization does not obscure others' tragic experiences but makes room for them all, demanding that each individual be recognized as a human being with a history, life, and dreams. Claudia's image does not further efface the many people that systematic violence and the US immigration system would render nameless entities because they, too, are part of the story that only corporeal experience can tell. Instead, a confluence of parties establish presence alongside her memory, sharing her aim to survive the persistent pressures of colonial domination.

Even now, her memory unites people across social, political, and temporal geographies, people who demand answers and justice, ever lacking in cases of state violence against migrants and Indigenous peoples. Thus, our understanding of collective memorialization must recognize how traditional views of ethos and exigence can perpetuate the colonial goals of empire, promoting an individualist and ephemeral impression of speech that can work to muffle, if never quite silence, communal forms of counter-rhetoric and counter-memory. And, our analysis must ever begin by centering rhetors' material and corporeal circumstances as active elements in any rhetorical performance rather than regarding them as a mere backdrop for public speech.

Conclusion

Rigoberta and Claudia each embody a persona that reveals communal ways of speaking that stand in contrast to an individualist ethos bound by conventional exigence. Due to colonial pressures, the "exigence" they signify actually proves a constant, encapsulating the kairos of the Guatemalan Civil War and its afterlife as well as the chronos of the last 500 years of settler history. As a result, credibility hinges not just on being permitted speech by the dominant order to testify about these genocidal processes, but upon having a singular corporeal knowledge of them based on material circumstances, political status, and cultural identity. Privileged speakers—and researchers—may not have to take into account all of these concerns, but for members of colonized communities, these matters are ever-present constraints. This is *not* to say that Indigenous peoples should only be defined in relation to colonization and coloniality. However, existing in opposition to colonialism's genocidal regime necessarily affects how their rhetoricity is interpreted by dominant culture audiences via whose subjectivity notions of ethos and exigence are constructed. Thus, deploying concepts like ethos and exigence uncritically without accounting for the material and sociopolitical realities of colonized communities enables rhetorical erasure that often sanctions cultural and physical genocide.

Habituated language and practices can be harmful, especially when deeply embedded in our daily forms of discourse and behavior so that they go unnoticed. Words do not disappear into the ether but have very real consequences. Actions mold spaces mold attitudes mold bodies. Words and actions are interpreted through epistemological frameworks that determine what and who matters and what is simply matter upon which to impose meaning. Rhetorical terms that exclude elements of communication crucial to oppressed peoples, whether in everyday cultural practice or in direct challenge to erasure, suggest that said oppression is attributable to failed entelechy rather than deliberate colonial design. Consequently, we must be conscientious when using concepts familiar to dominant culture audiences without interrogating how they might diminish or obscure the needs of marginalized people.[38] A commitment to listening and learning to appreciate vulnerable people's full humanity demands "understanding how rhetoric and culture are interconnecting concepts," and how material conditions determine credibility and kairos.[39] Colonial violence engenders counternarratives that survival compels be told, but they may be obscured by the interpretive frameworks we maintain, if they are based on privileged and exclusive understandings of the terms that organize our perception.

The afterlife of war continues to force refugees to flee their homes due to the enduring repercussions of US-funded violence even as legislative and media discourses render migrants' precarity a political inconvenience and reduce their humanity to a monstrous anonymous "surge" looming at the nation's borders. As feminist rhetoricians, we are called to make a humanizing intervention, beginning with recognizing that the rhetorical impositions imposed by our most basic disciplinary terms on Indigenous peoples' speech can advance the colonial goal of rendering Indigenous peoples transposable, exploitable, and vulnerable to genocide. When ethos as rhetorical authority and exigence as kairotic urgency fail to account for this amalgam of pressures, a person's credibility can easily be reduced to a matter of possessing the right documents (or not) and their humanity to that of an expedient political stereotype. Researchers must be careful to approach rhetorical concepts through an intersectional lens, recognizing that forces like colonialism and empire influence how we construe gender, speech, credibility, urgency, and effectiveness. As stated, this is just a start. This work is in itself not decolonial, centering academic practices and audiences. However, perhaps this methodology can make plain why basic comparative analysis or tracing of colonial networks are not enough; unless we center Indigenous peoples' material and corporeal conditions, goals, perspectives, and respective rhetorical sovereignty—their ability to determine their own "communicative goals, selected means of communication, and [ ] anticipated audiences"—even feminist and ostensibly liberatory praxes enact colonial erasure.[40] Therefore, we must begin by recognizing that Indigenous existence necessarily stands counter to colonialism, and how that opposition manifests rhetorically must be understood in critical relation to the restrictive, effacing disciplinary concepts we so often take for granted.

NOTES

1. Collins, "Intersectionality's Definition," 2.
2. See Browdy and Milu, "Global Black Rhetorics"; Royster and Kirsch, *Feminist Rhetorical Practices*; Schell and Rawson, *Rhetorica in Motion*.
3. Moorman, Blanton, and McLaughlin, "The Rhetoric," 319.
4. Halloran, "Aristotle's Concept," 60.
5. Griffin, "The Essentialist Roots," 21–39; Couture and Kent, *Private*.
6. McKeon, *The Secret History*, xix; Bullen, *The Myth*.
7. Hesford, "Ethos Righted," 199; Waite, "The Unavailable Means," 71–88.
8. Brownlee, "Decolonizing Composition," 55; Powell, "Rhetorics of Survivance," 396–434; Chowdhury, "Restriction," 47–56.
9. Ore, "Whiteness," 257.
10. Arboleda Quiñonez, "*Los afrocolombianos*," 213, 217; translations my own. While Arboleda Quiñonez doesn't discuss these problems in rhetorical terms, his materio-corporeal analysis of Afrocolombian sociopolitical erasure and presence underscores the rhetorical dimensions of state violence.
11. Reynolds, "Ethos as Location," 326.
12. Bizzell, "Frances Willard," 379.
13. Douglas Farah, "Indian from Guatemala Wins Nobel Peace Prize," *Washington Post*, October 17, 1992, http://www.washingtonpost.com/.
14. Menchú, *I, Rigoberta Menchú*, 262.
15. Stoll qtd. in Catherine Nolin, review of *Rigoberta Menchu*, 120.
16. Rogachevsky, "David Stoll," 2.
17. Aznárez, "*Los que me atacan*."
18. Yúdice, "Testimonio and Postmodernism," 15.
19. The Latina Feminist Group, Introduction, 2.
20. Reyes and Rodríguez, "*Testimonio*," 525.
21. Reyes and Rodríguez, "*Testimonio*," 526–27.
22. Larry Rohter, "Tarnished Laureate: A Special Report; Nobel Winner Finds Her Story Challenged," *New York Times*, December 15, 1998, https://archive.nytimes.com/.
23. Catherine Nolin, Review of *I, Rigoberta Menchú*, 120–22.
24. Rogachevsky, "David Stoll," 2.
25. Hartman, *Lose Your Mother*, 6.
26. See Rosenberg, "Genocide," 16–23.
27. See Adib and Emiljanowicz, "Colonial Time," 1221–238.
28. Michael Gould-Wartofsky and Kelly Lee, "Guatemala's Dirty War," *The Nation*, May 15, 2009, https://www.thenation.com/article/archive/guatemalas-dirty-war/;

Douglas Farah, "Papers Show U.S. Role in Guatemalan Abuses," *Washington Post*, March 11, 1999, https://www.washingtonpost.com/.

29. International Monetary Fund, *Guatemala: Selected Issues Paper*, June 8, 2018, https://www.imf.org/; Nina Lakhani and Tom Dart, "'Claudia Was a Good Girl. Why Did They Kill Her?' From a Guatemalan Village to Death in Texas," *The Guardian*, June 2, 2018, https://www.theguardian.com/.

30. César Rodriguez, "Court Records Reveal Details After Family of Woman Fatally Shot by BP Agent Near Laredo Files Suit," *LMTonline*, May 15, 2020, https://www.lmtonline.com/.

31. Associated Press, "Advocates Want $100 Million for Woman Killed by U.S. Border Agent," *NBC News*, May 24, 2019, https://www.nbcnews.com/; Rodriguez, "Court Records."

32. Roncero-Bellido, "*Testimoniando*," 37.

33. Roncero-Bellido, "*Testimoniando*," 36.

34. Caitlin Cruz, "People Are Outraged Over the Story of a 19-Year-Old Woman Shot & Killed by Border Patrol," *Bustle*, May 27, 2018, https://www.bustle.com/.

35. Daniella Silva, "Migrant Mom Details Daughter's Death After ICE Detention in Emotional Testimony," *NBC News*, July 10, 2019, https://www.nbcnews.com/.

36. Sara Sanchez and Aaron Montes, "Months After Jakelin Caal's Death, Medical Examiner Releases Autopsy Report," *El Paso Times*, March 19, 2019, https://www.elpasotimes.com/story/news/2019/03/29/jakelin-caal-autopsy-report-released-el-paso-medical-examiner-migrant-girl/3313850002/; Mara Sacchetti, "Official: Guatemalan Boy Who Died in U.S. Custody Tested Positive for Influenza B, Final Cause of Death Remains Under Investigation," *Washington Post*, December 28, 2018, https://www.washingtonpost.com/.

37. Bold, Knowles, and Leach, "Feminist Memorializing," 125–48.

38. Delgado, "The Silken Cord," 415–24.

39. Mukavetz, "Towards a Cultural Rhetorics Methodology," 109–10.

40. King, "Speaking Sovereignty," 77.

WORKS CITED

Adib, and Paul Emiljanowicz. "Colonial Time in Tension: Decolonizing Temporal Imaginaries." *Time & Society* 28, no. 3 (2019): 1221–238.

Arboleda Quiñonez, Santiago. "*Los afrocolombianos: Entre la retórica del multiculturalismo y el fuego cruzado del destierro*." *The Journal of Latin American and Caribbean Anthropology* 12, no. 1 (2007): 213–22.

Aznárez, Julian Jesús. "Los que me atacan humillan a las víctimas." *El País*, January 24, 1999. http://www1.udel.edu/leipzig/071198/elb250199.htm.

Bizzell, Patricia. "Frances Willard, Phoebe Palmer, and the Ethos of the Methodist Woman Preacher." *Rhetoric Society Quarterly* 36, no. 4 (2006): 377–98.

Bold, Christine, Ric Knowles, and Belinda Leach. "Feminist Memorializing and Cultural Countermemory: The Case of Marianne's Park." *Signs* 28, no. 1 (2002): 125–48.

Browdy Ronisha, and Esther Milu, eds. "Global Black Rhetorics: A New Framework for Engaging African and Afro Diasporic Rhetorical Traditions." *Rhetoric Society Quarterly* 52, no. 3 (2022): 219–41.

Brownlee, Yavanna M. "Decolonizing Composition and Rhetorics Programs: An Indigenous Rhetorics Model for Implementing Concepts of Relationship and Integrating Marginalized Rhetorics." PhD diss., Ohio University, 2018.

Bullen, J.B. *The Myth of the Renaissance in Nineteenth-Century Writing*. Oxford: Oxford University Press, 1994.

Chowdhury, Rowshan Jahan. "Restriction, Resistance, and Humility: A Feminist Approach to Anne Bradstreet and Phillis Wheatley's Literary Works." *A Journal of English Studies* 10 (2019): 47–56.

Collins, Patricia Hill. "Intersectionality's Definitional Dilemmas." *Annual Review of Sociology* 41 (2015): 1–20.

Couture, Barbara, and Thomas Kent, eds. *Private, the Public, and the Published: Reconciling Private Lives and Public Rhetoric*. Denver, CO: University Press of Colorado, 2004.

Delgado, Richard. "The Silken Cord: An Essay in Honor of Jane Hill." In *The Persistence of Language: Constructing and Confronting the Past and Present in the Voices of Jane H. Hill*, edited by Shannon T. Bischoff, Deborah Cole, Amy V. Fountain, and Mizuki Miyashita, 415–24. Amsterdam: John Benjamins Press, 2013.

Griffin, Cindy L. "The Essentialist Roots of the Public Sphere: A Feminist Critique." *Western Journal of Communication* 60, no. 1 (1996): 21–39.

Halloran, S. Michael. "Aristotle's Concept of Ethos, or If Not His Somebody Else's." *Rhetoric Review* 1, no. 1 (1982): 58–63.

Hartman, Saidiya. *Lose Your Mother: A Journey along the Atlantic Slave Route*. New York: Farrar, Straus and Giroux, 2008.

Hesford, Wendy S. "Ethos Righted: Transnational Feminist Analytics." In *Rethinking Ethos: A Feminist Ecological Approach to Rhetoric*, edited by Kathleen J. Ryan, Nancy Myers, and Rebecca Jones, 198–215. Carbondale, IL: Southern Illinois University Press, 2016.

King, Lisa. "Speaking Sovereignty and Communicating Change: Rhetorical Sovereignty and the Inaugural Exhibits at the NMAI." *American Indian Quarterly* 35, no. 1 (2011): 75–103.

The Latina Feminist Group. Introduction to *Telling to Live: Latina Feminist Testimonios*, edited by The Latina Feminist Group, 1–24. Durham, NC: Duke University Press, 2001.

McKeon, Michael. *The Secret History of Domesticity: Public, Private, and the Division of Knowledge*. Baltimore, MD: Johns Hopkins University Press, 2006.

Menchú, Rigoberta. *I, Rigoberta Menchú: An Indian Woman in Guatemala*, edited by Elisabeth Burgos-Debray. Translated by Ann Wright. New York: Verso Books, 2010.

Moorman, Gary B., William E. Blanton, and Thomas McLaughlin. "The Rhetoric of Whole Language." *Reading Research Quarterly* 29, no. 4 (1994): 308–29.

Mukavetz, Andrea M. Riley. "Towards a Cultural Rhetorics Methodology: Making Research Matter with Multi-generational Women from the Little Traverse Bay Band." *Rhetoric, Professional Communication, and Globalization* 5, no. 1 (2014): 108–25.

Nolin, Catherine. "Review of *Rigoberta Menchu and the Story of All Poor Guatemalans*, by David Stoll." *Journal of Latin American Geography* 3, no. 1 (2004): 120–22. https://doi.org/10.1353/lag.2005.0012.

Ore, Ersula. "Whiteness as Racialized Space: Obama and the Rhetorical Constraints of Phenotypical Blackness." In *Rhetorics of Whiteness: Postracial Hauntings in Popular Culture, Social Media, and Education*, edited by Tammie M. Kennedy, Joyce Irene Middleton, and Krista Ratcliffe, 256–70. Carbondale, IL: Southern Illinois University Press, 2016.

Powell, Malea. "Rhetorics of Survivance: How American Indians Use Writing." *College Composition and Communication* 53, no. 3 (2002): 396–434.

Reyes, Kathryn Blackmer, and Julia E. Curry Rodríguez. "*Testimonio:* Origins, Terms, and Resources." *Equity & Excellence in Education* 45, no. 3 (2012): 525–38.

Reynolds, Nedra. "Ethos as Location: New Sites for Understanding Discursive Authority." *Rhetoric Review* 11, no. 2 (1993): 325–38. https://doi.org/10.1080/073501 99309389009.

Rogachevsky, Jorge R. "David Stoll vs. Rigoberta Menchú: Indigenous Victims or Protagonists?" *Delaware Review of Latin American Studies* 2, no. 2 (2001). https://www1.udel.edu/LAS/Vol2-2Rogachevsky.html.

Roncero-Bellido, Ana. "*Testimoniando y comadreando* across Borders: *Latina/s Anónima/s* in *Telling to Live: Latina Feminist Testimonios.*" *Chicana/Latina Studies* 20, no. 1 (2020): 26–55.

Rosenberg, Sheri P. "Genocide Is a Process, Not an Event." *Genocide Studies and Prevention* 7, no. 1 (2012) 16–23.

Royster, Jacqueline Jones, and Gesa E. Kirsch. *Feminist Rhetorical Practices: New Horizons for Rhetoric, Composition, and Literacy Studies.* Carbondale, IL: Southern Illinois University Press, 2012.

Schell, Eileen E., and K.J. Rawson, eds. *Rhetorica in Motion: Feminist Rhetorical Methods and Methodologies.* Pittsburgh, PA: University of Pittsburgh Press, 2010.

Waite, Stacey. "The Unavailable Means of Persuasion: A Queer Ethos for Feminist Writers and Teachers." In *Rethinking Ethos: A Feminist Ecological Approach to Rhetoric,* edited by Kathleen J. Ryan, Nancy Myers, and Rebecca Jones, 71–88. Carbondale, IL: Southern Illinois University Press, 2016.

Yúdice, George. "Testimonio and Postmodernism." *Latin American Perspectives* 18, no. 3 (1991): 15–31.

FOUR

Against the Asylum

A Re-Rhetorica of Madness

sarah madoka currie and Ada Hubrig

For those of us living with severe mental illness,
the world is full of cages where we can be locked in. /
My Hope is that I'll stay out of those cages for the rest of my life.

—ESMÉ WEIJUN WANG, *THE COLLECTED SCHIZOPHRENIAS*

We are crip-mads: m/Mad, disabled people proud of who we are.[1]

Would you like to sit next to us? We can do something brave together, a fireside chat, a pathway investigation about what we do with mad rhythms and psychiatric translations—and what it might look like to translate less.

We, sarah and Ada, offer this crip-mad feminist methodology primer, centering crip-mad agency and ethical engagement with m/Madness.[2] Too often, non-Mad academics have written about us, over us, and even against us, using us as convenient anecdotes or low-hanging metaphors or have otherwise rhetorically figured our existence to mold into whatever adjacent project is at hand.

This is held and legitimized by the ways in which modern medicine, psychiatry, psychology, neuroscience, biology and eugenic research practices continue to treat people with mental illness; as recently demonstrable in 25–30% higher homelessness rates persisting pre- and post-pandemic,[3] two to three times lower life expectancy dependent on diagnosis,[4] and significantly higher education dropout rates dependent on diagnosis.[5] This list of continued mistreatments and secondary citizen status perpetuated by biased understandings of mental illness is absolutely non-exhaustive, and becomes ever more complicated when combined with comorbidities or intersectionality paradigms.

We Mad folk refuse to be your metaphor. In what follows, we offer a short overview of Mad Pride and offer three crip-mad, feminist methodological approaches: embracing realities, where we argue for the importance of believing crip-mads; disavowal of hierarchical logics, where we argue for the importance of dismantling academia's fastidious, oppressive obsession with "rationality" and "intelligence"; and practicing mad, radical consent, where we implore you to write *with* and *alongside* crip-mads, asking you to not engage in the epistemological violence of writing *over us* or *for us*.

In writing "Against the Asylum," we mean to write against the very conceptual frameworks that undergird ableist, socially constructed notions of able-mindedness and mental disability and madness that are weaponized against crip-mads, disproportionately impacting multiply marginalized crip-mads, following a history of Mad activists and scholars. We offer a truncated, necessarily abbreviated history of Mad activism, not as a definitive guide, but in hopes that you might take up these still unfolding conversations ethically in your own work (see our methodological suggestions later in this chapter).

crip-mads against the asylum, in academia

We write against the carceral rhetoric of the asylum, pathologizing "mental illness" to stigmatize and harm us and people like us, writing alongside the work of Mad Movements and Disability Justice to refigure feminist rhetorics as a methodology to resist the stigmatization and vilification of madness that has been a staple of asylum rhetorics permeating Western culture. We echo other scholars in underscoring how these framings of madness deny the rhetorical capacity of Mad subjects,[6] but we work towards a feminist rhetoric that embrace Madness, reclaiming space for Mad femmes like us to show up as our whole mad, disabled, neurodivergent selves.[7]

sarah: Toward the end of the 1960s to the mid-1980s, following reforms in post-WWII advancements in psychology that changed therapeutic discourse,[8] American and Canadian asylums began the process of deinstitutionalization, or decarcerating long-term mental illness "patients" with the hope of productively reintegrating them back into the community population.[9] At the time, there was no short-form or extended-term reintegration strategy, and insufficient resources were allocated to help these trapped bodyminds adjust to their new reality. As a predictable result, homelessness skyrocketed and huge pressure on social services caused catastrophically lengthy wait times for these individuals to have their basic needs met.[10]

Over time, these activists began advocating for their right to have their basic needs met in a legally enforceable way—and their humanity similarly legally and sociopolitically recognized—through the Mad Movement (capitalized), which post-millennium acquired additional aliases as "Mad Pride" or "mad mvmt" (decapitalized).[11] Core issues to the mad mvmt have included the ongoing critically stigmatizing practices of North American policy and healthcare, the right to autonomous treatment, the right to non-carceral care, the right to equal education, ensured access to quality of life resources, and the right to self-identify as mad or mentally ill without danger of inequitable treatment.[12]

Ada: Following a history of crip-Mad, feminist, and trans/queer activism, we seek to intervene in the rhetoric of the asylum that harms Mad people and multiply marginalized people. Writing alongside Mad and Disability Justice organizers and Queer/Trans activists, we underscore how negative frameworks of madness are leveraged as a white supremacist, colonialist project against Black and Indigenous femmes and queer/trans femmes. To write *alongside* (or speaking-with) as a decolonial project, we offer multiply marginalized, embodied experiences of madness as a way to push back against negative rhetorical framings of madness meant to exclude, isolate, and silence mad subjects.

sarah: Meanwhile, higher education and hospital-funded private research circles continue to profit from cure-based research on mad subjects, as if in defiance of mad distrust and withholding of autonomous permission.[13] In short, there have been hundreds of years of supposedly productive research problematizing, criminalizing, psychiatrizing, psychologizing, villainizing and medicalizing madness (inclusive of the creation of "mental illness" itself) as an undesirable, unproductive and unworthy aberration based on a simple and largely uncontested understanding that deviating too far from the majority's definition of (neuro) normative is an act of sociocultural aggression.

Ada: In carving out this crip-mad rhetorical space, we expand on Jay Dolmage and Cynthia Lewiecki-Wilson's assertion in the first iteration of *Rhetorica in Motion,* "that feminism and disability ought to be powerful allies,"[14] and we gesture to the false dichotomy between mental and physical disabilities.[15] We approach this work cautiously, asking our crip-mad allies to imagine with us what it might mean to do this activist, imperative, futuristic work in ways that respect crip-mad agency and foster ecosystems of co-operating crip-mad communities.

We write against both the literal asylums as well as the *logics* of asylums—a carceral framework that punishes crip-mad, multiply marginalized femmes who deviate from socially-constructed normativities. We recognize the privileges afforded to us as crip-mads in higher education, but we also point to how higher education is built on a foundation of able-minded mythos and its attendant concepts. As Margaret Price has argued, many of the topoi most central to academe itself "intersect problematically" with mental disability, including rationality, criticality, productivity, collegiality, and others.[16] Price takes up disability studies to reevaluate academic frameworks *through* the lens of mental disabilities, challenging academic discourse and classroom practices.

sarah: Truly, the biomedical and psychopharmaceutical hold on madness in its seemingly inextricable relationship with psychiatry is presented to us as the objective, research substantiated pathway: the Doctors believe this, so it must be true. The Doctors (or "experts," or keepers-of-knowledge) recognize neurodivergence as "illness" in need of rehabilitation or "cure," so I know this must be true. What's more, I feel an imperative to tell others that this telling and retelling of history is inescapably true—save for "exceptions," mads who "beat the odds" or present as "gifted" in otherwise abled, authorized, academicized spaces.

Ada: We write alongside Price in imagining how madness might serve as a method that makes the sanist, ableist rhetoric and practices often lurking just below the surface for our abled peers (but is the lived reality of crip-mads) explicit, especially noting where this ableist construction of madness has been disproportionately wielded against minoritized groups,[17] but especially against Femmes of color and LGBTQ folx who were pathologized, medicalized, and disproportionately institutionalized through asylum rhetorics.[18] We understand that these categories were invented as a means of social control in the in the late 1800s and continue to be rhetorically deployed to implement racist and otherwise oppressive social policies to this day and are used to pathologize and disbelieve femmes of color.[19] And we recognize that the threat of asylum—the cages so eagerly waiting for us that Weijun Wang has written about—is still very real, not just on far-away places but on our own campuses. We point to the pathologization of "mental health" and "mental illness" on college campuses.[20] Amy Gaeta notes the policing/surveillance function of university mental health centers, that operate so "the status quo of the university and its community partners remains intact and pristine."[21]

Whereas asylum rhetorics sought to speak *about* people like us, we build on the disability justice frameworks of Leah Lakshmi Piepzna-Samarasinha and the disability justice collective Sins Invalid, to reclaim Madness as a site of rhetorical invention, especially for multiply marginalized rhetors.

moving beyond context to mad-positive methodologies

To reimagine feminist rhetorics of Madness, we write alongside a constellation of others who have resisted the villainization of madness, tracing interventions like the Mad Queer Organizing of Eliot Fukui, the Disability Justice Framework created by queer, disabled of color collective Sins Invalid, the healing justice ethos of Fireweed Collective, and intersectional decarceral approaches to the mental health industrial complex; we turn to feminist rhetorics of madness as feminist coalition building, working to build a "collaboration of misfits," a Mad, feminist coalition between people of color, queer/trans people, and disabled people who have historically been targeted by the white supremacist, ableist misogynoir of asylum rhetorics.[22]

reject reality and embrace realities

In taking up a crip-mad feminist methodology, we point to the importance of *listening* to and *believing* crip-mads. We begin with the "Navigating Crisis" guide, published by Fireweed Collective (formerly the Icarus Project). The guide, meant to help beloved community members support each other in times of mad crisis, reminds the reader to listen to the person experiencing crisis without judgment, to be present with them and hear their feelings, emotions, and experiences. The guide reiterates the importance of the person in crisis communicating what they are feeling and experiencing, and for those supporting the person in crisis to listen without judgment. While we may have an altered sense of what reality is and be driven by anxieties to be hypercritical of ourselves—and may rely on loved ones to help us get a more accurate read on the situation—it is also necessary to acknowledge and understand our thoughts and feelings that we experience.

As crip-mads, we reject the notion that there is a single experienced, objective reality. Maybe that seems irrational to you, and that's precisely the point. What is *rational* is a sanist construct, already bound up and constructed from positions of power. Simply put, we draw on crip-mad wisdom that argues no two people experience the world the same way and there is no shared objective reality. As methodology, madness highlights these disjunctures between experiences.

Throughout *Bodyminds Reimagined: (Dis)Ability, Race, and Gender in Black Women's Speculative Fiction,* Sami Schalk establishes not only the racial and gender biases in who is and who isn't categorized as mentally disabled, mentally ill,[23] but explores how Black Women's speculative fiction highlight how the realities we experience "vary significantly by our cultural locations within the systems of (dis)ability, race, gender, class, sexuality, and more."[24] Schalk argues that there is no objective, stable line between able-mindedness and mental disability, because these are both subjective, culturally created categories that have been historically leveraged against racial, gender, sexual, and disabled minorities, often precisely when they point to injustices: "when marginalized individuals are accused of overreacting to, being too sensitive about, or reading too much into the actions and behaviors of those around them; when marginalized people who attempt to call out, name, and share their experiences with oppression are told that the way they experienced an event is not the way it really happened or the way that others experienced, that they are missing something, that their interpretation was not what was intended, and so on."[25]

As Schalk demonstrates, this gaslighting of Black Women and other minoritized people is directly tied to creating dividing lines around able-mindedness and mental disability, creating social and cultural implications for those deemed mad while affirming the lived realities of those with more power in oppressive systems while denying the lived realities of those with less.

We point to how madness is often leveraged against crip-mad and other minoritized people to deny their lived reality. As trans, disabled scholar V. Jo Hsu has argued about anti-trans zealots, their rhetorical strategy frequently hinges on circular logic that assumes: (a) trans people (and especially trans youth) are mentally ill for being trans (usually with no diagnosis, but assumed-to-be-mentally-ill because they are trans) and that (b) because trans people are de facto mentally ill, their experiences and opinion of their own bodies cannot be trusted,[26] going on to highlight how trans, racial, and disabled identities are pathologized. Hsu highlights how anti-trans rhetorics draws on mental disability as a means to discredit trans people, to deny their very lived experience of their own bodies.

Just as Schalk points to Black Women's speculative fiction as a site that deconstructs the notion of an objective, shared reality and Hsu pushes back against the pathologization of racial, transgender, and disabled identities, we highlight how crip-mad experiences illuminate the gaps between our lived realities, how we do not experience the world the same. This has, of course, serious implications for scholarship.

As feminist rhetorical methodology, rhetorics of madness ask us to tend to this gaslighting, to this denial of lived realities: to see rhetorical projects where people's lived experiences are denied because they simply don't align with the official version of things recorded that serves hierarchical power relationships. Writing against the carceral logics of the asylum and towards mad, feminist rhetorical methodology means better tending to these differences in lived realities.

But feminist methodology must extend beyond our research agendas: embracing realities as crip-mad feminist praxis also means applying this knowledge to the spaces we inhabit, noting when individual lived experiences are being displaced and replaced, when we are being gaslit in the service of upholding a single, assumed-to-be-objective viewpoint of reality—often for the sake of institutional agendas. In their article "#Triggered: The Invisible Labor of Traumatized Graduate Students," scholars Jesse Rice-Evans and Andrea Stella relay their experiences as disabled graduate students navigating academia. As part of this telling, Stella recalls a previous abusive relationship and notes some of the parallels between that relationship and having a neurocognitive disability as a graduate student, writing, "He insisted I was lying, it had not happened the way I claimed, and I knew this was false; but after the 30th time being told my memories aren't real, I began to question myself: *what had I actually done? Why couldn't I remember the awful things he said I did?*"[27] Stella's narrative, mirrored by Rice-Evans's experiences, demonstrates how even shared space and time is experienced quite differently by different bodyminds, and that claims about objective realities are often leveraged against crip-mads and other minoritized people. It is imperative that we listen to these accounts and work toward change in academia.

to hell with "high functioning," disavow hierarchical logics

Related to believing the accounts of crip-mads is the importance of delinking worthiness and what we perceive as intelligence and sanity, concepts often used to discriminate by gender, race, disability, class, sexuality, and maintain an array of such marginalizations. In *The Collected Schizophrenias*, Esmé Weijun Wang describes her time in a psychiatric hospital, writing "the psychiatric hierarchy decrees who can and cannot be high functioning and 'gifted.'"[28] Wang describes, throughout her experiences, how this hierarchy informs how different patients are both perceived and treated by hospital staff and especially by nurses and doctors. For Wang, this hierarchy relates directly to people's perceived abilities to *achieve* or make progress in socially intelligible goals. To be "high functioning" in this hierarchy means to be closest to the perceived normate, to be able to perform in closer proximity to the sanist version of reality, and ultimately to reinforce a binary that dictates who is acceptably sane or unacceptably mad based on ableist presuppositions.

As we've already argued, the construction of a singular reality is already at odds with a feminist, crip-mad justice framework. If we accept this to be the case, we suggest that other "ranking" systems, like notions of objective rankings of intelligence, of "self control," and sanity are also faulty, as they are based in the belief in an objective, baseline normativity that frankly doesn't exist, either. And these hierarchies are extensions of cisheteropatriarchal, white supremacist value systems. La Marr Jurelle Bruce describes the "psychonormative binary that casts madness as patently bad and Reason as inherently good on opposite sides of a metaphysical wall," tracing "discursive conflations, historical intersections, and phenomenal convergences of madness and blackness" that aligns whiteness with reason and Blackness with madness.[29]

We reject labels such as "high functioning" that we see as further stigmatizing those considered "lower functioning" and allow open discrimination against them while simultaneously using "high functioning" to deny support to crip-mads. Consider the encoding of "executive function" or "high functioning" (given as the opposite of "lower-order" thought) and what that signals to mad-identifying bodyminds. Mad studies as a discipline has been historically defined by its defiant polarization from the psychopharmacological and psychiatric definitions of mental "health" and "wellness," instead claiming madness by positing lived and living experience narratives that elide this simplistic terminology and question the equally simplistic conjuration of "normalcy" at the root of sci-comprehension. Pseudo-diagnostic terminology like "high functioning" is not an objective or sci-based assessment but a performative and highly subjective evaluation that has been roundly dismissed by the community the term was originally designed to service: predominantly the ASD community.[30]

As diagnostic language gained greater cultural currency in the second millennium's pharmacomedicalization complex and the concurrent rise of the new-wave "neurodiversity movement," "high functioning" was borrowed from its original home 'measuring' ASD ability and became cross-applicable for various mental illness diagnoses, particularly those known for manic cycling or intense episodes: articles about "high-functioning bi-polar rockstars,"[31] "medically reviewed high-functioning schizophrenia,"[32] "high-functioning" or "quiet" borderline personality disorder,"[33] and a study archived in the National Library of Medicine following three "high-func-tioning multiple personality [disorder] patients."[34] We reject this "higher" order is according to a non-neutral metric that takes for granted that "nor-mative" ordered thinking is a stable, readily identifiable concept that can be scaled frontwards and backwards based on eugenic, pseudoscientific notions of IQ that were designed *from the beginning* to be used as a tool to further stigmatize women and people of color as part of coercive function of asylum rhetorics.[35]

And we our "sane" counterparts doing their ableist algebra: as Remi Yergeau has described in their account of autism and neurological queer-ness, when Yergeau shares that they are autistic, this disclosure "provides entry for others to tally my symptoms, to compare the context of my dis-closure against their knowledge (or lack thereof) of autism's motions and means. That is, declaring one's neuroqueerness is often culturally read as an invitation for neurotypicals to theorize and assess what neuroqueerness is."[36] Claiming of neuroqueerness, of madness, of mental disability is not an invitation for further questions. We resist the "tally of symptoms" that sort us crip-mads into hierarchies. We resist "high functioning," because these labels are often pressed upon us crip-mads by external, usually sane, neuro-typical people who have no such qualification or frame of reference to un-derstand our positionalities. In conversation with Remi Yergeau's analysis of autism anecdotes, Margaret Price observes "we must resist facile conclusions about our students based upon their diagnosed, self-identified, *or* suspected neuroatypicalities, and focus instead on ways that their writing and ways of knowing might change and inform our practices."[37]

We see the ableist impulse to rank madness and sort crip-mads into a hierarchy of acceptable and unacceptable madness as part of the ableist categorizations that, as Shayda Kafai asserts, "uses the abnormal, the mad, to reinforce the potency and power of the center, the normal, the sane."[38] Kafai describes how ableist culture relies on these binaries, the ability to quickly sort the sane and mad, and takes up conversations about borders in Chicana/o Studies, Women's Studies, Queer Studies, and Disability Studies, creating her own framework of the mad border body, a proud reclamation of madness. Kafai captures the pressure of not wanting to be *read* a certain way, of lacking the ability to reason or be a person on her own terms but claims madness through this theorization of the mad border body, an embodied experience that demonstrates how the very binary created between sane/mad is subjective. Kafai writes, "by claiming madness, by stating that I am a mad border body, I am acknowledging the ways history is rewritten through language. I am taking apart what I have been taught of madness in order to create my own story."[39]

This reclamation, this being able to tell our own crip-mad stories against an ableist sorting function that creates acceptable and unacceptable madness that centers so-called sanity is at the heart of our rejection of hierarchical labels. Put another way, we crip-mads are considered "high functioning" until we're not: until we get to loud, too sad, have too many needs for an ableist system that deems our bodyminds too mad, too loud, too sad, too suicidal, too much. Hierarchical labels reinforce the binary by saying some mad people are acceptable and others are not.

mad kinship & radical consent through speaking-with dialectics

We study and center madness as a way to be in community with mad people and foster mad community. We point to Mad Queer organizer Elliott Fukui, who records his own mental health goal as "Remembering that capitalism is the true crisis I give myself permission to let go of the ableist notions of worthiness productivity and value instead centering and prioritizing my wholeness in the service of healing myself and my people."[40] At the same time, we worry about the academification of critical disability studies—the ways in which intersectionally complex dis/abled allies are permitted or deauthorized from imagining, creating, advocating for or otherwise legislating their right to exist on parity terms with abled individuals—compromises were made in terms of the language used to justify or otherwise make explicit the harms dealt to disabled bodyminds in the past and present. The paradoxical requirement for crip theory and methodology to "sound like" other fields of theory, and most especially the hyper-abled theory crafting of academia proper, comes in direct conflict with some of the overarching imperatives of authentic inclusivity. Namely, recognizability and acquiescence: noting what words I use when, and how my words must pass as sounding *as comfortably* coherent to broad-scoped academic mores as possible in order to be seen, heard and co-operated with.

This paradigm of passing as sane in order to discuss (never mind *ensure*) some level of inclusivity in prestige spaces manifests as a price of entry, a means by which certain crip audiences "deserve" to be heard while others are dismissed as "emotional,"[41] "non-academic,"[42] "unmedicated,"[43] or outright "incomprehensible."[44] Consider the methodology by which accessible learning centers decide which students are "deserving" of accommodations: they must re-legitimize their experiences through the subjective lens of psychiatry or biomedical logics, and re-present their case as told by another (the 'expert' who is tasked with reducing a lifetime of complex experiences to a readily-optimized paragraph). The Doctor adjudicates the student as a plethora of vague labels, passing down this verdict to accessibility centers who will match this vague label with a broad accommodation: "time and a half," "extended deadline," "scribe needed."[45] By passing as a ready diagnosis in need of a quick cure, accessible learning centers accomplish the too-easily optimized, streamlined practice of psychiatrizing students in order to control the ways they are permitted to pass in our classrooms. Isn't it interesting how closely this methodology matches screening mechanics for qual/quantitative interview processes, to which we assemble authoritative datasets on mad minds we then take responsibility for "advocating for"? Is it possible we do not award mad bodyminds enough respect and autonomy with which to comment on their pastness and futures unadulterated by us, the Doctors, the Experts and Adjudicators of coherence?

Disability studies as it existed in the early 1990s made the clever decision to pass as already "legitimized" avenues of theory crafting through careful deliberation by which their words and arguments could suitably *sound like* the acceptable, comfortable, coherent arguments already underway in such long-standing fields as film theory, in epistemology, in cultural rhetorics (non-exhaustively), until such time as we reached an era more willing to hear us out on our own terms (also see cripistemologies). Speaking-with dialectics emerge alongside standpoint theory and identity-based fields of articulation that force well-meaning researchers to ask difficult questions about how much we can really learn without ourselves experiencing the conditions under discussion: just as queer theorists, feminist liberators, and Black solidarity activists have spoken powerfully in the past, mad movement acolytes engender "nothing about us without us" as their call-in of conduct, of radically reminding experts that not everything subject to scrutiny can be so simply read, understood, and memorized. Some experiences will always manifest as a closed door, though carefully empathized with, and the stage must be relented to those whom the microphone can make melodies in the clearest, closest sense.

The speaking-with paradigm, or the right to self-advocate and write the story of one's own experiences in order to name one's own harms and subsequent needs, is of central concern for conversations about the relationship

between mental illness and higher education. Prior to deinstitutionalization, crip-mad imprisoned bodies were ostensibly free research material for
research think tanks, pharmaceutical labs and higher education institutions
in need of compliant human subjects.[46] The abled insistence to narrate or
overwrite the mad bodymind is produced through the mediated lens of
so-called normative ability. It's important to remember that mad history
is often mediated by someone abled—or the production of speaking-for
stories—and when we continue to allow published research on mental illness to proliferate primarily from this mediated lens, we are not honestly
interrogating what the research really reveals about ourselves and our overreliance on 'normativity' in evaluating acculturation. In the truest conjuring
of speaking-with, mad bodyminds are given parity space with those who
have the privileges associated with taking up, giving or otherwise designat-
ing space—on stages, in articles, in zines and journals and poetry cafes and
grassroots forums of protest.

Other speculative elements to consider when building-in speaking-with
visions of parity research could include the following questions, which could
be taken up in your own thought space or among research teams designing
well-meaning studies to uncover "truths" about the lived and living experiences of mental illness and psychopharmacology:

- Is this a madness safari envisioning of illness (am I rubbernecking or
  investigating?)?
- To ask this question another way, do my questions as written wish to
  understand mad rhetoric, or put it on display to others?
- If I showed my study to the subjects themselves, would they feel they
  are being accurately reflected (e.g., studies about schizophrenics that
  assume the subjects lack the capacity to read/interpret the quantitative results)?
- Are these questions as written asking to translate mad experiences
  authentically, or comfortably? Am I asking them to do translation
  work on my behalf?
- Have I used significant article space to "translate" answers provided
  in more comfortable words? Is it possible to reduce the translational
  imperative and allow their words used when and where they elected?
- Is my study built on an abled-adjacent envisioning of a solution (e.g.,
  assuming the ultimate goal of madness is cure/eradication, assuming
  you know what is "best for them")?

- Have I asked how the subjects might render or re-explain what we've uncovered together? This information and data are not solely mine, and lived experiences should not be simplistically mined as a resource to spend or swap in academic venues.
- To what extent is their lived experience being tokenized or quietly delegitimized? By this, I mean is it core to your methodology—or merely used as a "bonus" element?
- If the subject of my investigation were a close friend, would I have written about them or rendered their rhetoric in the same way? Am I participating in mad exceptionalism?

This list of questions is by no means exhaustive, and makes no attempt to be accusatory or otherwise derisive—my hope is by providing you with guiding questions with which to assess the speaking-with-ness of your research as considered by a mad traveler and truth-teller, you gain tools to do the well-meaning work you're envisioning in ways that do not come at the cost of legitimizing mad studies, mad rhetoric or crip-mad ways of knowing and being in the world. These are merely a starting place: this list is unending and open to remixing, reinterpretation and updating for your kaleidoscopic context. Ultimately, speaking-with asks for authentic and honest conversations about the rhetoric we so often take for granted: have I spoken with madness on parity terms, as someone to legitimize and empathize with? Or am I participating in yet another comfortable instantiation of spectacle dialectics, of madness safaris and pointing derisively at that which we cannot imagine or expect to become (itself a flawed line of reasoning)?

Out Loud, or gifting you with a Feminist re-rhetorica of m/Madness

We began this chapter by owning our madness. And throughout this chapter, in community with other crip-mads, we have dreamt up contours of mad, feminist rhetorical methodologies. While still an emerging list, we offer embracing multiple realities, disavowal of hierarchical logics, and writing in community as three moves *toward* a more just, mad-inclusive feminist praxis.

But more than that, we proudly claim madness in this chapter—knowing well the institutional violence faced by mad folx—because too-often, madness is erased from the narrative. We point to the work of Leah Lakshmi Piepzna-Samarasinha, writing of the legacy of Marsha P. Johnson and how her madness/mental disability was often removed from conversations about her. Piepzna-Samarasinha writes how too many "Movements that were neck deep in talking about trauma and chronic illness and the medical industrial complex" "didn't have an out-loud political understanding of how ableism, disability justice, and disability were all up in our lives."[47]

While we understand some of our crip-mad community cannot safely "out" themselves as we have here (and that complex choice must be respected, too), we ask for feminist methodologies that sees people in our full complexities, that addresses sanism and ableism *out loud,* that tends to how race, gender, disability, sexuality, and other embodied experiences are bound together and inseparable and how mad and especially multiply-marginalized mad folx are subject to cages of all kind. So, we ask you, especially those readers who do not identify as crip-mad, please do not speak for us. Do not speak over us. As the disability slogan has proclaimed: *nothing about us without us.*[48] Instead of writing *about* us, write *with* us. And *do not* assume crip-mads aren't reading your words. We are. If you don't want to engage the Mad community ethically, don't engage us at all.

We ask feminist rhetoricians to contend with the socially-constructed markers of sanity and their aggressive maintenance that serve as barriers to keep crip-mad bodyminds out of spaces—or to forcibly confine us to others. If, in the end, this chapter has pushed us to reconsider this dichotomy between madness and reason, to pause before we demean mentally disabled, crip-mads in our profession and beyond, we've done our work.

NOTES

1. Following the Mad Pride Movement, we reclaim madness. An umbrella term featuring a range of diagnosis and welcoming those without diagnosis, we move to destigmatize madness and mental disability and make clear the violent histories of psychiatry and psychiatric institutions—including their offshoots on college campuses—that continue to harm mad folks.
2. There are a *lot* of politics around the capitalization of M/madness, and both sides of this argument have salient evaluations of the circumstances by which they choose their grammar.
3. Aaron Lai, "The 'Crushing' Cycle of Homelessness and Mental Illness," *Breaktime,* May 28, 2021, https://www.breaktime.org/post/the-crushing-cycle-of-homelessness-and-mental-illness; Padgett, "Homelessness"; Canadian Observatory on Homelessness, "About Homelessness," https://preventhomelessness.ca/.
4. Center for Addiction and Mental Health (CAMH), "Mental Illness and Addiction: Facts and Statistics," 2022; Liu et al., "Volumetric Abnormalities."
5. Hjorth et al., "Mental Health"; University of Exeter, "Poor Mental Health 'Both Cause and Effect' of School Exclusion," January 22, 2020, https://news-archive.exeter.ac.uk/featurednews/title_774208_en.html.
6. Price, *Mad at School,* 33; Yergeau, *Authoring Autism,* 43.

7. sarah and Ada use "femme" in recognition of a spectrum of gender identities and expressions outside of a colonial-imposed gender binary, mirroring the ways Madness is gendered and racialized.

8. Menzies, LeFrançois, and Reaume, Introduction, 3.

9. Spagnolo, "Improving."

10. Disability Justice Network of Ontario (DJNO), "Cops Out of Care Work: A Summer Series," https://www.djno.ca/; Spagnolo, "Improving"; Finkler, "'They should not be allowed,'" 225.

11. Sealy and Whitehead, "Forty Years"; Greg Macdougall, "Call Us Crazy: Mad Movements Organize Against Ableism, Mentalism and More," *Equitable Education*, May 10, 2013, https://equitableeducation.ca/2013/call-us-crazy; Inclusion Canada, "Press Release: Discriminatory Disaster: Inclusion Canada Calls for Repeal of MAiD for Mental Illness and C-7," December 15, 2022, https://inclusion canada.ca/.

12. Sealy and Whitehead, "Forty Years"; Inclusion Canada, "Press Release."

13. CAMH, "Science & Research Staff Directory," https://www.camh.ca/en/science -and-research/science-and-research-staff-directory; Doblyte, "Power Dynamics."

14. Dolmage and Lewiecki-Wilson, "Refiguring Rhetorica," 23.

15. Price, "The Bodymind Problem," 269.

16. Price, *Mad at School*, 5.

17. Kafer, *Feminist, Queer, Crip*, 30.

18. Pickens, *Black Madness*, 27Piepzna-Samarasinha, "Disability Justice," Clare, *Exile and Pride*, 112; Gill-Peterson, *Histories*, 83.

19. Dolmage, *Disabled*, 25; Cedillo, "Unruly Borders," 12; Manivannan, "Hollow Me."

20. Anglesey and Hubrig, "Do You Feel," 189.

21. Gaeta, "There Is No 'Good Student.'"

22. Maier et al., "GET THE FRAC IN!"

23. Schalk, *Bodyminds Reimagined*, 64.

24. Schalk, *Bodyminds Reimagined*, 65.

25. Schalk, *Bodyminds Reimagined*, 65.

26. Hsu, "Irreducible Damage," 65–68.

27. Rice-Evans and Stella, "#Triggered."

28. Weijun Wang, *The Collected Schizophrenias*, 48.

29. Bruce, *How to Go Mad*, 21, 29.

30. Planning Across the Spectrum (PATS), "Here's Why You Should STOP Using Functioning Labels," August 2020, https://planningacrossthespectrum.com/blog /why-stop-using-functioning-labels/; Bottema-Beutel et al., "Avoiding Ableist Language."

31. Menlo Park Psychiatry & Sleep Medicine, "Agitated Depression and the High Functioning Bipolar Rockstar (of Silicon Valley)," https://siliconpsych.com/agitated -depression-and-the-high-functioning-bipolar-rockstar-of-silicon-valley/.

32. Karen Sosnoski and Christie Craft, "What It's Like Living with High Functioning Schizophrenia," *PsychCentral*, April 22, 2022, https://psychcentral.com/.

33. Imi Lo Ma, "The Struggles of Quiet BPD," *Psychology Today*, July 23, 2021, https:// www.psychologytoday.com/.

34. Kluft, "High-Functioning."

35. Kafer, *Feminist, Queer, Crip*; Schalk, *Bodyminds Reimagined*.

36. Yergeau, *Authoring Autism*, 139.

37. Price, *Mad at School*, 56.
38. Kafai, "The Mad Border Body."
39. Kafai, "The Mad Border Body."
40. Eliot Fukui, "Mad Queer Organizing Strategies," last modified 2022, https://madqueer.org/.
41. Greg Lukanioff and Jonathan Haidt, "The Coddling of the American Mind," *The Atlantic*, September 2015, https://www.theatlantic.com/magazine/archive/2015/09/the-coddling-of-the-american-mind/399356/.
42. Mark Mercer, "The Academic Irrelevance of Lived Experience," *The Society for Academic Freedom and Scholarship*, January 2019, https://www.safs.ca/newsletters/article.php?article=1004.
43. Canadian Psychiatric Association, *SchizoPhrenia: The Road to Recovery*, 2008, https://www.schizophrenia.ca/docs/RoadtoRecoveryschzhioph-web.pdf.
44. de Vries et al., "Self Disturbance."
45. Humber College Center for Accessibility Services, "Additional Resources for Faculty: Accessible Learning," last modified 2025, https://humber.ca/student-life/swac/accessible-learning/information-faculty/additional-resources/faculty-faqs.
46. As well documented in Dresser, "Mentally Disabled Research Subjects"; Dolmage, *Academic Ableism*; Jain et al., "Ethics"; Disability Justice Network of Ontario, "Sarah Jama Testimony at the Special Joint Committee on Medical Assistance in Dying (AMAD) on May 16," *YouTube*, June 3, 2022, https://www.youtube.com/watch?v=6jflFL8LAKo; Dakic, "No Research."
47. Piepzna-Samarasinha, The Future is Disabled, 57.
48. See Hubrig, "'We Move Together.'"

WORKS CITED

Anglesey, Leslie R., and Ada Hubrig. "'Do You Feel Like :(?' Discursive Interventions in University Mental Health Rhetorics." In *Strategic Interventions in Mental Health Rhetoric*, edited by Lisa Melonçon and Cathryn Molloy. New York: Routledge, 2020.
Barstow, Bonnie. *Psychiatry and the Business of Madness*. New York: Palgrave Macmillan, 2015.
Bottema-Beutel, Kristen, Steven K. Kapp, Jessica Nina Lester, Noah J. Sasson, and Brittany N. Hand. "Avoiding Ableist Language: Suggestions for Autism Researchers." *Autism in Adulthood* 3, no. 1 (2021). https://www.liebertpub.com/doi/10.1089/aut.2020.0014
Bruce, La Marr Jurelle. *How To Go Mad Without Losing Your Mind: Madness and Black Radical Creativity*. Durham, NC: Duke University Press, 2021.
Cedillo, Christina. "Unruly Borders, Bodies, and Blood: Mexican 'Mongrels' and the Eugenics of Empire." *Journal of the History of Rhetoric* 24, no. 1 (2021): 7–23.
Clare, Eli. *Exile and Pride: Disability, Queerness, and Liberation*. Durham, NC: Duke University Press. 2015.
Dakic, Tea. "No Research for the Decisionally-Impaired Mentally Ill: A View from Montenegro." *BNC Medical Ethics* 21, no. 1 (2020): 1–9.
De Vries, Rob, Henriette D. Heering, Lot Postmes, Saskia Goedhart, Herman N. Sno, and Lieuwe de Haan. "Self-Disturbance in Schizophrenia: A Phenomenological Approach to Better Understand Our Patients." *The Primary Care Companion for CNS Disorders* 15, no. 1 (2013). https://pmc.ncbi.nlm.nih.gov/articles/PMC3661330/.

Doblyte, "Power Dynamics of the Healthcare Field: Seeking Mental Care in Lithuania." *Journal of Baltic Studies* 52, no. 3 (2021): 357–72.

Dolmage, Jay Timothy. *Academic Ableism: Disability and Higher Education.* Ann Arbor: University of Michigan Press, 2017.

Dolmage, Jay. *Disabled Upon Arrival: Eugenics, Immigration, and the Construction of Race and Disability.* Columbus: Ohio State University Press, 2018.

Dolmage, Jay, and Cynthia Lewiecki-Wilson. "Refiguring Rhetorica: Linking Feminist Rhetoric with Disability Studies." In *Rhetorica in Motion: Feminist Rhetorical Methods and Methodologies*, edited by Eileen E. Schell and K.J. Rawson. Pittsburgh, PA: University of Pittsburgh Press, 2010.

Dresser, Rebecca. "Mentally Disabled Research Subjects: The Enduring Policy Issue." *JAMA* 276, no. 1 (1996): 67–72.

Finkler, Lilith 'Chava'. "'They should not be allowed to do this to the homeless and mentally ill': Minimum Separation Distance Bylaws Reconsidered." In *Mad Matters: A Critical Reader in Canadian Mad Studies*, edited by Brenda A. LeFrançois, Robert Menzies, and Geoffrey Reaume. Toronto, ON: Canadian Scholars' Press, 2013.

Gaeta, Amy. "There Is No 'Good Student': The Role of Mental Health Services in the University." *Spark: A 4C4Equality Journal* 4 (2022). https://sparkactivism.com/.

Gill-Peterson, Jules. *Histories of the Transgender Child.* Minneapolis, MN: University of Minnesota Press, 2018.

Hjorth, Cathrine F. et al. "Mental Health and School Dropout Across Educational Levels and Genders: A 4.8-Year Follow-Up Study." *BMC Public Health* 16, no. 976 (2016).

Hsu, V. Jo. "Irreducible Damage: The Affective Drift of Race, Gender, and Disability in Anti-Trans Rhetorics." *Rhetoric Society Quarterly* 52, no. 1 (2022): 62–77.

Hubrig, Ada. "'We Move Together': Reckoning with Disability Justice in Community Literacy Studies." *Community Literacy Journal* 14, no. 2 (2020): 144–53.

Jain, Shobhit, Pooja Patnaik Kuppili, Raman Deep Pattanayak, and Rajesh Sagar. "Ethics in Psychiatric Research: Issues and Recommendations." *Indian Journal of Psychological Medicine* 39, no. 1 (2017): 558–65.

Kafai, Shayda. "The Mad Border Body: A Political In-Betweeness." *Disability Studies Quarterly* 33, no. 1 (2012), https://doi.org/10.18061/dsq.v33i1.3438.

Kafer, Alison. *Feminist, Queer, Crip.* Bloomington, IN: Indiana University Press, 2013.

Kluft, Richard P. "High-Functioning Multiple Personality Patients: Three Cases." *Journal of Nervous and Mental Disease* 174, no. 12 (1986): 722–26.

Liu, FengJu, Yang Shao, Xin Li, et al. "Volumetric Abnormalities in Violent Schizophrenic Patients on the General Psychiatric Ward." *Frontiers in Psychiatry* 11, no. 1 (2020). https://doi.org/10.3389/fpsyt.2020.00788.

Maier, Sophia, V. Jo Hsu, Christina V. Cedillo, and M. Remi Yergeau. "GET THE FRAC IN! Or, The Fractal Many-Festo: A (Trans)(Crip)t." *Peitho* 22, no. 4 (2020). https://wac.colostate.edu/docs/peitho/article/get-the-frac-in-or-the-fractal-many-festo-a-transcript/.

Manivannan, Vyshali. "Hollow Me, Hollow Me, Until Only You Remain." *Spark: A 4C4Equality Journal* 4 (2022). https://sparkactivism.com/.

Menzies, Robert, Brenda A. LeFrançois, and Geoffrey Reaume, eds. Introduction to *Mad Matters: A Critical Reader in Canadian Mad Studies*, 39–48. Toronto, ON: Canadian Scholars' Press, 2013.

Padgett, Deborah K. "Homelessness, Housing Instability and Mental Health: Making the Connections." *BJPsych Bulletin* 44, no. 5 (2020): 197–201.

Pickens, Therí A. *Black Madness :: Mad Blackness*. Durham, NC: Duke University Press, 2019.

Piepzna-Samarasinha, Leah Lakshmi. *The Future is Disabled: Prophecies, Love Notes, and Mourning Songs*. Vancouver, Canada: Arsenal Pulp Press, 2022.

Price, Margaret. "The Bodymind Problem and the Possibilities of Pain." *Hypatia* 20, no. 1 (November 2014): 268–84.

Price, Margaret. *Mad at School: Rhetorics of Mental Disability and Academic Life*. Ann Arbor, MI: University of Michigan Press, 2011.

Rice-Evans, Jesse, and Andréa Stella. "#Triggered: The Invisible Labor of Traumatized Doctoral Students." *Journal of Multimodal Rhetoric* 5, no. 1 (2021): 20–32.

Schalk, Sami. *Bodyminds Reimagined: (Dis)ability, Race, and Gender in Black Women's Speculative Fiction*. Durham, NC: Duke University Press, 2018.

Sealy, Patrici, and Paul C. Whitehead. "Forty Years of Deinstitutionalization of Psychiatric Services in Canada: An Empiral Asesssment." *The Canadian Journal of Psychiatry* 49, no. 4 (2004): 249–57.

Spagnolo, Jessica. "Improving First-Line Mental Health Services in Canada: Addressing Two Challenges Caused by the Deinstitutionalization Movement." *Healthcare Quarterly* 17, no. 4 (2014): 41–5.

Weijun Wang, Esmé. *The Collected Schizophrenias*. Minneapolis, MN: Graywolf Press, 2019.

Yergeau, Remi. *Authoring Autism: On Rhetoric and Neurological Queerness*. Durham, NC: Duke University Press, 2017.

PART II

Enacting Care in Ethical Research Relationships

In a world often defined by vulnerability, trauma, and precarity, how can researchers undertake ethical research methods and methodologies that are built around the care of individuals and communities? Drawing on a range of perspectives from feminist theory, queer theory, and prison abolition, chapters in this part consider ways we, as researchers, can approach the perspectives and stories of specific communities with care and respect. The authors offer specific guidance on researcher ethics, including designing trauma-informed research methodologies; interrogating consent, vulnerability, and trust in response to power imbalances that shape research relationships; negotiating researcher desire, positionality, and intentionality; and collecting and curating stories in digital and multilingual environments. Ethical research demands that we approach dynamic and often shifting research relationships through trauma-informed research methodologies that are sensitive to the ways that participants can be triggered or harmed by questions and interactions (Schoettler). Moreover, contributors consider how we, as researchers, can be open and transparent about the idea of consent in research relationships, seeking to understand how our own desire may be made manifest in our encounters with those individuals, groups, and communities with which we are conducting research (Restaino and Oleksiak). Vulnerability must be factored into research relationships, especially when working with at-risk communities, such as incarcerated sexual and gender minorities (Lewis). Negotiating agency and representation in incarcerated spaces must be done carefully and in ways that allow prisoners to speak and represent themselves in environments that provide limited agency (Lewis). Finally, how we curate and share stories in digital environments matters. Developing ethical research practices for representing community stories and activism is a process of negotiating what can and can't be shared, building trust, and navigating multilingual environments (Bloom-Pojar and Koepke). This part demonstrates how implementing feminist research design principles is not only transformative for researchers and the participants we work with, but how these principles become the fabric of the academic and public scholarship we produce.

FIVE

Lessons from Advocacy

A Feminist and Trauma-Informed Methodology

Megan Schoettler

On a winter morning in her office at the Midwest Rape Crisis Organization (MRCO), I interviewed Rebecca as part of a study of the rhetorical strategies and literacy practices of feminist activists and advocates. Rebecca is a feminist activist and advocate and a survivor of sexual assault. As soon as this research participant began to tell me her survival story, I began the process of networking my training in feminist research methodologies with trauma-informed care I learned as a sexual assault survivor advocate at MRCO, a nonprofit that serves survivors of sexual assault, domestic violence, and stalking. While my practices as a feminist researcher already emphasized respect, reciprocity, and reflection, my training as an advocate brought an awareness of trauma and how my responses to Rebecca's story could impact her self-perceptions. This meant I paid extra attention to how I was responding to her story: honoring her decision-making and resilience and ceding even more power in the session for her to own how she told her story.

This chapter presents a feminist and trauma-informed methodology that emerged from networking my training as a feminist researcher and the lessons I have learned as a sexual assault survivor advocate. I will begin this chapter by providing context for the study for which I developed this methodology. Next, I will introduce key ideas of trauma-informed care, including how trauma-informed approaches have already been taken up in Writing and Rhetoric. Then, I will share five principles of my feminist trauma-informed methodology that helped me minimize the possibility of retraumatizing my participants. Finally, I will share the guiding questions that helped me to enact this methodology. I hope that the methodology presented in this chapter, including its principles and guiding questions, inspires and helps feminist researchers to bring trauma-informed care to their own work.

Context

I developed this feminist trauma-informed methodology for a study of feminist affective resistance and the transformative rhetorics and literacy practices feminists employ in challenging dominant pedagogies of emotion. For this study, I interviewed eleven feminist activists and conducted an ethnographic case study of MRCO, which included interviews with six organization leaders and advocates, observation of 40 hours of advocate training, a survey of 36 volunteer advocates' experiences, and analysis of advocacy materials and public-facing writing–artifacts composed for a general public audience.[1] My experiences as an advocate and research partnership with MRCO were essential to the development of this methodology.

Everyone carries positions from which they interpret the world, and as a researcher, I am limited to my situated knowledges.[2] As part of strategic contemplation in my study, I considered how my positioning influenced how I was interpreting the experiences of my participants.[3] I reflected on how my experiences as a white, cisgender, middle-class, bisexual woman, survivor advocate, and trauma survivor influenced my views. I do not know first-hand what it is like to be both a woman of color and sexual assault survivor. Through carefully listening and extended reflection, I avoided quick judgments that would place my visions and positions over those of my participants.

Trauma-Informed Care

Trauma-informed care is an approach originally designed by and for mental health and substance abuse service providers. Agencies such as the US federal government's Substance Abuse and Mental Health Services Administration (SAMHSA) and MRCO use trauma-informed care as a guiding approach to their services and decision making, and states such as Ohio are unrolling initiatives to encourage trauma-informed care among practitioners, facilities, and agencies.[4] Best practices in rape-crisis organizations, such as the MRCO, are to anticipate that any person might be a trauma survivor, recognizing that a trauma-informed approach can be growth-promoting for all people involved.[5] Literature on trauma-informed care centers on these principles—safety, trustworthiness and transparency, collaboration and peer support, empowerment, choice, and researcher attention to the intersectionality of identity characteristics.[6] These principles align well with values of feminist research in contemporary writing and rhetoric.

Trauma-Informed Work in Writing and Rhetoric

In the field of writing and rhetoric, there has been rich trove of research on the rhetorics and writings of trauma.[7] In their important article on research as care, John T. Gagon and Maria Novotny remind researchers that the process of sharing a trauma narrative can be retraumatizing itself and call on us to decolonize our scholarship on trauma, including paying attention to the embodiment of trauma. The methodology shared in this chapter pours attention into potentials for re-traumatization and the embodied nature of trauma. From the perspective of trauma in the writing classroom, Kendall Gerdes argues that "violence can happen without the striking of a single physical blow . . . 'violence' . . . may not be physical, but that does not make it less literal."[8] Violence in this sense can take on the form of retraumatizing participants, taking advantage of vulnerable populations, manipulating participants to give certain labor toward a study, and perpetuating discrimination and oppression that participants already face. Researchers should tread thoughtfully into any study related to trauma and consider researchers' own capacities for violence.

Though trauma-related work has been abundant, explicitly "trauma-informed" work is only beginning to emerge and has been focused on pedagogy. In Melissa Tayles's 2021 article on trauma-informed writing pedagogy, she argues that a trauma-informed lens can help teachers anticipate and examine "the trauma responses that may threaten a student's success and connection in the writing classroom."[9] Though I am using a trauma-informed approach to build a methodology rather than a pedagogy, I borrow Tayles's standing that anyone can be a trauma survivor and Gerdes's attention to the possibility of violence. Teachers or researchers have a responsibility to minimize the possibility of re-traumatizing those with whom they work.

Trauma-informed care complements the goals and aims of existing feminist rhetorical methodologies. As argued by Gesa Kirsch, feminist research is distinguished by its "focus on gender combined with an emphasis on emancipatory goals."[10] A trauma-informed approach can help feminist researchers become even more emancipatory, empathetic, and attentive to the needs and desires of our participants, especially women and other trauma survivors. According to the National Sexual Violence Resource Center, "81% of women and 43% of men reported experiencing some form of sexual harassment and/or assault in their lifetime."[11] The idea of thinking about research participants as survivors of assault might sound scary, but it is important that researchers intentionally design their practices to minimize the possibility of retraumatizing participants. As I will discuss in Principle 1 of my methodology, any research participant could potentially be a trauma survivor, and a feminist and trauma-informed methodology helps researchers support participants. The risk of not using a trauma-informed approach is that of retraumatizing the participants and perpetuating systems of oppression, such as white supremacy, misogyny, and homophobia.

Principles of Feminist and Trauma-Informed Methodology

Building from existing feminist methodologies, trauma-informed scholarship, and the lessons I learned as a rape crisis advocate, I developed the following principles to guide my methodology: (1) Anticipate that all participants may be survivors of trauma; (2) Honor participants' expertise in their own lives; (3) Cede power and control to participants; (4) Respond intentionally to disclosures of trauma; and (5) Respect personal capacities for trauma as a researcher. Firm lines do not necessarily separate each of these principles from one another—they interlink, inform each other, and build into a feminist and trauma-informed methodology.

Principle 1. Anticipate That All Participants May Be Trauma Survivors

Important to my feminist trauma-informed methodology is treating each research participant as if they might be a survivor of trauma. This does not mean avoiding sensitive topics or treating people as if they are fragile—it means recognizing that anyone could have the capacity of being retraumatized and that my study design lessens the likelihood of that happening. SAMHSA describes that individual trauma results from "an event, series of events, or set of circumstances that is experienced by an individual as physically or emotionally harmful or life threatening and that has lasting adverse effects on the individual's functioning and mental, physical, social, emotional, or spiritual well-being."[12] Though people may have assumptions about who is more likely to be a survivor of trauma, "trauma has no boundaries with regard to age, gender, socioeconomic status, race, ethnicity, or sexual orientation."[13] In other words, it is possible that *anyone* can be a trauma survivor who could potentially be retraumatized as a result of research sessions. However, disability scholar Angela Carter reminds researchers that "the vast majority of potentially traumatizing experiences are rooted in systems of power and oppression. The forces of racism/white supremacy, colonization, and global capitalism continuously instigate enumerable violences worldwide."[14] Therefore, it is important to consider these systems of oppression when considering the trauma and potential triggers of participants.

Carter says to be triggered means to "mentally and physically re-experience a past trauma in such an embodied manner that one's affective response literally takes over the ability to be present in one's bodymind."[15] There are many potentially uncomfortable and disruptive effects of being triggered, including but not limited to—increased heart rate, difficulty breathing, dissociation and/or dysphoria; forgetfulness; chronic fatigue or immune system problems; and reduced capacity for managing stress and anxiety.[16] A trauma-informed approach helps prevent research participants from being triggered, but researchers should not assume they know what being triggered looks like for a given individual. Instead, they should respect the expertise of their participants in their own lives, as discussed in Principle 2 below. Awareness of re-traumatization can help researchers to review their practices, but as argued by Tayles, it is "impossible to completely eliminate the risk of re-traumatization."[17]

A simple step that trauma-informed researchers can take is to create safer research spaces. One of the top priorities of a trauma-informed approach is that people feel "physically and psychologically safe" and this includes researchers providing a safe physical space.[18] This safety is defined by those being served. Before any of my interviews started, I took steps to consider the physical environment of the research space to promote participant comfort. Trauma-informed design, or trauma-informed environments, is an area emerging from the behavioral sciences, architecture, and interior design fields.[19] At its core, trauma-informed design is about creating spaces from principles of trauma-informed care–specifically, paying attention to how environments can potentially create or reduce stress or lead to re-traumatization. SAMHSA encourages attention to "triggers such as lighting, access to exits, seating arrangements, emotionality within a group, or visual or auditory stimuli" to help minimize the risk of re-traumatization.[20] More specifically, the Vermont-based nonprofit COTS (Committee on Temporary Shelter) encourages a trauma-informed design that is mindful of furniture and proximity. COTS encourages those serving trauma survivors to avoid "sitting face-to-face across a desk or table" as this "may be perceived as confrontational, whereas sitting corner to corner invites conversation and interaction."[21] Participants' perspectives, of course, are culturally informed.

COTS also encourages survivor control over the room arrangement, including opportunities for choice, such as moving furniture around in a room as desired.

I applied concepts of trauma-informed design when choosing and setting up research spaces. When arranging interviews with participants, I let participants choose the physical locations of our meetings, offering a variety of options for their comfort. Most local participants chose to meet me at public library study rooms, but many also chose Zoom meetings, especially after the COVID-19 pandemic began. For participants I met in-person, I arrived early and arranged the meeting space in a way that was trauma-informed. I made sure there were clear exits, multiple seating options, space to move around and shift furniture, and I made efforts to not seem "established" in my spot when they arrived so that I could move based on their preferences. I also made sure to not sit between the participant and the room exit so that they did not feel cornered or forced to be in an unwanted space. I explicitly directed my participants to arrange the space to their comfort, with additional attention to where my recording devices were placed. Assault survivors who have been through formal investigative processes may be particularly sensitive to atmospheres that feel like a probing interview about their experiences.

Trauma-informed approaches reduce survivor pressure to "conform" to interview expectations and emphasize survivor's rights to make decisions about their participation.[22] The design of my IRB also helped me minimize the possibility of retraumatizing participants and enhance their agency in the research process. In my interviews with feminist activists and advocates, I emphasized with participants that their participation in the study was voluntary and that they could withdraw at any time—they had full control of what experiences they wanted to share and the power to decline to answer any questions. I encouraged participants to tell me when they needed breaks—which several did for mental health reasons and child care responsibilities—and encouraged silence if they wanted to think through an idea. I also told my participants I did not want them to feel like they had to respond to anything immediately—they could take what steps they needed, including writing down on paper what they wanted to say. When participants delved into personal experiences, including stories of trauma, some of them apologized for taking up time and talking a lot. In these instances, I reminded participants that I was there to listen to whatever they wanted to share, intentionally sitting back and actively listening to where they wanted to bring the interview. I also conducted member checks with participants, which will be discussed more in Principle 3. Altogether, these are small, intentional steps that trauma-informed researchers can take to help all participants feel comfortable in their space and reduce stress that could contribute to re-traumatization.

Principle 2. Honor Participants' Expertise in Their Own Lives

Throughout advocate training at MRCO, the facilitators remind new advocates that "we are not the expert in the life of the survivor. The survivor is the expert in their own life." This approach is also reinforced by trauma-informed scholars such as Denise E. Elliott, Paula Bjelajac, Roger D. Fallot, Laurie S. Markoff, and Beth Glover Reed, who argue that people should be seen as the "experts" in their own lives and there should not be assumptions about their experiences, feelings, or needs.[23] A trauma-informed approach means listening to the survivor and trying to better understand their experiences through their cultural context instead of applying one's own experiences, needs, and goals to someone else's life. Even if I think I know what a participant needs, it is better to trust their own insights about their desires and goals.

A trauma-informed methodology can enhance how we attend to the embodied and intersectional experiences of participants. Those who practice trauma-informed care "strive to be culturally competent and understand each woman in the context of her life experiences and cultural background."[24] Denise E. Elliott and fellow scholars argue that cultural competence in trauma-informed care does not mean someone has "detailed knowledge of every culture" but rather that someone recognizes "the importance of cultural context."[25] Trauma-informed researchers should be "open to being educated" to try to understand a person's "experience and responses through the lens of her cultural context."[26] Member checks, a process of validating research as described by Patti Lather, is an important tool for trusting the expertise of research participants.[27]

In my training as a trauma-informed survivor advocate, I was taught to trust the life experiences and expertise of survivors and not challenge them on their decision making. Each survivor's situation is different, and an advocate and researcher can never know the whole context of someone's trauma. As an advocate and a researcher, I do not ask assault survivors questions such as "Why didn't you go to the police?" or demand "You need to report this so that the perpetrator is held accountable and doesn't do this again." Survivors are experts in their own lives, and there can be many reasons behind decisions such as not calling police—many communities feel they cannot trust police. In my interviews with feminists, activists and advocates, if they disclosed an assault, I listened to their stories and refrained from prescribing any sort of solution or "right" thing to do. At the end of my interviews, I also asked each participant to share their advice for other feminist activists and advocates. This practice also honored their expertise and allowed them a reflective moment to think toward the future and cultural progress toward feminist goals.

Principle 3. Cede Power and Control to Participants

The third principle, cede power and control to participants, is closely tied to the second principle of my feminist, trauma-informed methodology— that of honoring participants' expertise in their own lives. Researchers can honor participant expertise by ceding power and control in the research process to them. In trauma-informed advocate training at MRCO, a facilitator explained to new advocates that, "We walk alongside survivors." This is a helpful metaphor for a trauma-informed approach; however, advocates and researchers must recognize that there is always a power dynamic. Advocates almost always exist within a frame of a helper/helped relationship— advocates have the resources and expertise that can help survivors toward their goals. Researchers are also in a context in which they inherently have more power—the researcher typically has taken a leading role in designing the study, has research expertise in their specialty, and the interview format often puts the researcher in control, asking most of—if not all of—the questions.

Nevertheless, researchers can take steps to try and cede some power involved in the researcher/participant relationship. Ceding power means listening to what participants need, following their requests, honoring their decision-making, and creating an atmosphere of safety, choice, and respect. As argued by Powell et al, "studying culture is a relational practice, requiring interaction with and investment in the communities whose practices are being investigated."[28] Meaningful research relationships require investment in participant needs and attention to power dynamics. This approach directly resists traditional positivist approaches to social science research. Higher education scholars Christine Halse and Anne Honey observe how typical IRB processes encourage a "hierarchical power relationship between researchers and participants when it constructs researchers as objective, dispassionate scientists with the knowledge and expertise to reveal 'truths' about their research 'subjects.'"[29] In designing my research study, a trauma-informed approach helped me cede power and control to participants in ways that challenged the typical binary of "researcher" and "researched." However, it is important to note that it may be impossible to completely flip the power structure between researcher and participant—researchers will always carry a certain authority and control in study contexts that participants do not.

Trauma-informed approaches describe the importance of destabilizing power imbalances to bolster the agency of survivors. Social work experts Elizabeth A. Bowen and Nadine Shaanta Murshid argue that when a trauma-informed perspective is applied, there should not just be a "rhetoric of liberation" but "actual shared power in terms of extending decision-making ability."[30] This approach can help tackle the "inherent power imbalance" between a survivor and those who are hearing their story, especially if the survivor sees the interaction as a "helper-helped relationship."[31] If a survivor sees the interaction within this frame, they may be less inclined to enact their own agency and decision making.

Feminist researchers including Patti Lather, Chris Smithies, Gesa Kirsch and Jacqueline Jones Royster argue for dialectical and reciprocal relationships with participants to break down power hierarchies. Seeing participants as experts in their own lives helped me cede power and enact reciprocity. In the advocate training at MRCO, a facilitator explained that with a trauma-informed approach, "If we're listening to the survivor, we should hear the needs and questions they have, not the problems we think should be solved." This involves equal attention to listening and reflexivity about positionality as a researcher. Elliot and fellow authors also argue that in trauma-informed work, "the goals of the work are mutual and established collaboratively."[32] These approaches resonate with feminist perspectives on research collaboration, such as Kirsch's call to "begin to collaborate with participants in the development of research questions, the design of research studies, and the interpretation of data if they want to ensure that feminist research contributes toward enhancing—and not interfering with—the lives of others."[33]

One of the ways I ceded power to my participants was by letting them guide the disclosures of their stories and have control over how they were represented in my writing. As mentioned earlier in this chapter, I conducted member checks with each research participant, allowing everyone an opportunity to provide feedback on how I represented them and their stories. Part of this process was allowing participants to revise or suggest their own pseudonyms. As described by Burgess-Proctor, the simple act of allowing participants to choose pseudonyms accomplishes several feminist aims: "first, it affords women control over their participation in the interview process and gives them agency, thereby reducing the researcher-subject power differential. Second, and perhaps more importantly, it allows women to govern their identity in the developing interview narrative. Finally, it can allow women to impart particular meaning to the interview process."[34] My participants described the process of member-checks as "empowering" and took opportunities to create their own pseudonyms and suggest changes to my writing to better reflect their realities.

Principle 4. Respond Intentionally to Disclosures of Trauma

The next principle of my feminist trauma-informed methodology combines the previous three principles—recognizing survivors, honoring expertise, and ceding power—and adds specific approaches to responding to disclosures of trauma. A trauma-informed methodology can help researchers recognize the effects of violence on the lives of participants as well as help them discuss that violence with participants and write about their stories. Feminist scholarship recognizes the impact of violence on women's lives, from patriarchal structures, to racism, homophobia, and assault.[35] However, methodologies of feminist work in writing and rhetoric do not often provide direct advice on discussing and writing about the violence—particularly sexual violence—that participants experience.

In this study, I combined dialogic, flexible interview practices that prioritize participants' voices with a trauma-informed approach to respond intentionally to disclosures of trauma. I use the word "intentionally," because I believe that most feminist researchers come to projects with participants' best interests at heart, but that it takes specific, intentional planning to design a study that is trauma-informed. Researchers should not pry into the lives of the participants looking for stories of trauma, unless the participant is well informed that they are being asked to share these stories, as related to research questions, and have consented to the process with knowledge that they can always withhold information and withdraw after the interview.

When interviewing feminist activists and advocates for this project, many participants shared experiences of trauma that influenced their activism. During each interview and disclosure, I remained actively aware and reflective of how I was taking in the story and the intentions behind any questions. My training in trauma-informed care steered me away from unnecessary and harmful questions, such as asking about the context of sexual assaults, such as "Were you drinking?", "Who was with you?", "Where were you?", because these questions were not relevant to my research questions.

The answers to these questions were only relevant if the participant who was an assault survivor brought these up themselves. Though a simple question such as "Were you drinking?" may seem benign, questions such as these can be interpreted by the participant as blaming them for their own assault.

Throughout my research, I also checked in with my participants about the role of their stories in relation to my research project. I would ask the participant, "When you are telling me this story, is it in my role as a researcher or just someone to listen?", and I received a variety of responses that I respected. Participants would also tell me during interviews, "This is not for your research, but . . . ", and then I would listen to their experiences without judgment, keeping in mind that this story was not for my research project. These types of disclosures and stories were deleted from recordings and transcripts, so I did not inadvertently include them in my coding and writing. In a trauma-informed methodology, every action should be "consistent with the recovery process and [reduce] the possibility of re-traumatization."[36] This means respecting participant goals and boundaries, and when applicable, referring participants to professional services, such as the National Sexual Assault Telephone Hotline, for help. However, it is important for researchers to consider how "certain referrals might be perceived as a way to extend surveillance on those who are already institutionalized."[37]

In an interview in which a participant discloses a traumatic event, such as sexual assault, a feminist researcher may feel at a loss for words. Positivist traditions of research tell scholars that we are removed from the lives and emotions of our participants, but feminist researchers understand that researchers and participants form relationships and emotions are part of knowledge-making.[38] In difficult moments of disclosure, validation is an important quality of trauma-informed care that can help decrease participant guilt and shame.[39] Researchers can validate the resilience of the participants in small, supportive ways during interviews. These responses should avoid judgment and assessment and focus on honoring past choices of participants—as mentioned earlier, participants are the experts in their own lives. Researchers can also "express and reciprocate emotion with participants," which "not only forges connections with participants that improve rapport, which can enhance their comfort with disclosure, but also helps affirm the importance of them telling their stories."[40]

In advocate training in crisis intervention at MRCO, the facilitator explained the importance of "attuning" emotionally with survivors. For example, she explained, "If someone's talking about how frustrated they were, or how scared they were, we're reflecting that. That we acknowledge, we see that. Of course, how frustrating it is to be violated by someone you trusted." Trauma-informed practitioners—whether they are advocates, researchers, or teachers—acknowledge and validate emotions expressed by survivors. In advocate training at MRCO, the facilitator provided examples of how an advocate can respond to a survivor who is telling their story. In addition to just listening, a trauma-informed researcher can respond to disclosures in these ways:

- "I believe you."
- "I'm glad you're safe [now]."
- "Help and support is available."
- "It's not your fault that this happened."
- "You're responding normally to a situation you shouldn't have to be going through in the first place."

These trauma-informed approaches informed how I responded to disclosures of sexual assault and trauma in my interviews. In my responses, I showed participants that I believed their stories, valued their safety and decision making, was willing to connect them to resources, did not believe they were responsible for their own assaults, and validated their confusing emotions. Trauma-informed strategies—such as validating the emotions and choices of survivors, telling them we believe them, and honoring their safety—can help researchers build healthy and liberatory relationships with participants who trust us with their most private stories.

Principle 5. Respect Personal Capacities for Trauma as a Researcher

The final principle of this methodology recognizes that researchers may be survivors of trauma themselves and have thresholds for how much vicarious trauma they can experience before it becomes too much. Participants can come to see researchers—especially ethnographers—as "sources of stability and normalcy,"[41] and "complicated interpersonal relationships emerge as researchers walk the delicate line between maintaining healthy professional boundaries and being compassionate listeners and confidants."[42] To help navigate this line, researchers can turn to feminist theory that engages the need for selfcare and community care. Audre Lorde established that caring for ourselves "is not self-indulgence, it is self-preservation, and that is an act of political warfare."[43] Self-care is not selfish; if we want to continue to do the work, we need to survive. In *Living a Feminist Life*, Sara Ahmed includes her "killjoy survival kit, which includes "some permission notes to step back when it is too much."[44] Ahmed argues that having the permission notes, as a way to "give yourself permission to exit a situation, can make the situation more bearable. You can leave; you can grieve."[45] In the process of caring for themselves, feminist researchers need to respect their own capacities for trauma and recognize when they need to step back, even if just for a moment.

Researchers' boundaries are just as important as those of participants. Trauma-informed ethnographer Taylor Paige Winfield argues that "in order to keep the investigators and participants safe, it is critical that researchers are competent in creating and maintaining professional boundaries . . . [these] can include physical limits on where a researcher will meet with participants (i.e., keeping an office door cracked, or being aware of increased risk in certain private locations) and symbolic borders such as imagining an emotional wall erected to ensure the investigator is not taking on participants' emotional states."[46] This is hard work; senior research mentors, peers, and mental health professionals can help feminist trauma-informed researchers make sure they are attending to their own needs.

The final principle of my methodology was most important when I began drafting the chapters of my research project which focused on the rhetorics of advocacy at MRCO. During the work day, I would listen to interviews with advocates, code their experiences, and write about the important rhetorical strategies they used when communicating with survivors across various settings, including emergency rooms and domestic relations court. Thursday was my typical volunteer advocacy day for MRCO, so after research writing during the day, I would spend a 6-hour shift serving survivors through the MRCO chat/text line. At the end of one of these long days, I realized the affective labor and exposure to trauma I was putting myself through was unsustainable. I could feel the toll the emotional stress was putting on my body. If I wanted to finish this project, I needed to respect my own capacities for trauma. I talked with my advocacy and research mentors and decided to step back from some of my volunteer responsibilities. This allowed me to continue my research project, which involved answering research questions I developed with my community partner. I felt some guilt, stepping back from the direct advocacy that I had been doing for several years, but also reminded myself that I was still contributing to the mission of the organization through my research and making deliverables for MRCO. In the long term, recognizing how much trauma I was exposing myself to and adjusting based on my needs and limits was important to continuing the project and my career as a feminist scholar.

Conclusion

In this chapter, I explained how I networked my experiences as an advocate, including lessons in trauma-informed care, with relationships with my research participants and methodologies from writing and rhetoric to develop a feminist trauma-informed methodology. I hope that readers find the principles of my methodology generative for thinking about their study designs and relationships with their own participants. A trauma-informed methodology can help us address the embodied experiences, unique identities, and needs of our research partners. A trauma-informed approach is by no means easy—it requires levels of reflexivity, reflection, and reciprocity that are unique to each researcher-participant relationship.

I want to conclude this chapter with guiding questions that helped me to enact the principles of my methodology. Feminist and trauma-informed researchers should be constantly reflective about their own goals, values, and curiosity. When I conducted this study, I consistently asked myself:

Principle 1. Anticipate That All Participants May Be Survivors of Trauma

- Am I assuming, based on someone's age, gender, socioeconomic status, race, ethnicity, or sexual orientation, that they are not a survivor of trauma?
- In what ways have systems of power and oppression impacted my participants?
- Am I assuming I know what being triggered looks like?
- Am I arranging physical spaces in a way that prioritizes survivor safety and decision-making?
- Am I demonstrating flexibility and encouraging participants to express their needs?

Principle 2. Honor Participants' Expertise in Their Own Lives

- Am I making any assumptions about participants' experiences, feelings, or needs?
- Do my words and actions privilege the expertise of the survivor in their own life?
- Am I open to being educated and understanding my participants through the context of their life experiences?

Principle 3. Cede Power and Control to Participants

- Are the goals of this research relationship mutual and established collaboratively?
- Am I hearing the needs and questions participants have, not the problems I think should be solved?
- Am I reflecting on the power dynamic of my research partnership and placing power and control in the hands of my participants when possible?
- Am I conducting member checks and allowing participants to choose pseudonyms?

Principle 4. Respond Intentionally to Disclosures of Trauma

- Am I listening to what the participant wants to share, or pushing them into telling a certain kind of story?
- Am I asking about this trauma because of my research questions and genuine desire to learn about my participant, or am I drawn to the sensationalism of this trauma and my personal curiosity about this event?
- Is the context clear for the disclosure of this traumatic event? Is the participant talking to me at this moment as a researcher or just as a listener and real (or imagined) friend?

Principle 5. Respect Personal Capacities for Trauma as a Researcher

- Am I respecting my own capacities for trauma?
- When might I need to step back?
- How do I make this project accomplishable and sustainable? Where do I need to make room for my own needs?
- What am I willing to sacrifice to complete this feminist project? What am I unwilling to sacrifice?
- How might my own experiences with trauma impact how I design, analyze, process, and share results of this study?

NOTES

1. This study was approved by the Research Ethics & Integrity Program at Miami University (IRB protocol #01912).

2. Haraway, "Situated Knowledges."

3. Royster and Kirsch, *Feminist Rhetorical Practices*.

4. Ohio Mental Health & Addiction Services, "Ohio's Trauma-Competent Care (TCC) Initiative," https://mha.ohio.gov/get-help/treatment-services/.

5. Elliott et al., "Trauma-Informed or Trauma-Denied," 463.

6. Bowen and Murshid, "Trauma-Informed Social Policy," 224.

7. Fayard, "Rape, Trauma, and Shame"; Gagnon and Novotny, "Revisiting Research"; Gerdes, "Trauma"; Larson, "Survivors"; Tayles, "Trauma-Informed Writing."

8. Gerdes, "Trauma," 15–16.

9. Tayles, "Trauma-Informed Writing," 300.

10. Kirsch, *Ethical Dilemmas*, 7.

11. National Sexual Violence Resource Center, "Statistics," https://www.nsvrc.org/statistics.

12. Substance Abuse and Mental Health Services Administration (SAMHSA), "Trauma and Violence," https://www.samhsa.gov/.

13. SAMHSA, "Trauma and Violence," https://www.samhsa.gov/.

14. Carter, "Teaching," 7.

15. Carter, "Teaching," 4.

16. Carter, "Teaching."

17. Tayles, "Trauma-Informed Writing," 302.

18. SAMHSA, "SAMHSA's Concept of Trauma and Guidance for a Trauma-Informed Approach." https://ncsacw.acf.hhs.gov/userfiles/files/SAMHSA_Trauma.pdf, 10.

19. Committee on Temporary Shelter (COTS), "Trauma Informed Design," https://cotsonline.org/mission-and-approach; Hopper, Bassuk, and Olivet, "Shelter"; SAMHSA, "SAMHSA's Concept.

20. SAMHSA, "SAMHSA's Concept."

21. COTS, "Trauma Informed Design," https://cotsonline.org/mission-and-approach.

22. Elliott et al., "Trauma-Informed or Trauma-Denied," 466.

23. Elliott et al., "Trauma-Informed or Trauma-Denied," 474.

24. Elliott et al., "Trauma-Informed or Trauma-Denied," 468.

25. Elliott et al., "Trauma-Informed or Trauma-Denied," 248.

26. Elliott et al., "Trauma-Informed or Trauma-Denied," 468.

27. Lather, *Getting Smart*.

28. Powell et al., "Our Story."

29. Halse and Honey, "Unraveling Ethics," 2154–55.

30. Bowen and Murshid, "Trauma-Informed Social Policy," 226.

31. Elliott et al., "Trauma-Informed or Trauma-Denied," 466.

32. Elliott et al., "Trauma-Informed or Trauma-Denied," 465.

33. Kirsch, *Ethical Dilemmas*, x.

34. Burgess-Proctor, "Methodological and Ethical Issues," 130.

35. Lather and Smithies, *Troubling the Angels*; Mendes, Ringrose, and Keller, *Digital Feminist Activism*; Moraga and Anzaldúa, *This Bridge*; Stenberg, "'Tweet Me.'"

36. Elliott et al., "Trauma-Informed or Trauma-Denied," 462.

37. Winfield, "Vulnerable Research," 149.

38. Jaggar, "Love and Knowledge"; Mendes, Ringrose, and Keller, *Digital Feminist Activism*; Restaino, *Surrender*.

39. Elliott et al., "Trauma-Informed or Trauma-Denied."

40. Burgess-Proctor, "Methodological and Ethical Issues," 132.
41. Winfield, "Vulnerable Research," 137.
42. Winfield, "Vulnerable Research," 138.
43. Lorde, *A Burst of Light*, 131.
44. Ahmed, *Living*, 224.
45. Ahmed, *Living*, 244.
46. Winfield, "Vulnerable Research," 150.

WORKS CITED

Ahmed, Sara. *Living a Feminist Life*. Durham, NC: Duke University Press, 2017.

Bowen, Elizabeth A., and Nadine Shaanta Murshid. "Trauma-Informed Social Policy: A Conceptual Framework for Policy Analysis and Advocacy." *American Journal of Public Health* 106, no. 2 (2016): 223–29.

Burgess-Proctor, Amanda. "Methodological and Ethical Issues in Feminist Research with Abused Women: Reflections on Participants' Vulnerability and Empowerment." *Women's Studies International Forum* 48 (2015): 124–34.

Carter, Angela. "Teaching with Trauma: Trigger Warnings, Feminism, and Disability Pedagogy." *Disability Studies Quarterly* 35, no. 2 (2015): https://doi.org/10.18061/dsq.v35i2.4652.

Elliott, Denise E., Paula Bjelajac, Roger D. Fallot, Laurie S. Markoff, and Beth Glover Reed. "Trauma-Informed or Trauma-Denied: Principles and Implementation of Trauma-Informed Services for Women." *Journal of Community Psychology* 33, no. 4 (2005): 461–77.

Fayard, Nicole. "Rape, Trauma, and Shame in Samira Bellil's Dans L'enfer Des Tournantes." In *The Female Face of Shame*, edited by Erica L. Johnson and Patricia Moran, 34–47. Bloomington, IN: Indiana University Press, 2013.

Gagnon, John T., and Maria Novotny. "Revisiting Research as Care: A Call to Decolonize Narratives of Trauma." *Rhetoric Review* 39, no. 4 (2020): 486–501.

Gerdes, Kendall. "Trauma, Trigger Warnings, and the Rhetoric of Sensitivity." *Rhetoric Society Quarterly* 49, no. 1 (2019): 3–24.

Halse, Christine, and Anne Honey. "Unraveling Ethics: Illuminating the Moral Dilemmas of Research Ethics." *Signs* 30, no. 4 (2005): 2141–62.

Haraway, Donna. "Situated Knowledges: The Science Question in Feminism and the Privilege of Partial Perspective." *Feminist Studies* 14, no. 3 (1988): 575–99.

Hopper, Elizabeth K., Ellen L. Bassuk, and Jeffrey Olivet. "Shelter from the Storm: Trauma-Informed Care in Homelessness Services Settings." *The Open Health Services and Policy Journal* 3, no. 1 (2010): 80–100.

Jaggar, Alison M. "Love and Knowledge: Emotion in Feminist Epistemology." *Inquiry* 32, no. 2 (1989): 151–76.

Kirsch, Gesa E. *Ethical Dilemmas in Feminist Research: The Politics of Location, Interpretation, and Publication*. Albany, NY: SUNY Press, 1999.

Larson, Stephanie R. "Survivors, Liars, and Unfit Minds: Rhetorical Impossibility and Rape Trauma Disclosure." *Hypatia* 33, no. 4 (2018): 681–99.

Lather, Patricia A. *Getting Smart: Feminist Research and Pedagogy Within/in the Postmodern*. New York: Routledge, 1991.

Lather, Patricia A., and Christine S. Smithies. *Troubling the Angels: Women Living with HIV/AIDS*. Boulder, CO: Westview Press, 1997.

Lorde, Audre. *A Burst of Light: Essays*. Ithaca, NY: Firebrand, 1988.

Mendes, Kaitlynn, Jessica Ringrose, and Jessalynn Keller. *Digital Feminist Activism: Girls and Women Fight Back Against Rape Culture*. Oxford: Oxford University Press, 2019.

Moraga, Cherríe, and Gloria Anzaldúa, eds. *This Bridge Called My Back: Writings by Radical Women of Color*. 4th ed. Albany: SUNY Press, 2015.

Powell, Malea, Daisy Levy, Andrea Riley Mukavetz, Marilee Brooks-Gillies, and Jennifer Fisch-Ferguson. "Our Story Begins Here: Constellating Cultural Rhetorics." *Enculturation: A Journal of Rhetoric, Writing, and Culture* 18 (2014). https://enculturation.net/our-story-begins-here.

Restaino, Jessica. *Surrender: Feminist Rhetoric and Ethics in Love and Illness*. Carbondale, IL: Southern Illinois University Press, 2019.

Royster, Jacqueline Jones, and Gesa E. Kirsch. *Feminist Rhetorical Practices: New Horizons for Rhetoric, Composition, and Literacy Studies*. Carbondale, IL: Southern Illinois University Press, 2012.

Stenberg, Shari J. "'Tweet Me Your First Assaults': Writing Shame and the Rhetorical Work of #NotOkay." *Rhetoric Society Quarterly* 28, no. 2 (2018): 119–38.

Tayles, Melissa. "Trauma-Informed Writing Pedagogy: Ways to Support Student Writers Affected by Trauma and Traumatic Stress." *Teaching English in the Two Year College* 48, no. 3 (2021): 295–313.

Winfield, Taylor Paige. "Vulnerable Research: Competencies for Trauma and Justice-Informed Ethnography." *Journal of Contemporary Ethnography* 51, no. 2 (2022): 135–70.

SIX

Desiring Consent

A Reflexive Methodology for Feminist Research

Jessica Restaino and Timothy Oleksiak

In his work on queer rhetorics, Jonathan Alexander notes the textual nature of desire which, we argue here, may underlay the pursuit of consent—for data, for participation, for the text itself.[1] Indeed, what desire can offer writing, for Alexander and numerous others, has to do with relationality, a merging of materiality and queerness that might yield the next text, an alterity. More than a theory of invention, however, for feminist researchers desire creates a space to think methodologically about the process of consent among researchers and their human participants. The work we set to do here is to advance a theoretical framework for learning to recognize desire as it functions within the research relationship. From this theorizing, methods can emerge.

Psychoanalytic writers have long acknowledged both the presence of and typical resistances to desire and longing between therapist and patient in the consulting room. In his 1996 review of such work, which stretches from Freud's notorious and problematic struggles to Searles's desirous fantasies toward patients across genders, Stanley Coen argues that desire is fundamental to therapeutic progress though often unacknowledged: "Therapists tend to avoid experiencing the full range of loving and hating feelings between themselves and their patients. They do so because such intense passions make them feel anxious and guilty. Therapists' ego ideals still hold that therapists are not to feel such passions in the therapeutic setting." However, for Coen, it is the therapist's capacity for access to exactly such depth of feeling that 'help[s] patients achieve maximum autonomy from conflict and from the therapeutic relationship."[2] We find Coen's description between therapist and patient similar to the feminist researcher and her participants. Emotional attachment and depth of feeling is paradoxically valued in most feminist literature while being denied in research contexts precisely when those feelings for more are extended toward each other, across the no one's land of soliciting and offering data for analysis.

Here, we focus on the relationality that emerges from a desire to be together within the research context and we call for a feminist methodology of close reading for its cues. We bring up desire in methodology because it can reflect a core drive behind the discovery of new knowledge about writing and literacy—we simply need each other and so often come to desire each other in a variety of iterations, often in ways that disrupt traditional power dynamics and hierarchical roles. And yet desire is often checkered with uncertainties. Desire for more can overwhelm the research process to such an extent that continued pursuit for more—more reciprocity, more data, more knowledge-making, more intimacy—could lead all involved into an imprecisely articulated but deeply felt trouble.

This felt trouble is precisely why feminist researchers have taken great care to make reflexivity a fundamental practice.[3] These are the questions brought forth from the reflexivity imperative in feminist research: Have we researchers done harm in our reaching? Have we asked one question too far? Have we squeezed ourselves into spaces we are not fully welcomed (or welcomed at all)? How did we arrive at this longing in the first place? Why did we deem such longing and searching permissible at all? The work of reflecting on *desiring* consent in the research relationship, above and beyond what we have perhaps "successfully" collected in terms of data, is essential feminist work encouraged by the demand to maintain the bodily autonomy and self-determination of our participants. Reflecting on the impact of desire often leads feminist researchers to better and more sophisticated methods for working with human participants. In this way, methods are developed to protect researchers from the knowable and unknowable desires of our participants and to protect participants from a researcher's desires. In her beautifully crafted reflection about her own researcher positionality, Kate Vieira asserts, "And it is right to avoid constructing a narrative that fetishizes the pain of marginalized people, as does much 'damage-centered' research. But it is also right to use the tools of story to bring to light injustice, struggle, beauty, strength. On good days, I believe I used narrative as a kind of historically situated, empirically grounded, aesthetic reckoning with power. Other days I'm not so sure. What I do know is that my eventual analysis was a close, if neurotic, kind of listening that to me felt something like love."[4]

Vieira engages her own discomfort with this very drive to write *about* others and the inevitability of objectification "no matter how my participants sought me out expressly to be heard."[5] For Vieira, methodological "specificity," following as closely as possible the rules of careful coding and research design, becomes a way for researchers to show their respect for their participants. When thinking about the complexity of desire in the research moment, we simply say that fidelity to methods is necessary.[6] However, such fidelity is not enough. While methods do provide a process for interacting with human participants, strict adherence to methods in the design and data collection phase runs the risk of ignoring or being unable to see the shifts and turns that take place during moments of contact. As Bob Broad maintains, "choices among research methods are not as purely rationalistic and strategic as we might wish, believe, or pretend. Deep-seated intellectual desires and predilections are also in play."[7] One way to track shifts and turns is to sensitize ourselves to participant's uses of modal qualifiers: linguistic cues such as "may" or "might" that indicate an openness or a diminishment of certainty by those who use them. We affirm Wendy Bishop's insight that researchers notice ethical issues in their prose "after the fact: during the writing-it-up phase, during the next project as [they] attempt to teach others to go into territories [they] have only just begun to explore."[8] Our intention in this chapter is to enact the work of a feminist model for looking back and, hopefully, charting ways forward that are informed by attunements to cues of consent given by researchers *and* participants that resist reductive, decisive lines toward consent as certainty.

We pause here to reflect on both Bishop's "after the fact" and what it means to need each other in relation to the work we have set out to accomplish in this chapter as co-authors. Jess saw Timothy's[9] work with modal qualification in "Composing Consent as a Response to the Challenge of Openness" as important for reflexive praxis and we both agreed to dialogue about these ideas. As our Zoom conversations extended beyond admiration for each other's work, we began to recognize a development of ideas that moved from being our own into something collaborative. However, we find ourselves needing to explain this as a co-authored piece rather than as the work of one scholar, Jess, citing another's, Timothy, to do a different kind of reflexive work. In reflecting on the work needed, we both saw a vulnerability and exposure that emerged from wanting to be seen and understood by each other and by those who read this work as good people. The questions we ask above expose us, and we found ourselves needing support in the process regardless of what the effects of this effort look like on the page. To put the matter of co-authorship and voice in academic writing more directly—we determined that the vulnerability we shared with each other necessitated co-authorship. We recognize, as Jacqueline Jones Royster did years ago, that we speak with a multiplicity of voices, each as authentic (as vexed as that term is) as the next.[10] If we recognize that in ourselves, can we also not see this multivocality in this chapter as well? Not Jess. Not Timothy. Just us.

To locate desire in research methodology is to bring an awareness of the shifting dynamics of openness for more insight into the research process. Body language, tone of voice, hesitancy in speech, or writing around an issue or idea during writing prompts have been typical cues for researchers that participants might say more. Modal qualifiers may also function similarly. In "Composing Consent," Timothy theorizes rhetorical consent within the context of persuasion and argumentation. He suggests that modal qualification offers cues for consent that function as touchpoints of contact that "expand the range of contact that writers hope to achieve and readers hope to recognize."[11] These touchpoints invite further contact because they signal an openness for more. Words like "sometimes" or "often" or "may" or "almost" point us toward a space of "more" or, at least "possible," because they suggest that the rhetor believes there *could be* exceptions, pockets of unknown or unexpected information. A lack of qualification implies a lack of consent for engagement, that the author's claims cannot be challenged. The consequences for rhetors who wish to respond is that they need to shift audiences and move toward an analysis of why such a closed position is harmful. As a cue for consent, modal qualifiers expand the range of contact and engagement. They dislodge the claim as the primary focus of interest. Modal qualifiers are a more precise way of understanding how rhetors open themselves up for more contact. We argue here that they also illustrate markers that feminist researchers can use to trace the evolving degrees of engagement within the research relationship, where the "researcher" and the "researched" each work (struggle?) to read and respond to other's cues (or lack thereof) that might deepen collaboration itself.

We choose modal qualifiers as a location for analysis and theorization precisely because they are *textualized* cues. While it is impossible to know the precise direction of human communication, modal qualifiers provide a grounding between researchers and their participants and a location where all might reflect on the felt nature of contact. We can point to a textual moment of openness, one recognized among all those involved. Textualized cues for consent expressed through modal qualification are a location where those working within a research study can return should misunderstanding occur.

We now turn our attention to a reflexive methodology for rhetorical consent in *Surrender,* Jess's ethnographic study of friend and collaborator Susan Lundy Maute's last two years of living and dying with breast cancer. Together, we present a queer feminist reflexive methodological practice made possible via rhetorical consent.

Desire and Consent in Surrender: Feminist Rhetorics and Ethics in Love and Illness

Jess: I'm guessing you're staying in the hospital through tomorrow? I'm around in the morning and plan to come by. Need anything?

Sue: I may get out of here late morning. I won't know until tomorrow. Would love to see you.

Jess: Ok well text me if you're getting out . . . If I don't hear from you, I'll turn up at hospital.

Sue: K . . . should still be here . . . but I will let you know.[12]

In her introduction to *Rhetorica in Motion,* later quoted in *Surrender,* Schell writes of "feminist rhetorical methods and methodologies as movement, as motion, and as action."[13] We continue to embrace the idea of motion, though want to suggest it often happens in starts and stops, hesitations and backslides. Modal qualifiers help us identify such movements methodologically, as potential openings and closings. At times, desire and consent seem to happen as a kind of push pull: "desire" as the assertion—"[I] . . . plan to come by"—and consent as a control on desire's enactment—"K . . . should still be here . . . but I will let you know."[14] Notably we sometimes fail to ask explicitly for consent to act—*Can I come by?*—perhaps because the selfish heft of desire—*I want to see you*—itself takes centerstage. Using modal qualifiers, our audience can respond in a way that both complicates and inserts the necessity of permission: "I won't know *until . . . should* still . . . *but* I will let you know." They may even share our desire—"would love to see you"— but that does not mean they will grant us permission to act. The door is both open and potentially closed; we must wait. Tracking such modal qualifications in our research relationships chart a methodological map for relationship building, one grounded in power-sharing and patience.

To the extent that *Surrender* is a work about method, it is also a work about movement. There are bursts of energy, of leaning towards and perhaps even real reaching, and there are moments of impasse, fear, and impossibility. In between is a dance within a research partnership and friendship, as Jess and Sue relay and negotiate desire and consent to be together (or not) for Sue's progressing illness and also, perhaps most importantly for our purposes here, *do* research in the form of writing and recording Sue's experiences. Ultimately, in the scenario captured above Jess is granted permission, but only because Sue has established her authority as the one who must consent—regardless of the presence of desire—to Jess's reach, perhaps indeed her overstep: "If I don't hear from you, I'll turn up." Sue essentially qualifies: "You will hear from me *and* I will let you know whether or not to turn up." In other words, *you are not yet granted permission to just turn up, however much you might want to be present. Maybe permission will be granted; maybe it will not. I will let you know.* This negotiation is one of many in which the use of modal qualifiers facilitated Jess and Sue's movement through her illness and their joint project, all following Sue's signing of formal consent paperwork that granted Jess full use of the artifacts she collected as part of their collaboration.

Timothy's modal qualifiers, cues in the context of rhetorical argument, provide a theoretical frame for reading the dance of this research relationship. Their presence allows us to track openings in this exchange between Jess and Sue, but not certainty, not the sort of "strong and enthusiastic consent" models that are sought after by informed consent paperwork and predetermined interview questions. The insertion of cues on Sue's part establishes control of an otherwise potentially unregulated situation (i.e., Jess's "showing up"), creating both order and possibility. Sue qualifies with "may," "until," "would," and "should." These words open engagement, suggest the need for more time and thus a refusal of the immediacy of access Jess seeks to establish. It's worth noting, however, that even in Jess's move, which feels in retrospect overly assertive and perhaps even domineering, there is slippage and uncertainty. Timothy explains: "The transactional 'offer: consent or reject' imagines a universal subjectivity prior to the engagement where participants act within predefined roles and expectations in an idealized setting. Such an approach assumes clear lines of power."[15] While Jess's movement-as-researcher towards Sue might suggest a *wish* for such a clear line of power, we learn quickly by tracking modal qualifiers that she, as researcher and even as friend, does not possess it. Further, too, we ought to imagine the hospital Jess seeks to enter as far from Timothy's "idealized setting." It is a fraught space, one steeped in its remove from everyday rules for coming and going that govern ordinary life. Indeed, Rita Charon describes the subjective space of illness for its very loss of recognizable "role"—"The seriously ill people for whom we care in clinical practice are marooned between stable states. They are no longer defined by their work role, family role, or state role and not yet defined as simply awaiting death but de-differentiated by cotton hospital gowns and plastic wristbands to be side by side only with others who, too, find themselves in the limbo regions of sickness."[16]

We thus have in the rhetorical, text-based negotiation between Jess and Sue, "researcher" and "researched," an absence of stability in setting and in role. The instability in role is true for both: Sue is as Charon describes, "marooned" and not defined, while in the hospital, by the typical roles we occupy when we are well enough to be out in the world; Jess is researcher but also friend, unsure which role might be more deserving or legitimate in its rights to access. Either way and perhaps most poignantly, Jess desires consent and attempts to confirm it by claiming Sue's potential silence *as* consent, assigning meaning in a way Jess has predefined; in this move she attempts to close off engagement to fulfill her own desire. We see this in Jess's, "If I don't hear from you, I'll turn up at the hospital." Of "closed positions," Timothy tell us: "[they] are rhetorical dead ends."[17] Indeed in Jess's move here we have only one reason for why she might not hear from Sue—because it is okay for her to show up. We lose any of the *other* possibilities for why Jess *might not* hear from Sue—her illness has worsened; her phone is misplaced or the battery has died; she has other visitors; or her doctors are actively treating her. In her response, "I will let you know," Sue establishes her authority as the one who will grant permission, and she shifts the exchange to one of openness, of possibility. In Sue's new configuration, time will tell whether or not she has been discharged, and a host of possibilities around whether or not she will grant Jess access to her in the hospital are reinvigorated. To the extent that there is possibility, there are qualifiers. A queer feminist methodology values both the absence of certainty as well as the presence of possibility. There are no direct lines here, but we have a way of reading methodologically for want, hope, and need, and that includes Sue's potential need to control Jess's movements.

In this exchange between Jess and Sue, the researcher seems the most urgently desiring, working to arrange a visit with some degree of disregard for potential opposition. Coming to terms with the researcher as desirer, we admit that we may often want our research participants more desperately than they want us. There are, of course, shades of gray to this dynamic, exceptions to the rule. Certainly, in Sue's case there was often a drive to "get things down" as her illness worsened and, for Jess's part, attachment to Sue as her friend and an urgency to be present for her, including as her witness or recorder. Nevertheless, the researcher's longing for that content, for "data," as we might think of it contextually, does stand to invert assumptions about who has the most power and authority in the dynamic. And, in fact, in her outward efforts to "arrange" consent for her visit, Jess appears the more desirous one and power shifts profoundly. Sue, clearly authorized, uses modal qualifiers to undo the potential for conflict (Jess showing up without permission) and demonstrates her autonomy and decision-making power within the dynamic *despite* being in the position of seemingly less power, that of "researched" and also terminally ill. We might consider at this juncture, too, the way in which the presence of marginalized identities, particularly among our research participants, may complicate the very inversion that Sue is able to realize—she is a white, cishet-identified woman who is navigating medical institutions and treatment with these identity advantages amid her status as terminally ill. Camara Phyllis Jones's work in anti-racist medical practice challenges us to take up the ways in which the social determinants of health function to further disadvantage someone with Sue's condition whose identity markers might be less privileged; these considerations are essential in the reflexive work of trying to understand power dynamics as they play out within a research collaboration. Further, too, as we do this feminist work, we must consider the ways in which the researcher's authority and role might be further destabilized by their own marginalized identities. Being similar in age, gender, and race may have functioned to quiet some of these potential dynamics between Jess and Sue, though differences between them endured. As Jess now has the space to consider some of the very push-pull between them in their interactions, she must wrangle with the spaces of uncertainty and risk that ultimately drove the work itself.

Perhaps one of the most poignant written artifacts and, indeed, writing "events" in *Surrender* is the coauthoring of Sue's wishes in the weeks before her death. This is a scene we return to now, equipped with previously unpublished communications that worked to arrange that event, to use modal qualifiers to better understand the interplay between desire and consent in the relationship and in the text(s) produced. In *Surrender*, Jess casts the original scene thus: "Exactly three weeks before her death, when each day seemed to bring news of another serious medical issue, Sue whispered to me in her hospital room that maybe it'd be a good idea to write some things down: 'I've decided something . . . ' And I understood immediately, despite her difficulty with asking for much of anything, that this writing-things-down was my province, that this was my role. *Of course I will do this with you.*"[18]

Surrender is complex methodologically for its subversive mixing of friendship and research, and this scene is a fine example of the challenges such a mix might bring—the dialogue here does not emerge from a formal transcript, captured via audio recording, saved and printed for analysis. Rather this is a scene from inside a friendship and a memory, one in which Jess's ethnographic skills play a role in creating a space for Sue to talk and think about her illness and her death, to—as Jim Corder writes—"get things down right"—even as there is a slipperiness, an impossibility to precision.[19] This lack of precision might be true for all our work, but perhaps it is especially true in our relationships that engage love and attachment which, we suggest, can be within the province of our research relationships. Still, even in Jess's recollection we can see evidence of qualifiers—*seemed, maybe, it'd, some.* But with all the qualifiers leading up to what Jess experiences as a proposition—that she write down Sue's wishes for her approaching death—we do not get, as readers, even Timothy's "offer: accept reject" frame. Instead, Jess moves from a partial quotation from Sue, "'I've decided something . . .'" into her own "I understood immediately." Some of this move, for Jess, is rooted in her understanding (accurately or not) of Sue's personality ("her difficulty with asking for much of anything") as well as a firm commitment to notions of her own role, "writing-things-down was my province . . . my role." Because we know how this story ends, we know that not only did Jess record Sue's wishes, but she did so amid great support and clarity from Sue: "She had her arm around me, happy and confident: just as she had become so physically frail by this point, the creation of this text seemed to embolden her and she had become the stronger of the two of us. She squeezed me tighter, looked directly at me, and said, 'I know. I won.'"[20]

The text that was produced ultimately guided Sue's services following her death, directed the distribution of materials and messages among some of Sue's intimates, including her children, and established her values, especially about how she wanted those she loved to think about her death. In many ways, the document represents Sue's own desire, not only for what she wishes will happen beyond her death, but also how she would like to behave in the days leading up to her death. For example, under a section titled, "Things I Want to Get Done," she dictates to Jess a wish "when there's nothing more they can do for me," to give each of her children something they can carry with them so they might feel her continued presence. This is an active wish for physical contact with each of her four children, not a directive to be carried out after she is gone: "In that process I want to be able to then hand them these things."[21] At the time of this composing, Sue's cancer had already exceeded the capacities of medical treatment and she would live just nearly another three weeks. In that time, she would not enact her stated desire here. In part, we might wonder about Sue's own notions of consent as it might apply to her children. Despite her desires for how *she* might act, would her children accept—indeed consent, in their way—to receiving from their mother an acknowledgement of her certain, approaching death? Might they refuse whatever material memorabilia or trinket she tries to place into their grasp? We can imagine maternal restraint here, a fear of or resistance to causing her children anticipatory grief, even though their suffering would ultimately be inevitable. Wrapped around these questions is Jess's very possession of this text in the first place, her decision to write about it in an ethnographic context that tracks Sue's struggle in words and body.

Jess's desire to not only tell the story but to study the words themselves, to cast them as meaningful for others, looms large. We will never know the extent to which *Surrender*, published five years after her death, realizes what Sue wished for when she explained that "to give back" was her motivation for doing the project. At the same time, we all search for a satisfying experience of our subjectivity out in the world. Sue seeks a life "purpose" or value as a person who is also dying. As researchers we, too, desire a version of ourselves we can live with, even when we know our failures and slippages will be inevitable. Sue releases herself and us: "I keep waiting for it to look a certain way, but maybe I stop looking for this 'aha' moment."[22]

Concluding Thoughts

In our analysis, reading for modal qualifiers provides us with a tool for listening harder and committing to reflexivity as a practice that endures beyond the research event itself. For most of us this inevitably means accepting ourselves in starts and stops, a series of hesitations. This is as true for us as researchers as it was for Sue as she was dying. Whatever the ethically good researcher may yet be, she is at least this.

Our goal was to bring the complicated messiness of desire into the research process. The theorizing we have begun here works with an existing research project to help us create a set of questions other feminist researchers might want to take up and refine. We are opening a call for feminist methods that do this work. We are unsure what a methodology based on attending to the cues of consent offered by modal qualification might look like as a method for data analysis. How can we code modal qualifiers with the spirit of the methodology we have developed here? We believe, too, that the questions we have posed throughout can help teach us how to do more careful and responsible research and writing. We hope that social movement scholars might carry our practice into their work as well and that we learn from what they might offer us. Ultimately, we understand this chapter as a call for feminist researchers to begin this work. The questions, we hope, invite a diverse multitude of feminist, queer reckonings.

NOTES

1. Alexander, "Materiality," 9.
2. Coen, "Love," 25.
3. See, for example, Lather, *Getting Smart*; Chiseri-Strater, "Turning In"; Royster and Kirsch, *Feminist Rhetorical Practices*.
4. Vieira, "Writing About Others," 56.
5. Vieira, "Writing About Others," 53.
6. See, e.g., Smagorinsky, "The Methods Section," 8.
7. Broad, "Strategies," 200.
8. Bishop, *Ethnographic Writing*, 148–49.
9. We wish to retain the more familiar and less formal first name use of "Jess" and "Timothy" rather than "Restaino" and "Oleksiak" (or "Sue" for "Maute"). We find it no less academic in style or tone or purpose to include the more familiar, conversational first-name references to each other.
10. Royster, "When the First Voice You Hear," 37; Royster then develops this idea throughout *Traces* within the context of African American women rhetors.
11. Oleksiak, "Composing Consent," 442.
12. Susan Lundy Maute and Jessica Restaino, text messages, May 2014.
13. Schell and Rawson, *Rhetorica in Motion*, 6.
14. Susan Lundy Maute and Jessica Restaino, text messages, May 2014.
15. Oleksiak, "Composing Consent," 436.
16. Charon, *Narrative Medicine*, 220.
17. Oleksiak, "Composing Consent," 431.
18. Restaino, *Surrender*, 58.
19. Corder, "I in Mine," 260.
20. Restaino, *Surrender*, 58.
21. Lundy Maute, "What I Want."
22. Susan Lundy Maute qtd. in Restaino, *Surrender*, 158.

WORKS CITED

Alexander, Jonathan. "Materiality, Queerness, and a Theory of Desire for Writing Studies." *College English* 83, no. 1 (2020): 7–41.

Bishop, Wendy. *Ethnographic Writing Research: Writing it Down, Writing it Up, and Reading It*. Portsmouth, NH: Boynton/Cook, 1999.

Broad, Bob. "Strategies and Passions in Empirical Qualitative Research." In *Writing Studies Research in Practice*, edited by Gesa E. Kirsch, 197–209. Carbondale, IL: Southern Illinois University Press, 2012.

Charon, Rita. *Narrative Medicine: Honoring the Stories of Illness*. Oxford: Oxford University Press, 2006.

Chiseri-Strater, Elizabeth. "Turning In Upon Ourselves: Positionality, Subjectivity, and Reflexivity in Case Study and Ethnographic Research." In *Ethics and Representation in Qualitative Studies of Literacy*, edited by Peter Mortensen and Gesa E. Kirsch, 115–33. Champaign, IL: National Council of Teachers of English, 1996.

Coen, Stanley. "Love between Therapist and Patient: A Review." *American Journal of Psychotherapy* 50, no. 1 (1996): 14–27.

Corder, Jim W. "I in Mine, You Elsewhere." In *Selected Essays of Jim W. Corder: Pursuing the Personal in Scholarship, Teaching, and Writing*, edited by James S. Baumlin and Keith D. Miller, 243–562. Champaign, IL: National Council of Teachers of English, 2004.

Lather, Patricia A. *Getting Smart: Feminist Research and Pedagogy With/in the Postmodern*. New York: Routledge, 1991.

Maute, Susan Lundy. "What I Want." Unpublished manuscript. August 8, 2014.

Oleksiak, Timothy. "Composing Consent as a Response to the Challenge of Openness." *College English* 84, no. 5 (2022): 429–46.

Restaino, Jessica. *Surrender: Feminist Rhetoric and Ethics in Love and Illness*. Carbondale, IL: Southern Illinois University Press, 2019.

Royster, Jacqueline Jones. *Traces of a Stream: Literacy and Social Change Among African American Women*. Pittsburgh, PA: University of Pittsburgh Press, 2000.

Royster, Jacqueline Jones. "When the First Voice You Hear Is Not Your Own." *College Composition and Communication* 47, no. 1 (1996): 29–40.

Royster, Jacqueline Jones, and Gesa E. Kirsch. *Feminist Rhetorical Practices: New Horizons for Rhetoric, Composition, and Literacy Studies*. Carbondale, IL: Southern Illinois University Press, 2012.

Schell, Eileen E., and K.J. Rawson, eds. *Rhetorica in Motion: Feminist Rhetorical Methods and Methodologies*. Pittsburgh, PA: University of Pittsburgh Press, 2010.

Smagorinsky, Peter. "The Method Section as Conceptual Epicenter in Constructing Social Science Research Reports." *Written Communication* 25, no. 3 (2008): 389–411.

Vieira, Kate. "Writing About Others Writing: Some Field Notes." In *Rhetorics Elsewhere and Otherwise: Contested Modernities, Decolonial Visions*, edited by Romeo Garcia and Damian Baca, 49–61. Champaign, IL: SWR/NCTE, 2019.

SEVEN

Collective Identity in Feminist Rhetorical Research

Un/representing Incarceration and Queerness through Abolition Feminism

Rachel Lewis

Prisons are not Feminist.

—MARIAME KABA, "TOWARDS THE HORIZON OF ABOLITION"

Historically—and rhetorically—speaking, there is a gap between the political goals of prison abolition and feminist rhetorical advocacy. Abolition feminists, like Kaba, argue that gendered violence cannot be ended through carceral means,[1] while feminist advocacy against domestic and sexual violence has historically yielded movements that often imagine extensions of the carceral state to protect survivors through the increased criminalization of domestic and sexual violence.[2] In *Abolition. Feminism. Now.*, abolition feminists Angela Davis, Gina Dent, Erika Meiners, and Beth Ritchie call such conflicts "as old as they are familiar." Of modern feminist and abolitionist movement history, they write that "precisely at the moment domestic violence and sexual assault were being recognized as crimes, thus presumably requiring carceral responses, contemporary abolitionists were effectively challenging a criminal legal system that naturalized retributive punishment."[3] In this chapter, I make room in feminist rhetorical research for abolition feminism—feminism defined by a rejection of carceral means to both end gender violence and promote gender equality—by drawing on the generative commitments feminist rhetorical methodologies have made to expanding the subjects of feminist research and to the lived experiences of feminist subjects. Intersectional in approach, abolition feminism centers lived experience, material disparity and scarcity, and many subjects of liberation at once. In short, gender equality is not a single stake in competition with other social freedoms but enmeshed with the rights of all. Like feminist rhetorical research, abolition feminism has a vested interest in marginalized subjects (including queer, trans, queer of color, Black, disabled, Indigenous, and low-income people). However, unlike most feminist projects (rhetorical and otherwise), abolition feminism does not take the workings of the prison industrial complex (PIC) as beneficial when it does the purported work of feminism (e.g., punishing acts of violence against women by carceral means) and harmful only when it does not (e.g., a lack of carceral punishment for violence against women or an increased incarceration of women with non-violent offenses due to drug policy/mandatory minimums).

As a lens that values the lived realities of people in the most stringent of material circumstances (incarcerated people), and who are also in isolation from each other and the rest of free society, abolition feminism is integral to the rhetorical reading and analytical processes I engage as a facilitator and researcher of community texts written by incarcerated LGBTQ+ writers. I present these texts to connect abolition feminism to feminist rhetorical methodologies, surfacing readings of collective identity that resist simple representations and rhetorical signifiers, such as "landmark" protections (safety legislation linked to a particular figure or narrative, e.g. "Megan's Law" or "the Brady Act") and "key" rhetorical figures as the defining nexus between the individual/self (or selves) and the collective/other(s). In the history of feminist rhetorical reclamation and recovery work, primary figures and their texts have been a central and essential focus. A consequence of this work is that collective identity is often figured through a singular figure rather than through community voices being represented as a collective spectrum, though work in this mode has broadened via community literacy studies.[4]

The exclusionary practices of the PIC are relevant to a wide range of contexts and contribute to the foundational logics of exclusion that frame many spheres of inquiry and research in feminist rhetorical methodologies, as they do across multiple fields and sites of study. The lived, material experiences of incarcerated people are dominated by the privations and disciplinary logics of incarceration, as well as by civic exclusions. Applied together, abolition feminism and feminist rhetorical methodologies emphasize collective identification and representation, as well as the necessity of grounding scholarship in lived materiality. Through these frames, we might read incarcerated LGBTQ+ writers as drawing on collectivity and interdependence as a form of material survival, world-building, and sustenance inside and outside of institutional life. In my analysis, identification, representation, and local/lived experience in feminist rhetorical methodologies are attenuated to the dimensions of identity expressed in the writing of incarcerated LGBTQ+ writers—collective and fluid.

I am drawn to feminist rhetorical methodologies through Jaqueline Jones Royster's "passionate attachments"—an excavation of connections to research that are bound in lived experiences and sense of self.[5] Acknowledging the specific position that one has as a researcher to subjects of research, Royster notes, is integral to creating ethical methods and the reflection necessary to articulate a "kaleidoscopic"[6] perspective across insiders and outsiders in a community. Multiple research perspectives, like multiple narratives and subjects, are part of feminist knowledge-making. Nancy Myers writes that "feminist rhetorical studies circulates around and critically engages the material conditions of all women's work, no matter the time or place. It is about all of us—then, now, and coming." Myers illuminates an openness, not only to diverse identities, but to feminist identities and subjects as explicitly futuristic, looking forward to new iterations of the "us—then, now, and coming."[7] Broad invitations to new perspectives, new subjects, and new ways of reading that make them visible are embedded in feminist rhetorical methodologies, and as a queer person with a growing critical consciousness of my family history of incarceration, I sought a community space that would make sense of both forms of othering: first, the class unconsciousness that pervades Queer Studies, alongside many other disciplines, as Matt Brim reminds us, by "locating the problem somewhere beyond its field,"[8] and, second, the exclusions of queer life across class contexts, in academic departments as well as in nuclear family life. To build a political home, I began organizing alongside a collective of activists in a queer abolitionist community organization. Weekly, we responded to letters from incarcerated LGBTQ+ writers, sometimes transcribing them, if the writer asked, for publication in the organizational newspaper, a national publication with (at the time) nearly 8,000 subscribers, the majority of whom were receiving and reading the newspaper in prison or jail. By regularly publishing letters by readers, the newspaper offered incarcerated LGBTQ+ writers a platform through which to engage and compare lived experiences generally characterized by isolation—imprisonment, existing inside a perceived LGBTQ+ umbrella, and especially the combination of those two identifiers.

The newspaper letters to/from readers and writers provided practical perspectives from the everyday lives of LGBTQ+ incarcerated people.

Individual writers noted the intersections of criminalization and queerness through narratives of lived experience and material realities. These epistolary exchanges were soon dubbed "letters to family" or "family letters" due to the frequency of "family" used in the salutation.[9] Writers often attributed the motivations to write letters at all to the realization that their experiences and insights were not only materially useful to other readers but might inspire specific actions and feelings in others with political and communal consequences. Single stories became enmeshed in references to others, both cited and uncited, and writers wrote about themselves and their audiences as a collective, political bloc with no dominant voice, and necessary conflicts and contradictions due to the isolation and distance between each letter added to a literary family portrait.

These two threads—the sharing of both materially specific, embodied experience and a collective political identity—offer insight into the horizons of feminist rhetorical methodologies, where "we are compelled to recast our whole ways of thinking and doing and to situate ourselves more deliberately in the company of others as we reach for more-comprehensive and more-nimble views, attitudes, and expectations. . . ."[10] Alternative, expansive ways of reading and recognizing feminist subjects and identities is a founding motion of feminist rhetorical methodologies, and the field continues to seek multiplicity in the standpoints it represents and the subjects it constitutes, as well as interrogate assumptions about the gendered character of such subjects.[11] Abolition feminism takes as its subjects, participants, and researchers all who have been impacted by the PIC, and its attendant rhetoric of punishment, individualism, and exceptionalism. I draw on feminist rhetorical methodologies along with abolition feminism to address the material conditions embedded in these "family letters," and how material perspectives are negotiated into community conversations, exchanges, and a collective queer identity that resists a fully shared politic, even as it seeks to build "shared power." These writers emphasize the nuances of their experiences in prison but simultaneously and rhetorically demonstrate collective identity.

Researcher Subjectivity in Text Analysis

Those researching incarceration, as well as those directly impacted by it, benefit from asking Krista Ratcliffe's vivid question about identification in *Rhetorical Listening: Identification, Gender, Whiteness*—"The questions that haunt such identification and disidentification are: How accurate are mental images that drive our identifications and disidentifications?"[12] Ratcliffe describes inaccurate mental images as inclinations toward inequitable assessments of self and other. In her example, xenophobia is produced by a dominant culture's "freedom to choose" whether to learn about nondominant cultures, as well as the *privilege to choose* to recognize that *dominant* and *nondominant* are cultural constructs and that the identities of each group are always interdependent. . . ."[13] The centrality of a representative individual—a figure, a narrator—to characterize a large and diverse group of people is a common rhetorical practice among advocates and antagonists of prison reform generally, usually invoked with an explicitly political purpose. The lived specifics of material conditions form the "commonalities and differences that we analyze, reify, and/or disrupt as researchers."[14]

In one description of these physical effects, Mira Shimabukuro compellingly describes her physical encounters with the literacy artifacts of writers incarcerated in Japanese internment camps,[15] "handwritten and wide-ruled, tiny drawings filling in space between all the text. On some documents, crossed-out text and handwritten notes projected images in my mind of real hands writing, committed to making the words perform the writer's intent."[16] In Skimabukuro's account, attention to the physical response— the material conditions—of the researcher places the locus of the "literacy-in-action" to the narrating mind of the researcher, perhaps particularly because a single individuated and authoritative voice does not necessarily emerge from archives that span diverse, historically marginalized communities. "Reading" the activities of writers—their engagements, relationships, and identities—becomes the primary focus. The individual reader/researcher must ignite these possibilities while acknowledging their own position and subjectivity, thus further situating the knowledge that emerges from/through lived experience.

Addressing Material Collectivity

Despite working within the restrictions of the PIC (an isolating apparatus that criminalizes various books, sex and sexual expression, same-gender relationships, transgender expression and gender fluidity, and many forms of mail, including mail between two incarcerated people in the same or separate institutions), the incarcerated writers who wrote to us persisted in reading themselves collectively alongside other readers and writers connected to the newspaper. As the readership of the newspaper increased, pages and pages of family letters were published in each monthly issue, with a chorus of voices seeking support, belonging, and identity within a similarly situated audience. Moreover, the writers consistently responded to other letters and compared experiences by noting explicit commonalities and differences, a practice explicitly linked, in rhetorical listening, to establishing dis/identifications between the self and other.

These moments of identification and disidentification built, to my mind, a shifting and contradictory, but nonetheless collective identity, highlighting a simultaneous and multidirectional diversity of voices. Writers imagined their letters as resonating with, persuading, and even agitating different strands of readership, all while emphasizing the deep material connections that networked them as incarcerated LGBTQ+ peers. Communications *between* incarcerated people, especially across various prisons and jails, is prohibited and/or strictly monitored, and the publication of a newspaper was interpreted, by both readers and writers, as an act of material and cultural resistance. A newspaper for LGBTQ+ incarcerated people provides a space for solidarity-against-the-machine.

However, the individuated writing practices embedded in these letters also focus on possibilities of collective identity through differences and differentiated experience, rather than collective difference cast as a singular political resistance to a mainstream. Drawing on the social concerns of Black, queer, and disabled abolition feminists, I suggest that centering collective subjectivity, rather than individual subjects, in my reading practices helped me figure subjects not just as multiple, but as fluid and "shape-shifting," as C. Jan Swearingen termed the archetypal figure of Dame Rhetorica.[17] Reading these texts as a constitutive of collective identity brings collective literacy practices[18] into conversation with formations of the queer subject, who is cast often as deliberately uncomposed in composition theory. My aim is to connect feminist rhetorical subjectivity with rhetoric and composition's analysis of a queer/ed subject, that is, one that does not easily or singularly speak, signify, or compose,[19] but establishes a "collective consciousness."[20]

Abolition Feminism, Collectivity, and Interdependence

In abolition feminism, collective identities are prioritized for their relationship to social interdependence and sustainability, as well as resisting the burden placed on singular leaders and leadership models. Transformative justice facilitator, author, and activist adrienne maree brown describes the damaging effect of individual figures in activist movements. "So far, we in movements for justice only make it collectively as far as our individual leaders can survive the onslaught," she observes.[21] "We mistakenly operate as individuals when we are already ecosystem—this is keeping us from the growth we and our communities desperately need."[22] The power (and exhaustion) of singular, charismatic leaders of justice movements are familiar features in activist structure/struggle and celebrated in a wide spectrum of ways—some that promote collectivity as essential to the individual's representative force, and some that uplift a monolithic figure as a unified voice for diverse peoples and experiences. brown continues, "One side effect of this hyper individualization of movement leaders is that the many small parts of our movement—our local organizers and chapters, our youth leaders, our community groups, our collectives—struggle to sustain themselves within our collaborative mass efforts."[23] Collective identity provides functional spaces for dissent and diversity, rather than a commitment to political unity. Voices affected by multiple marginalizations, Christina V. Cedillo writes, are excluded explicitly through the "material and physical conditions" that are left out of singular political visions.[24]

brown's emphasis on the "many small parts of our movement" echoes the concerns of Mia Mingus, a prison abolitionist and creator of the Disability Justice Framework, when she describes the role of "interdependence" in an accessible society: "Interdependency is both 'you and I' and 'we.' It is solidarity, in the best sense of the word. It is inscribing *community on our skin* over and over and over again. It is truly moving together in an oppressive world towards liberation and refusing to let the personal be a scapegoat for the political. It is knowing that one organization, one student or community group is not a movement. It is working in coalition and collaboration."[25] Though frequently missing from conversations about abolition and mass incarceration, the framework of disability justice figures significantly in abolition feminism, due to both the "disabling nature" of incarceration and the carceral treatment of many people with disabilities over time.[26] In disability justice, the space between individuality and community is smaller because of the material needs interdependence addresses— suggesting that disability frameworks teach material survival strategies, possible only through a physical cooperation and intimacy that supports access.[27]

Emphasis on an embodied subject position is significant in the intersection between disability and feminist rhetorical methodologies, Jay Dolmage and Cynthia Lewiecki-Wilson have explained, because "female embodiment [. . .] was figured as "dis-abled; to be a woman was to be disqualified from civic debate."[28] Dolmage and Lewiecki-Wilson reject disability as a limit of feminist rhetorics only if "monolithic and uniform [. . .] ways that the body is conceptualized" are similarly resisted.[29] Take this point alongside Mingus's directive to look at the varied impacts inaccessibility has made on the material lives of disabled people, rather than to denounce ablism as a political category. Feminist rhetorical methodologies must also remain flexible, contradictory, and, in keeping with those first two descriptors, necessarily collective when theorizing embodied experience. Methods of reading and analyzing that emphasize collective identity should account for the clear material differences across individual writers while holding contradictions, conflicts, and differences to be tools of cohesion and plurality.

While reading and coding nearly 500 family letters, I employed practices of critical discourse analysis, a system of reading that codes a text corpus by looking intentionally for language patterns that depict, suggest, or reference locations of sociopolitical power invoked by the corresponding discourse community. In composition studies, critical discourse analysis (CDA) surfaces power dynamics in ostensibly neutral or apolitical texts, or texts that have suasive intent but less visible loci of power embedded in language and use.[30] In my reading practice, I identified common broad rhetorical commitments to "unity" and desire for a coherent community among the letters and contrasted these unifying rhetorical gestures with a closer reading of specific material experiences and commitments writers made. Where and how did the resistant urge to build community or grassroots power invest in homogenizing narratives of unity as *sameness* and where or how did it invest in difference, conflict, and contrast? In short, CDA was applicable to this project because it held up as a method to examine the erasures of difference that come with community politics and identities designed to center the margins,[31] rather than to expose hierarchical and mainstream biases in a given text corpus. I identified an abundance of language stressing the urgency of forming a coherent community among incarcerated LGBTQ+ people, that is, of becoming a recognizable political subject through a constellation of varied experiences that are not always similar, but nevertheless are bound up in each writer's interest in collective, shifting queer identity. I found that writers made explicit use of material dis/identifications to expand, understand, and participate in a growing collective identity—incarcerated LGBTQ+ writers—that was always in a process of becoming, and of becoming revealed.

"Unity" as Political Imperative

Perhaps unsurprisingly, letter-writers often emphasized, even celebrated, the presence of voices that detailed similar experiences. From solitary confinement, one writes, "It seems like almost every month, there's another letter from one of my brothers or sisters who is spending a lengthy time in the Hole[32] (and not the good one). I, too, have spent time in the Hole and am there now. I would like to offer some words of encouragement for those of us who are dealing with this sucky experience."[33]

This writer aligns their lived experience with the writing of others, speaking directly to a subset of the audience ("those of us who are dealing with this sucky experience") as well as to explain how this specific material experience can benefit from wider attention in the newspaper readership. These specific identifications are rooted in shared material investments (the challenges of living in solitary confinement), while others sought advice from "someone out there who has been through this or knows someone who went through it,"[34] consciously seeking shared experiences. Indeed, these moments of identification are contingent on other writers and readers, inviting prospective identifying responses.

However, writers also used disidentifications to illustrate the diversity within the collective voices they established, not to signal definitive distinctions or separations from others (in Ratcliffe's reading of Kenneth Burke, the "not me" of "me").[35] In recounting their own unjust treatment in prison, another letter-writer shares that "I've been accosted by almost every staff member, even the Assistant Warden, and been kicked out of the chapel because I have no religion noted on my computer file."[36] Taking into account the many narratives of abuse and trauma published in the newspaper, they add, "I know these issues are minimal compared to the many I've read about in the amazing Newspaper, but they are real and damaging."[37] Here, a writer contextualizes their experience as inherently different in material terms but reinforces their role in a shared consciousness-raising via lived experience.

Above all, writers identified unity and collectivity as necessary not just to establish a political voice but to consolidate and leverage power that might sustain a diverse network of LGBTQ+ people behind walls. In a direct response to other readers and a writer in another state ("Versace"), a letter claims that "Idaho and Florida seem to share an approach/ideology. Versace could have been writing about Idaho DOC. I wish I could reach out through the distance and hug and hold you. I too have lost my family—I am an orphan. I wish we could all unite as one loving family, supporting and lifting each other up."[38] Many of these gestures are common throughout the family letters—the recognition of similarity or difference in lived experience, a strong sense of connection, and the desire for more connection and networking with other incarcerated LGBTQ+ people. Most writers put a high premium on "unity" in this communication. "When I think of a movement shaped by the prisoners for the liberation of all incarcerated people," one letter begins, "I imagine Pure Unity."[39] Nevertheless, writers regularly reinforce the differences and difficulties within a collective identity (incarcerated LGBTQ+ people), citing both un/shared material conditions, and by engaging both identification and disidentification practices when contextualizing their contributions to those collective identities.

In *Getting Specific,* Shane Phelan discusses the relationship between individual identity and collective identity as a mutually constitutive process. Collective and individual identity, Phelan says, do not exist outside of one another—instead, "we are still constituted by community, but community does not thereby acquire a prior, separate existence, for community is simultaneously constituted by us."[40] Thus, it is the compulsion to see "community" as a unifying set of commonalities that causes difficulty. Resisting a definition of community that seeks "common knowledges from a common identity," Phelan points to the inherent difference within collectivity as a necessary component of its function. "Being in common is the continual denial of community in favor of oneness," she writes, "Community in fact works to destabilize identity, as our being with others brings us face to face with multiplicity and differences. Thus, community is not a place of refuge, of sameness, but is its opposite."[41]

Taking that "opposite" of sameness seriously, decentering individual voices and turning to collective identities that are an amalgamation of "fragments" collected through time, community, and relationship, allows differences to come into focus, and to become clarified through their relationship to other forms of intragroup difference.[42] For example, when a writer connects their experiences to a common theme but describes both the departure from a commonality ("I know these issues are minimal compared to the many . . .") and the necessity of including it anyway (". . . but they are real and damaging"). Despite an emphasis on unity (as one writer put it, "power in numbers"), writers of family letters took care to construct a mosaic of material differences, underscoring the variety of experiences that attend to incarcerated LGBTQ+ identities. In the following examples, collective identity is illustrated by the flexible and fluid nature of queer gender and sexuality depicted in self-description from writers, and the social and material relations queer gender and sexuality make possible between readers, writers, and queer selves.

Collective Subjects across Carceral/Material Time and Space

Material descriptions of prison's spaces and times figure prominently in the shared literacy network provided by the newspaper. Letters open with a similar formula—sharing one's name, a particular identity within a queer framework, and a material measurement of carceral life, most commonly, time spent in prison, the age of the writer, the amount of time left before possible release, and/or a physical description of the prison space. Incarcerated writers describe the intricacies of their prison experience not because of their individual meanings, but because of the generative contrasts to be made between material differences. Take, for example, Cameron's self-description: "My name is Cameron, aka Cail. I'm 24 years old. I'm bisexual. I have 2 years and 8 months left in prison."[43] Cail presents a few identifiers that might resonate with readers, but more importantly, these identifiers position Cail in a wider queer network, where their material experience is necessary to create a point on a shared spectrum. Most letters begin with self-descriptions. In another example from 2010, a writer called Chestnut writes: "My name is John, aka 'Chestnut,' I'm 31 years old, a Black male. I'm incarcerated at Florida State Prison in a one man cell. I only get to shower and shave 3 times a week and also get to go to the Rec yard 3 times a week for 2 hours. I've been living like this since 2003."[44] Chestnut details his experience not because it might be immediately recognizable to other readers, but because it illustrates the material reality of one life in relation to others. When he notes he has been "living like this since 2003," Chestnut calls attention not just to the difficulty of his material experience, but of the time spent in that difficulty, heightening the material detail of his experience for other readers.

By collating a variety of material details about their lives in prison, incarcerated writers set the scene for others to respond with recognition or lack thereof, while detailing the specifics of queer and incarcerated life. "I'm a 25 year old bisexual male who is currently sitting in a 6X9 Ad-Seg[45] cell," another writer notes, "I have been in prison since the age of 13 and have been on Ad-Seg for 20 months."[46] In this example, time is figured in multiple material ways—time spent inside prison, time spent in solitary, and the time of the writing itself—incarcerated readers can appreciate the physical story these smaller details carry. Taken collectively, these writers demonstrate there is no singular incarcerated subject in terms of perspective.

Mapping the material contours of the prison through a diversity of coordinates in space and time unfixes subject positions. Many positionalities are folded into one comprehensive ecosystem of subjectivity. In *Fugitive Life*, Stephen Dillon reads the texts of 1960s leftist feminist and queer social movements as anticipatory of and challenging to the growing carceral state. Time is an undervalued aspect of this critique, he writes, because it gestures to race and gender as essential frameworks for understanding resistance to the emerging PIC.[47] Raced and gendered readings of time reject the idea of a future (lower crime rates, less social and interpersonal violence) that is not supported by the present (mass incarceration and metastasizing state violence). In detailing the violent present of carceral life, writers partially interpret stolen time as a devaluing of queer and queer of color lives, as well as describe their material lives in a manner legible to other incarcerated people. "20 months" in an Ad-Seg cell evokes a sense of confinement known to others who have moved or are moving through their own sentences and are attuned to the wear of institutional confinement over time.

Self-Definition as Flexible Practice

Much of incarcerated expression hinges on speaking upward to authority, being put in a beseeching position, pleading, explaining, and identifying for and as an individual entity, especially as one that is *uniquely* and individually contrite, innocent, or misjudged. The audience of recognizable peers in the newspaper setting allows speaking *across* differences to function as a form of power-building and collective identification. The self-in-relation to others persists even in the description of individuated sexuality. For example, terms used by incarcerated writers when laying claim to a particular queer identity included, "Openly feminine gay," "Bisexual," "Bi," "Gay male," "Transgender," "Trans-queen," "Masculine man," "Gay, though still in the closet," "I don't consider myself Gay or Bi, I'm Tri, 'cause I'll try anything :)," "Transgender woman," "Transsexual," "Transgender womyn," "Homosexual," "Gay," "I'm Bi 'cause at this time I still like females too. I like all gay people, but I'm attracted to the feminine type. But like I said, I like all my team-mates," "Queer," "Trans/gender and happy to be such," "Pre-operative transsexual," "Transgender man preparing to be released from a female Florida prison," "Male-2-female (m-2-f) pre-op transsexual," "Happy Gay Queen," "Two Spirit," "Revolutionary feminist transwoman prisoner," "Black male bisexual; mostly gay."

Even a first pass of this list might reveal the challenges of excavating common terms of sexual orientation (e.g., "gay," "bi," or "queer"—the most commonly occurring ways writers described sexual identity). In the early stages of coding, my intent was merely to understand the most accurate terms by which to describe family letter writers. However, as these terms accumulated, so did a blurring of how and when to code a stated sexual identity from other constitutive descriptors. At what point, in looking for this language, is it productive to sever "happy" from "gay" (or from "queen")? At what point does a writer stop describing their orientation? How, for example, does "preparing to be released from a female Florida prison" deepen the reader's identity of the "transgender man," by adding context, texture, and location? Where does the "prison" end and the assumption of "female" begin in that phrasing? As a researcher, this description moves me to consider my own relationship to freedom, access, and resources, understanding that my own identity, as well as my research standpoint, is mediated through material contexts, not just access to community research materials (like these) or to an un/shared identity category with research subjects or participants (although categories of queer and carceral experiences seeded my research interest). Material conditions inform an immediate understanding, not just of what one's gender, race, or sexuality is, but how it shifts to respond to immediate and material contexts, the realities of what Saidiya Hartman terms "everyday anarchy."[48]

In these expressions of identity, imprisonment and material conditions are a necessary expansion of queer prisoner identities. "Revolutionary feminist transwoman prisoner" locates the position and politics of the queer self/subject as necessary to understanding the essential LGBTQ identity label ("trans") that creates the queer belonging. Indeed, multiple writers took this approach, relating, comparing, and contrasting self-description as part of a larger way of relating to each other ("like I said, I like all my teammates").

The assertions of identity described here stand to moderate the strong desires for unity or oneness present in those same letters. By adding their own specifications to self-description of queer identity, writers seek productive identifications (and, to a lesser degree, disidentifications) in the family letters. Descriptions of the self are set in contexts that increase the legibility of these identities while emphasizing their flexibility on a microlevel. Importantly, writers collaged self-representations by collectively developing the convention of "introducing" oneself with an attention to changes and conditions, e.g., "still bi," "mostly gay," and "still in the closet."

Collective Identity and Feminist Rhetorical Research

The textual features that constellate collective subjects depict multiple material truths and subject positions at once. They are more powerful in their plurality than any one example, not because inspiring, passionate prose is lacking in prison writing, but because the accumulation and collective arrangement of our (always fragmented in the singular) identities offer sites of intersection between queer, feminist, and carceral subjectivities. For example, theorizing subjectivity as collective and dependent on networks of relationships to be assembled re-opens important questions of harm, care work, and abolition—essential concepts in contemporary activist rhetorics. "It takes unity to make a change for the better," notes one family letter, "and through all of us we can [. . .] work to close all the prisons [. . .] social environments do affect decisions of individuals and can lead to crime."[49] In this instance, unity gives way to a larger understanding of social interdependence, wherein a broader commitment to a more just society highlights the collective position that incarcerated LGBTQ+ people have to each other.

Just as multiple accounts of queer, material life in prison illuminate a collective terrain of experience through time and space, collective subjects might sketch new possibilities for understanding cycles, rather than individual acts of harm in communities, and the cultural contexts that produce singular (rhetorical) figures capable of great harm or great repair (and the histories we have learned through them).

Collective identities compose themselves in relation to each other by careful, distinct, and often intentional interstitial comparisons, contrasts, and other forms of co-constituency. Centering collectivity gives insight into the material networks of scarcity, availability, and distribution of resources, raising critical questions of access and justice in carceral rhetorical situations. Abolition feminism in rhetorical studies deepens the engagements between self and other already entered in feminist rhetorical practice and creates more politically significant opportunities to question a status quo.

The formulas of representation that force a few (usually "deserving," or the opposite, depending on political expediency) subjects to depict the many is limiting practice. Multiply marginalized people are vulnerable to criminalization and state violence, and to relationships with criminalization and state violence that complicate typical narratives and are less legible to others. Singular exemplars of success, or at least exceptions to an understood trend, are common representational forms of counter-narrative. Ushering in methods and methodologies that attend to collectivity as less-than-representable, and especially to material culture's effects on broad categories of identity, stand to advance a strong subjectivity[50] in feminist rhetorical methodologies.

NOTES

1. Kaba, *We Do This*, 3.
2. Kim, "From Carceral Feminism," 223; see also Gubar, *The Feminist War on Crime*.
3. Davis et al., *Abolition*, v.
4. See Pritchard, *Fashioning Lives*, 102–52; Shimabukuro, *Relocating Authority*, 57–76.
5. Royster, Traces, 277.

6. Royster, "When the First Voice," 29.

7. Myers, "Pieces," 347.

8. Although Brim also writes that queer studies, possibly before other disciplines, ought to mark the exclusions that come from a lack of access to education and scholarship as a "field-defining, field-constituting problem" (Brim, *Poor Queer Studies*, 65).

9. Note both the older uses of "family" or "in the family" to code recognition between LGBTQ+ people, as well as more recent uses of "chosen family" to describe queer communities (sometimes as a replacement for one's homophobic biological family).

10. Royster and Kirsch, *Feminist Rhetorical Practices*, 39.

11. Schell and Rawson, *Rhetorica*, 41–2.

12. Ratcliffe, Rhetorical Listening, 62.

13. Ratcliffe, Rhetorical Listening, 63.

14. Royster and Kirsch, *Feminist Rhetorical Practices*, 657.

15. Shimabukuro, *Relocating Authority*, 51.

16. Shimabukuro, *Relocating Authority*, 51.

17. Swearingen, qtd. in Ritchie and Ronald, *Available Means*, ix.

18. See Moss, *A Community Text*, 73–74.

19. Alexander and Rhodes, "Queer," 181–83.

20. Phelan, *Getting Specific*, 78.

21. adrienne maree brown, "Disrupting the Pattern: A Call for Love and Solidarity," April 17, 2021, https://adriennemareebrown.net/2021/04/17/.

22. brown, "Disrupting the Pattern."

23. brown, "Disrupting the Pattern."

24. Cedillo, "#DisabilityTooWhite."

25. Mingus, "Access Intimacy: The Missing Link," *Leaving Evidence*, May 5, 2011, https://leavingevidence.wordpress.com/2011/05/05/access-intimacy-the-missing-link/.

26. Ben-Moshe, Decarcerating Disability, 3.

27. Mingus, "Interdependence (excerpts from several talks)," *Leaving Evidence*, January 22, 2010, https://leavingevidence.wordpress.com/.

28. Dolmage and Lewiecki-Wilson, "Refiguring Rhetorica," 23.

29. Dolmage and Lewiecki-Wilson, "Refiguring Rhetorica," 27.

30. See Huckin, Andrus, and Clary-Lemon, "Critical Discourse Analysis," 111.

31. hooks, *Feminist Theory*, 163.

32. A term for solitary confinement.

33. "sucky experience," *Black and Pink National Newsletter*, December 2011.

34. "someone out here," *Black and Pink National Newsletter*, December 2011.

35. Ratcliffe, Rhetorical Listening, 57

36. "no religion," *Black and Pink National Newsletter*, August 2013.

37. "real and damaging," *Black and Pink National Newsletter*, August 2013.

38. "I am an orphan," *Black and Pink National Newsletter*, April 2011.

39. "I imagine pure unity," *Black and Pink National Newsletter*, January 2011.

40. Phelan, *Getting Specific*, 81.

41. Phelan, *Getting Specific*, 84.

42. Royster and Kirsch, *Feminist Rhetorical Practices*, 640.

43. "My name is Cameron," *Black and Pink National Newsletter*, December 2010.

44. "AKA Chestnut," *Black and Pink National Newsletter*, December 2010.

45. Administrative segregation, a form of solitary confinement.
46. "Ad-Seg," *Black and Pink National Newsletter*, February 2011.
47. Dillon, *Fugitive Life*, 42–50.
48. Hartman. *Wayward Lives*, xiv.
49. "work to close all the prisons," *Black and Pink National Newsletter*, March 2011.
50. Just as Sandra Harding notes that articulating subject positions in research is a form of "strong objectivity," collective identity and the methods that probe it might create for us a sense of strong subjectivity, where discrete categories of identity are inapplicable. See Cudd and Andreasen, *Feminist Theory*.

WORKS CITED

Alexander, Jonathan, and Jacqueline Rhodes. "Queer: An Impossible Subject for Composition." *JAC* 31, no. 1/2 (2011): 177–206.

Ben-Moshe, Liat. *Decarcerating Disability: Deinstitutionalization and Prison Abolition*. Minneapolis, MN: University of Minnesota Press, 2020.

Brim, Matt. *Poor Queer Studies: Confronting Elitism in the University*. Durham, NC: Duke University Press, 2020.

Cedillo, Christina V. "#DisabilityTooWhite: On Erasure's Material and Physical Dimensions." *Spark: A 4C4Equality Journal* 4 (September 2022): https://sparkactivism.com/.

Cudd, Ann, and Robin Andreasen, eds. *Feminist Theory: A Philosophical Anthology*. Oxford: Blackwell, 2005.

Davis, Angela Y., Gina Dent, Erica R. Meiners, and Beth E. Richie. *Abolition. Feminism. Now.* Chicago, IL: Haymarket Books, 2022.

Dillon, Stephen. *Fugitive Life: The Queer Politics of the Prison State*. Durham, NC: Duke University Press, 2018.

Dolmage, Jay, and Cynthia Lewiecki-Wilson. "Refiguring Rhetorica: Linking Feminist Rhetoric with Disability Studies." In *Rhetorica in Motion: Feminist Rhetorical Methods and Methodologies*, edited by Eileen E. Schell and K.J. Rawson, 23–38. Pittsburgh, PA: University of Pittsburgh Press, 2010.

Gubar, Aya. *The Feminist War on Crime: The Unexpected Role of Women's Liberation in Mass Incarceration*. Oakland: University of California Press, 2020.

Hartman, Saidiya. *Wayward Lives, Beautiful Experiments: Intimate Histories of Social Upheaval*. New York: Norton, 2019.

hooks, bell. *Feminist Theory from Margin to Center*. Boston, MA: South End Press, 1984.

Huckin, Thomas, Jennifer Andrus, and Jennifer Clary-Lemon. "Critical Discourse Analysis and Rhetoric and Composition." *College Composition and Communication* 64, no. 1 (2012): 107–29.

Kaba, Mariame. "Towards the Horizon of Abolition." *The Next System Project*, November 9, 2017, https://thenextsystem.org/learn/stories/towards-horizon-abolition-conversation-mariame-kaba.

Kaba, Mariame. *We Do This 'Til We Free Us: Abolitionist Organizing and Transforming Justice*. Chicago, IL: Haymarket Books, 2021.

Kim, Mimi E. "From Carceral Feminism to Transformative Justice." *Journal of Ethnic and Cultural Diversity in Social Work* 27, no. 3 (2018): 219–33.

Moss, Beverly. *A Community Text Arises: A Literate Text and a Literacy Tradition in African-American Churches*. New York: Hampton Press, 2002.

Myers, Nancy. "Pieces of the Puzzle: Feminist Rhetorical Studies and the Material Conditions of Women's Work." *College Composition and Communication* 65, no. 2 (2013): 345–65.

Phelan, Shane. *Getting Specific: Postmodern Lesbian Politics*. Minneapolis, MN: University of Minnesota Press, 1994.

Pritchard, Eric. *Fashioning Lives: Black Queers and the Politics of Literacy*. Carbondale, IL: Southern Illinois University Press, 2016.

Ratcliffe, Krista. *Rhetorical Listening: Identification, Gender, Whiteness*. Carbondale, IL: Southern Illinois University Press, 2005.

Ritchie, Joy S., and Katharine J. Ronald, eds. *Available Means: An Anthology of Women's Rhetoric(s)*. Pittsburgh, PA: University of Pittsburgh Press, 2001.

Royster, Jacqueline Jones. *Traces of a Stream: Literacy and Social Change Among African American Women*. Pittsburgh, PA: University of Pittsburgh Press, 2000.

Royster, Jacqueline Jones. "When the First Voice You Hear Is Not Your Own." *College Composition and Communication* 47, no. 1 (1996): 29–40.

Royster, Jacqueline Jones, and Gesa E. Kirsch, eds. *Feminist Rhetorical Practices: New Horizons for Rhetoric, Composition, and Literacy Studies*. Carbondale, IL: Southern Illinois University Press, 2012.

Schell, Eileen E., and K.J. Rawson, eds. *Rhetorica in Motion: Feminist Rhetorical Methods and Methodologies*. Pittsburgh, PA: University of Pittsburgh Press, 2010.

Shimabukuro, Mira. *Relocating Authority: Japanese Americans Writing to Redress Mass Incarceration*. Boulder, CO: University Press of Colorado, 2015.

EIGHT

Caring for *Cuentos* of Reproductive (In)Justice

Feminist Methods for Confianza, Curation, and Care-ful Digital Design

Rachel Bloom-Pojar and Danielle Koepke

> Como les dije [a mis participantes], "Esto es mi regalo más grande para ustedes, denle el valor que le quieran dar, pero no tengo más que ofrecerles. Esta es mi historia."
>
> **—ANGELES**

The practice of sharing stories has long been a core component to feminist methodologies and movements for social justice.[1] Whether it is through qualitative interviews or public testimonies, stories are often invited, shared, and circulated in community-engaged, feminist work. Personal, vulnerable stories also speak to the embodied nature of feminist rhetorical research, theory, and practice.[2] The reproductive justice movement has had a particular focus on stories that center on Black women's and women of color's lived experiences. As Loretta J. Ross explains, "Storytelling is a crucial part of reproductive justice theory, an act of reclamation and resistance, because our theories grow from our activist locations. . . . The role of oral history and storytelling is vital to our survival."[3] Black women, Indigenous women, women of color, and trans individuals have historically endured reproductive injustices across a range of issues at the hands of racist and patriarchal ideologies and policies. From the early days of colonization and chattel slavery in the US, Indigenous, Black, and immigrant women have wrongfully had their children taken away.[4] Women across Latin America and the Caribbean have endured reproductive and gender-based violence that too often ends in murder.[5] Black women and women of color have been coerced into a variety of sterilization and birth control experimentations.[6] These cruel and violent experiences are often erased from official historical accounts or are not widely recognized as integral to understanding reproductive injustice. They also reflect how any project that engages reproductive justice will involve at least some stories of trauma, vulnerability, and loss.

Reproductive justice is a movement distinct from the mainstream women's rights movement that has grown out of this history of injustice and oppression. As long as there has been a mainstream women's rights movement, there have been those fighting against racism and exclusion, such as Sojourner Truth, Harriet Tubman, and Ida B. Wells Barnett.[7] Activist groups such as the Combahee River Collective[8] and the Young Lords paved the way for the reproductive justice movement to be more officially formulated in the 1990s, during which time a group of Black women addressed the need to center their perspectives and experiences in advocacy for reproductive rights and social justice. Drawing from a human rights framework, they coined the term reproductive justice, which advocates for the rights to not have a child, to have a child, to parent children in safe and healthy environments, to sexual autonomy, and gender freedom.[9] The group later took the name SisterSong and today it is "the largest national multi-ethnic Reproductive Justice collective. [Their] membership includes and represents Indigenous, African American, Arab and Middle Eastern, Asian and Pacific Islander, and Latina women and LGBTQ people."[10] At its core, reproductive justice is rooted in community, not academia. It centers the most marginalized voices and disrupts mainstream white women's rights activism that is too often focused primarily on rhetorics of choice and abortion.

When doing community-engaged research that leads to sharing peoples' stories in public or digital spaces, especially regarding vulnerable experiences such as reproductive injustices, feminist rhetoricians must keep in mind how quickly stories can circulate online. Digital stories, seemingly abstract in form, are always connected to people's bodies, relationships, and material realities. Therefore, when feminist researchers participate in the process of curating digital spaces to circulate or display stories that were shared with them, they must engage methods that reflect the care that stories and storytellers deserve. In *Feminist Rhetorical Practices,* Jacqueline Royster and Gesa Kirsch describe an ethic of care as a responsible rhetorical action that "requires a commitment to be open, flexible, welcoming, patient, introspective, and reflective. [. . .] [I]t is an attitude, a stance, an inclination to discover well-embodied truths and to revise old truths." This feminist ethic of care includes an intention not to push desired results onto research findings and an obligation to "partner with [communities] as we join our world to theirs and work with them to set in motion a different, more fully rendered sense of rhetoric."[11]

As community-engaged researchers, we (Rachel and Danielle) have made a conscious effort to incorporate a feminist ethic of care in all that we do with the stories that our community partners share with us. As two white, cis women engaging in work related to reproductive justice, we have grappled with how we can leverage resources and privileges to create caring spaces that center the perspectives and leadership of a group of Latina[12] promotores de salud (health promoters) and decenter ourselves. In this chapter, we describe our experiences with such methods within the context of a community-engaged project that began as a research endeavor and led to the collaborative creation of a bilingual (Spanish-English) website called *Cuentos de Confianza* that features stories written by promotores de salud. We also share some reflections from our community and student collaborators who helped make *Cuentos* into what it is today.[13]

In our efforts to center story and relationships, the guiding principles of cultural rhetorics have informed our orientation to rhetorical research— story as theory, relationality, constellation, and connection with decolonial practices.[14] The first principle centers storytelling as important theory-building work and draws heavily on Indigenous theories.[15] It emphasizes that theories are stories that people use to explain the world and has connections to feminist theories of lived experience. The second principle, relationality, draws attention to a person's relation to their body, their embodied experiences, and other material connections. It guides researchers to practice more mindful and responsible engagement that is built on slow-grown relationships and offers co-ownership of research data to participants.[16] The third principle, constellation, is a practice of building connections between concepts, perspectives, individuals, and communities. Imagined as a web or a literal constellation in the sky, this principle offers the potential for "multiply-situated subjects to connect to multiple discourses at the same time."[17] The fourth principle, decolonial practices, is an active call to create something beyond critique. Decolonial research practices are honored as meaningful ways of knowing and enacting justice in the world as academics.[18] While we acknowledge and keep constellation and decolonial practices in mind, we heavily rely on story and relationships in our community-engaged work with the promotores.

Acerca del Proyecto[19]

Cuentos de Confianza is a community writing project that creates space for promotores de salud to reflect on how their life experiences and community work have impacted their understanding of reproductive justice. *Cuentos* began as a community writing class that Rachel taught for a small group of promotores affiliated with Planned Parenthood of Wisconsin (PPWI).[20] Through conversations with, and input from, the writers in this class, we developed a bilingual website (https://www.cuentosdeconfianza.com) that now hosts thirteen stories and has been used in community programming in Wisconsin, Puerto Rico, and Perú.

To understand the project, it is important to understand the relationships that made it possible. The focus on confianza in the *Cuentos* project emerged from the ethnographic research Rachel has been doing with the PPWI promotores and their program director, Maria Barker, for the past five years. She first learned about how multidimensional and important *confianza* was for the promotores through focus groups in 2019. Then in subsequent years as her relationship with many of them deepened, she recognized that confianza was integral both to the promotores' work and her methods as a community-engaged researcher. Translated into English as trust or confidence, confianza for the promotores is at the core of the work they do as community-based educators and advocates for sexual and reproductive health. It is something they create, build, sustain, and enter into with others. In a co-authored piece with Rachel, Maria Barker explains, "Confianza is something you earn over time by all the good deeds you do, not only for one person but for a family and a community, and not to gain notoriety but to simply help. . . . Respect for someone else's humanity is much more involved in confianza than niceness. Respect is something in confianza that does not come from titles or degrees; it comes from 'being part of' something with others."[21]

This chapter describes some of the ways we have been "part of something" with the writers and translators of *Cuentos*. During Fall 2020, Maria asked Rachel if she would consider teaching a writing class for the promotores. With a desire to let her research "agenda" be driven by community partner interests, she worked with Maria to plan for a class that could support the promotores in writing and sharing stories related to reproductive justice.

Danielle and Rachel began working together as a graduate student and faculty advisor during Danielle's MA and PhD programs at University of

Wisconsin-Milwaukee (UWM). In Spring 2021, Danielle did an internship with Rachel to help plan for programming related to her research. Maria's request led to their co-designing the community writing class, which Rachel taught and Danielle assisted through weekly meetings to evaluate how the class was going and how it might continue to be responsive to the priorities of reproductive justice pedagogy.[22] At first, this community writing class felt distinct from Rachel's initial research project because of the traditional ways "teaching" and "research" are separated in the academy. But over time, it was clear that this was an extension of the research in the ways *Cuentos* is a practical, public deliverable that centers the promotores' voices to address key issues that had surfaced in the focus groups from 2019.

During the community writing class, Danielle was finishing her PhD program and figuring out how she might write about the unfolding work with *Cuentos* in her dissertation in an ethical manner. She navigated questions and doubts about what counts as dissertation-level research, and when to refuse doing a traditional study.[23] She concluded that her community-engaged work with this class and website entailed a *lot* of research activities that were driven by community interests and needs, and that it would be better to focus her dissertation on describing the process of this work and how she incorporated it into her teaching. As Rachel and Danielle regularly reflected on their work and the methodologies guiding them, a few methods (discussed below) stood out as essential for this type of care-ful, community-engaged work.

Metodos Feministas (Feminist Methods)

For community-engaged research that invites and shares vulnerable stories, we recommend three feminist methods: (1) creating confianza, (2) collaborative curation, and (3) care-ful digital design. These methods are iterative and interwoven through different stages of a project, but they are all essential for feminist research that aims to invite and circulate stories in digital spaces to advocate for social justice. While our project is specifically informed by work in reproductive justice, researchers engaging in other justice-related issues should look to relevant scholarship and community-based experts in those areas. In the following sections, we weave together writing from multiple perspectives—ours as research-partners, the project translators, and some of the escritoras de *Cuentos*[24] to address how feminist methods of confianza, collaboration, and care were integral to this partnership and project.

Method 1. Creating Confianza (Rachel)

The primary method I have engaged in this process has been the practice of creating confianza with my community partners. I have come to recognize the act of "creating confianza" as a feminist method for community engagement that creates trusting spaces to share stories and recognizes relationality between people and stories, thus providing an exigence for rhetorical ethics of care in what people do with stories that are shared with them *en confianza*. My pedagogical approach for working with the writers for *Cuentos* was guided by Loretta J. Ross's work on how reproductive justice pedagogy "is most suitably experienced as a partnership process in which the teachers serve more as facilitators than professors, helping the group achieve desired outcomes that enrich and enhance their lives, rather than fixating on a rigid syllabus that perfunctorily marches through selected topics."[25] Throughout this project, the promotores navigated varied levels of trust with each other, with me, and with what they felt community members had entrusted in them not to share with others. To demonstrate respect and care for that confianza, I paused and prioritized different things along the path of my research project to focus my time and energy on this emerging storytelling project. I slowed down writing about my "research findings" and instead wrote course materials, proposals for funding, feedback for the promotores, and website content for *Cuentos*. In response to the writers' busy schedules and hesitance toward sharing stories with a big group, I pivoted from a full class format to one-on-one meetings so each writer could work at their own pace and develop their stories with me as they desired. While the first class formally ended in December 2021, my work with the writers continued until June 2022 when they completed their stories for the *Cuentos de Confianza* community launch event. We held that event at a high school on the south side of Milwaukee and celebrated the writers with over 70 of their friends, family, and supporters. Rather than rush to set up public programming in English to engage secondary audiences, we have focused on a slower process that started with the promotores' family and friends at our launch event and their community members at home health parties.

I navigated a lot of uncertainty about whether I was doing things right, whether the promotores were having a positive experience with the class, and whether anything tangible would come out of our efforts in the end. In a group interview I had with some of the writers about this process, they shared that they also felt that uncertainty. Elida explains how it was starting this process when we didn't really know what would come out of it:

Cuando empezamos pensamos que era algo chiquito. Ahorita como ya va avanzando realmente es algo grande. Como siempre, a los primeros siempre nos toca lo más difícil porque tenemos que empezar a descifrar cómo lo vamos a hacer, qué vamos a hacer, qué quieren, qué sirve, qué no sirve.[26]

Between September 2021 and June 2022, I spent countless hours in conversation with the six writers featured on the *Cuentos de Confianza* website—Angeles, Elida, Joshy, Gaby, Maria, and Kendy. They told me many more stories than what ended up on the site, and various phone calls included tears and descriptions of difficult moments in their lives.

Elida shares:

"[R]ecuerdo que me empecé a reunir contigo y me hacías así ciertas preguntas y respuestas que la verdad habían pasado muchos años que yo no había pensado en esas cosas hasta que tú me empezaste a preguntar. . . . Yo te había comentado, Rachel, varias veces que trataba de hablar, antes de hablar, tenía que llorar para poder escribir."[27]

Angeles adds:

"fuiste buena guía en relación de cómo deberíamos de irlo narrando porque estaba descompuesto muchas cosas. Unas palabras iban arriba, otras abajo. . . . Viste que me desmoroné también cuando estaba hablando de mis miscarriages y la posición de mi esposo, en ese dolor que también sentía . . . Eso me hacía sentir como triste a la vez, por estar recordando todo lo vivido en esa época de querer ser madre y todas las barreras que tuve para serlo. Fue algo bien difícil."[28]

Each of the writers opened up to me about deep and difficult topics with their own experiences concerning relationships, immigration, motherhood, and/or reproductive injustice. We discussed what relationships they wanted to care for in the process of writing, editing, and circulating their stories. We also discussed the risks that come with publishing information online and having stories shared publicly. Each writer decided what they felt comfortable sharing with these risks in mind from their names to photos to details from their stories.

Each of the cuentos describe different relationships—with partners, children, parents, and themselves. The messages they share are meant to resonate with others in their communities. In my relationship with the writers, I had to be cognizant of, and care for, all those different relationships as we made decisions about how to develop the site and share it with different audiences. Any steps I have taken to invite other people into the project have also been made cautiously. But building on our relationships and inviting others onto the team who cared for the stories has proven to be key to our success in launching a bilingual, multi-layered website that is easy for the promotores to use in their community work.

Method 2. Collaborative Curation

Feminist methods of curation, such as participatory curation, strive to bring together multiple and sometimes conflicting voices, often from marginalized communities, in efforts to support their lived experiences and learn from their stories through various art and creative works.[29] In curating *Cuentos,* we sought to critically engage with what it means to *care for stories about reproductive justice in digital spaces.* Digital rhetoric scholars are explicit about how digital design often burdens many while privileging a few due to the deeply ingrained influences of white supremacy, heteropatriarchy, ableism, and other structures of inequality in America.[30] Danielle tried to design the *Cuentos* site in a way that lessened the burden of technical work required of the writers while also integrating their input in conceptualizing how their stories would be displayed and shared. Stories can do important theory-building work, and in digital spaces, they have the capacity to impact larger, more public audiences. Design justice calls for scholars to create deliverables that will be used by a community alongside that community. Through this process, community members are legitimate co-developers who can ensure that their rhetorical and cultural values are adhered to in a project.[31] Co-curating digital content and design with community collaborators can keep the ownership and decision-making power within communities themselves.[32] Danielle strives to do similar work with the creation and management of *Cuentos.* While the promotores wrote their own stories, they and our website team engaged in collaborative curation for translating stories, creating content across the web pages, editing, and making design decisions.

From the start of this project, we decided to have all content written in both Spanish and English with a preference for Spanish. This was intentional to challenge the ways that the internet and US institutions prioritize English and the interests of US-based English-speaking audiences. All written content is in both languages, and the audio files of the writers reading their cuento are only in Spanish for the first cohort. We collaborated across multiple digital platforms, including Wix, Google Drive, phone calls, and Zoom. Working across varied relationships and institutional contexts,

Rachel served as a central point of connection between the writers and students involved in the project. Maria notes, "tú de veras fuiste como el intérprete de lo que [Danielle] necesitaba de nosotros y lo que el website necesitaba de ella."[33]

During the spring 2022 semester, Juan Arevalo, an undergraduate, bilingual English major, joined the team to help translate content for the digital site. With funding from the UWM Office of Undergraduate Research, Juan translated content between Spanish and English for the stories and various parts of the site. He also connected with each of the writers so they could review his translations and offer feedback or corrections. Gaby notes in an email, "I really appreciate Juan, such a nice, kind person who is very patient and appreciates his translation as he was there to listen and really translate the message of my story." That same grant was renewed to support the work of Alejandra González, an undergraduate Spanish linguistics major, over the 2022–2023 academic year. Alejandra helped with various translation needs as the promotores began training and planning to use the project in their community education spaces. She also developed a list of national and statewide resources for issues that come up in the stories, and that list is now featured on the Recursos/Resources page. In an email to Rachel, Alejandra shares, "Collaborating with women health promoters that empowered themselves and their communities is something I will never forget. . . . Expanding confianza and building a community by making issues comprehensible and resources accessible to a Spanish speaking community was a highlight of our collaboration and I will forever cherish it."

This experience taught us the value of a multi-layered process of collaboration, curation, and writing when working on community projects, especially if the projects are digital and multilingual in nature and if collaboration is happening virtually. Whenever a new version of the site was ready for review, Danielle and Rachel would share it with the writers and invite their feedback on how to continue improving it and whether it reflected what they wanted for their stories. In an email, Gaby noted that Danielle "worked so hard putting our website together and she just made our stories even glow more as it's so important to have a very good professional presentation on the internet." Collaborating like this on the curation of the public site kept the decision-making power and ownership of the curation within the community.[34] It's also important to note that Danielle was paid for time on this project with programming support from a Mellon/ACLS Scholars and Society fellowship that Rachel received. By dedicating resources toward this project, Danielle was able to focus on technical details like building a website while the promotores could focus on the content of their stories. This work has been done with the intended audience always at the forefront of our rhetorical decision-making—the promotores' communities.

Method 3. Care-ful Digital Design (Danielle)

As I collaborated on this digital community project that sought to highlight stories of reproductive injustice, design justice was an important component to my digital design practices. Design justice seeks to center the needs and knowledges of marginalized communities and to create deliverables that support or improve equity for those communities.[35] It also calls attention to what will be left behind for the community to use after a partnership ends. As a white woman in academia partnering with a community of Latina women, I sought to use my skills, expertise, and resources to support their goals, needs, and the target users of the digital deliverable I was designing for them. I also shared information about digital literacy topics such as privacy and security in online spaces so that the writers could make their own informed decisions about what they consented to share publicly. These practices, rooted in design justice and a feminist ethic of care, allowed the writers to make choices that cared for themselves. Care for oneself, after all, is part of reproductive justice.[36] Below, I reflect on three choices that exemplify how I actively practiced care for the writers and their stories throughout the digital design process.

First, I designed the *Cuentos* site to be bilingual (Spanish-English) from scratch. While doing this work has not involved hard coding, it has involved tedious layout changes and updates; creation and movement of page items like container boxes, text, and decorative elements; and lots of trial and error on everything from color schemes to font type to formatting and layout of the individual pages. Because of the bilingual audience, unique purpose, and planned circulation of the site, a template just wouldn't work for *Cuentos*. Most templates come with a goal like selling merchandise, promoting a business, or displaying art exhibits. Our concept didn't fit any of their pre-designed templates as we needed to be able to customize everything across the pages. The first version I designed was simple and like an art exhibit site. The second had many more page ideas including a page to explain the promotores' home health parties, one for civic engagement, and one with a pedagogical statement for the community writing class. But neither of these earlier designs prioritized Spanish because I was still researching and brainstorming how to best do that. For our current iteration, I collaborated with the student translators and the writers to design the Spanish and English elements at the same time to avoid force-fitting content from English to Spanish. While this led to more time-consuming work, it has allowed me to create a deliverable that the promotores feel is theirs to have for themselves, to share with their target audience, and to use at their fiestas caseras.[37]

Second, I prioritized the design of the mobile version for the site. The writers emphasized that their initial target audience, close friends and family members, would likely access the site on their mobile devices and the site would circulate publicly based on community sharing. As such, it was imperative that page lengths were shorter and that the content and design worked well for phones. Keeping the target audience and community context in mind, I tested navigation specifically for phone users and tried to keep pages with background information brief but helpful if visitors to the site wanted to read it. Initially, I had Spanish and English on every page. But we found that it was confusing and overwhelming to read on the mobile version. So, I separated the Spanish and the English, always privileging Spanish. I created tabs at the top of the site in Spanish, accompanied by English sub tabs that appear when you hover over each tab. One issue this created was more pages to navigate, so I created a guided navigation through buttons to help users move through the site.

Third, through experimentation and research, I created a semi-guided navigation for the site, which also served as a form of protection for the stories. The goal was to create a digital exhibit that users would move through in a certain page order—from Inicio, to Confianza, to Cuentos, and then into the individual stories. While visitors can navigate to other places using the menu across the top of the site, such as the pages under Acerca del Proyecto: Eventos, Comparte un Cuento, and Justicia Reproductiva, we recommend following our suggested navigation so that visitors read about confianza and our care statement before reading the stories. We hope this prepares them to thoughtfully and carefully engage with the stories and that it will reduce any confusion about how to find things on the site. After reading the care statement, visitors are directed to click on Cuentos, which leads to the page hosting the writer bios, images, and access to their stories. Once on a page, users can also click on the pink button in the upper right-hand side of the screen to toggle between the Spanish and English versions.

This process wasn't always perfect and didn't fit any design blueprint or scholarship I'd read about community-engaged work. However, in being responsive to feedback and to the unique expertise of the writers, translators, and Rachel, I was able to design a digital deliverable that fulfilled the vision of the community and would be used by them for their own purposes.

Una Invitación

Since the site launched, the promotores have shared the stories in conversations with individuals and at home health parties. They've noted that it is making a positive impact and that many people identify with the stories and writers. It has helped community members see the promotores as people who have gone through similar struggles and it has inspired conversations about mental health, relationships, parenting, infertility, gender equity, and more. Research partnerships that are driven by confianza, collaboration, and care can lead to outcomes that look different from traditional deliverables, but that may make more meaningful contributions for community partners. We're still learning what all *Cuentos* might do in the world, but so far, it's making a far greater impact than any of the presentations or summary reports Rachel has shared on her research. To conclude, we invite you to consider how the feminist methods we discussed can be applied to your own feminist rhetorical research.

The process of *creating confianza* begins before any partnership even starts to take shape. As a researcher, you must determine whether you value and are dedicated to nurturing the trust and confidence of your community partner. That means taking steps more than just identifying what can be "mutually beneficial" in a partnership. It means you'll show up as a full, genuine, and caring person who is ready to listen, learn, and work alongside others. It also means you're willing to share parts of yourself and to trust others with some of your own story. As Maria notes, confianza and respect do not come from fancy titles or degrees. They come from showing up and respecting others' humanity. They come from being a researcher who respects and cares for the trust and stories others share with them. Feminist researchers who want to create confianza must be willing to let go of preconceived (or institutionally sanctioned) notions about what is the most valuable outcome for their project and be open to figuring that out along the way with others.

As Angeles notes at the start of this chapter, sharing one's story is a gift. What others do with that gift says something about who they are and how they treat others. It has been a tremendous gift to have Angeles and the other promotores share their stories with us in various forms throughout our work together. Rachel first heard a version of Angeles's story during a focus group in 2019. At that time, Angeles shared more details than she ended up keeping in her story for the website. She also added details, such as the mention of her miscarriages, which were not part of her first telling of the story to Rachel as a researcher. Two years, a deepened relationship, and more confianza may have helped her open up about this. Or it might have simply been a different context where she thought it was relevant to share for her intended audience. Either way, el Cuento de Angeles on the website is the first time that story has been published in any form, and it will be the only one Rachel quotes from in any future writing about this part of her story. Any additional details, though approved by an IRB consent form, are not Rachel's to share now that she knows Angeles doesn't want them as part of her public story.

If you research entails any sort of storytelling, whether that be through the stories shared in interviews or a community writing project, consider how you will demonstrate care for those stories across multiple stages of a project through:

- your embodied and verbal response when the story is first shared with you,
- the ways you listen to, code, and analyze it,
- how you write about it and with whom you share it,
- how you account for your own positionality and framing of it, and
- the ways the original storytellers might receive and use it.

To navigate these stages with care and figure out the best approach for your own partnership, project, limitations, and resources, we encourage you to take on a form of *collaborative curation*. Community-engaged research cannot be done on your own. Take care when inviting others into spaces that you've already established confianza, but also open yourself up to new connections that might enhance the possibilities of your community-engaged work. Discuss ideas for collaboration early on in a partnership and review commitments, limits, hopes, and concerns periodically with everyone involved. Recognize when your academic interests and needs can coincide with community needs and when they do not. Explore multiple avenues for incorporating your collaborators' expertise and interests into the written account of what happened. Finally, come to consensus on when it is time to step away from something or how you might need to wrap up a project.

The last method mainly applies to researchers who have an interest in, or are currently engaging in, digitally published projects. For those, we hope Danielle's brief description of *care-ful digital design* and how design justice informed her process was helpful. Researchers engaging in digital projects that incorporate personal lived experiences should be transparent about concerns with sharing personal stories, photos, and identifying information in digital spaces. In our case, Danielle shared what she had read, researched, and experienced to inform the writers about these things. Then, each writer made their own decisions to care for their own stories. But we also were cautious and careful with which secondary audiences we shared *Cuentos* with as we didn't want these stories to be used or analyzed in ways that would be harmful or dishonorable to the promotores and their communities. Feminist researchers should take care to move slowly and design thoughtfully so that stories and storytellers are prioritized over academic goals or deadlines.

Finally, we invite you to experience *Cuentos* for yourself by going to www.cuentosdeconfianza.com. As you spend time with these stories, we also encourage you to implement what you learn from them into actionable responses of care and to recognize your own stories, your own body, and your own communities as worthy of care.

NOTES

1. Throughout this chapter, all Spanish quotes are translated to English in the notes. We encourage readers to look up words they don't know and consider how language preferences impact our experiences with stories and projects that may primarily be developed in languages other than English. Translation: "As I tell [my participants], 'This is my greatest gift for you, give it the value that you want to give, but I don't have more to offer you. This is my story.'" Angeles Soria, group interview, July 6, 2023.
2. Ahmed, *Living*; hooks, *Feminism*; Moraga and Anzaldúa, *This Bridge*, xliii–xlvii.
3. Ross et al., *Radical Reproductive Justice*, 203.
4. Briggs, *Taking Children*, 11–12.
5. Hernández and De Los Santos Upton, *Challenging Reproductive Control*.
6. Fixmer-Oraiz, *Homeland*; Sotomayor, "Reproductive Rights," 2–3
7. Davis, *Women, Race, and Class*, 53.
8. Taylor, *How We Get Free*, 15.
9. Ross and Solinger, *Reproductive Justice*, 65.
10. SisterSong: Women of Color Reproductive Justice Collective, "Reproductive Justice," https://www.sistersong.net/reproductive-justice.
11. Royster and Krisch, *Feminist Rhetorical Practices*, 146, 147.
12. The participants thus far in the project have identified as Latina. We welcome promotores de salud regardless of their gender identity and welcome those who may self-identify as Latine, Latinx, and Latino as well, primarily emphasizing writers with heritage and roots in Latin America or Latine culture in the United States.
13. While drafting this chapter, we invited participants from the first writing class and student translators to share reflections on their experience working on the project together to contribute to this piece. The quotes featured in this collection represent what was shared in a recorded gathering and email exchanges. Thanks to Elida Rebolledo, Angeles Soria, Maria Barker, Alejandra González, and Gaby Torres for their contributions!
14. Powell et al., "Our Story," https://enculturation.net/our-story-begins-here.

15. Kimmerer *Braiding Sweetgrass*, 30–31; King, *The Truth*, 95; Maracle, *Oratory*, 3.

16. Lindquist, "Time to Grow," 663–64; Riley Mukavetz, "Towards a Cultural Rhetorics Methodology," 114–15; Wilson, *Research as Ceremony*, 107.

17. Powell et al., "Our Story," https://enculturation.net/our-story-begins-here.

18. Smith, *Decolonizing Methodologies*, 214–15.

19. Translation: "About the Project."

20. The findings and conclusions in this article are those of the authors and do not necessarily represent the views of Planned Parenthood of Wisconsin, Inc.

21. Bloom-Pojar and Barker, "The Role," 92.

22. Ross, "Teaching Reproductive Justice," 170.

23. Tuck and Yang, "R-Words," 235.

24. Translation: "Cuentos writers."

25. Ross, "Teaching Reproductive Justice," 177.

26. Translation: "When we began, we thought it was something small. Now that it has developed, it really is something big. As always, the first ones are always going to have a more difficult time because we have to begin to decipher what we are going to do, what they want, what works, what doesn't work." Elida Rebolledo, group interview, July 6, 2023.

27. Translation: "I remember that I began to meet with you and you asked me certain questions and responses that truthfully it had been many years that I hadn't thought about these things until you started to ask. . . . I've commented to you, Rachel, many times that I tried to talk, but before talking, I had to cry to be able to write." Elida Rebolledo, group interview, July 6, 2023.

28. Translation: "You were a good guide in relation to how we should go about narrating because a lot of things were broken. Some words go above, others below. You also saw me break down when I was talking about my miscarriages and my husband's position, in this pain I also felt [in the process]. . . . This made me feel sad at the time, to be remembering everything that I had lived in this time of wanting to become a mother and all the barriers that I had to be one. It was very difficult." Angeles Soria, group interview, July 6, 2023.

29. Vinson and Dutta, "Participatory Curation," 242.

30. Haas, "Toward a Digital Cultural Rhetoric," 414.

31. Costanza-Chock, *Design Justice*, 6–7.

32. Vinson and Dutta, "Participatory Curation," 265.

33. Translation: "You were really like an interpreter for what she [Danielle] needed from us and what the website needed from her." Marina Barker, group interview, July 6, 2023.

34. Novotny and Horn-walker, "Art-i-facts," 59.

35. Design Justice Network, "Design Justice Network Principles," last modified 2018, https://designjustice.org/.

36. Bloom-Pojar and Barker, "The Role," 89–90.

37. Translation: "home health parties."

WORKS CITED

Ahmed, Sara. *Living a Feminist Life*. Durham, NC: Duke University Press, 2017.

Bloom-Pojar, Rachel, and Maria Barker. "The Role of Confianza in Community-Engaged Work for Reproductive Justice." *Reflections* 20, no. 2 (Fall/Winter 2020): 84–101.

Briggs, Laura. *Taking Children: A History of American Terror.* Oakland: University of California Press, 2021.

Costanza-Chock, Sasha. *Design Justice: Community-Led Practices to Build the Worlds We Need.* Cambridge, MA: The MIT Press, 2020.

Davis, Angela. *Women, Race, and Class.* London: The Women's Press, 1986.

Fixmer-Oraiz, Natalie. *Homeland Maternity: US Security Culture and the New Reproductive Regime.* Champaign, IL: University of Illinois Press, 2019.

Haas, Angela. "Toward a Digital Cultural Rhetoric." In *The Routledge Handbook of Digital Writing and Rhetoric,* edited by Jonathan Alexander and Jacqueline Rhodes, 412–22. New York: Routledge, 2018.

Hernandez, Leandra H., and Sara De Los Santos Upton. *Challenging Reproductive Control and Gendered Violence in the Américas: Intersectionality, Power, and Struggles for Rights.* Lanham, MD: Lexington Books, 2020.

hooks, bell. *Feminism Is for Everyone: Passionate Politics.* New York: Routledge, 2015.

Kimmerer, Robin Wall. *Braiding Sweetgrass: Indigenous Wisdom, Scientific Knowledge, and the Teaching of Plants.* Minneapolis, MN: Milkweed Editions, 2013.

King, Thomas. *The Truth About Stories: A Native Narrative.* Toronto, ON: House of Anansi Press, 2003.

Lindquist, Julie. "Time to Grow Them: Practicing Slow Research in a Fast Field." *Journal of Advanced Composition* 2, no. 3/4 (2012): 645–66.

Maracle, Lee. *Oratory: Coming to Theory.* Gallerie: Women Artists' Monographs. Vancouver, BC: Gallerie Publications, 1990.

Moraga, Cherríe, and Gloria Anzaldúa, eds. *This Bridge Called My Back: Writings by Radical Women of Color.* Albany, NY: SUNY Press, 2015.

Novotny, Maria, and Elizabeth Horn-Walker. "Art-i-facts: A Methodology for Circulating Infertility Counternarratives." In *Interrogating Gendered Pathologies,* edited by Erin A. Frost and Michelle F. Eble, 43–66. Logan, UT: Utah State University Press, 2020.

Powell, Malea, Daisy Levy, Andrea Riley Mukavetz, Marilee Brooks-Gillies, Maria Novotny, and Jennifer Fisch-Ferguson. "Our Story Begins Here: Constellating Cultural Rhetorics." *enculturation,* October 25, 2014. https://enculturation.net/our-story-begins-here.

Riley Mukavetz, Andrea M. "Towards a Cultural Rhetorics Methodology: Making Research Matter with Multi-Generational Women from Little Traverse Bay Band." *Rhetoric, Professional Communication and Globalization* 5, no. 1 (February 2014): 108–25.

Ross, Loretta. "Teaching Reproductive Justice: An Activist's Approach." *Black Women's Liberatory Pedagogies: Resistance, Transformations, and Healing within and Beyond the Academy,* edited by Olivia N. Perlow, Durene I. Wheeler, Sharon L. Bethea, and Barbara M. Scott, 159–80. New York: Palgrave Macmillan Publishing, 2018.

Ross, Loretta J., and Rickie Solinger. *Reproductive Justice: An Introduction.* Oakland: University of California Press, 2017.

Ross, Loretta J., Lynn Roberts, Erika Derkas, Whitney Peoples, and Pamela Bridgewater Toure, eds. *Radical Reproductive Justice: Foundations, Theories, Practices, Critique.* New York: Feminist Press, 2017.

Royster, Jacqueline Jones, and Gesa E. Kirsch. *Feminist Rhetorical Practices: New Horizons for Rhetoric, Composition, and Literacy Studies.* Carbondale, IL: Southern Illinois University Press, 2012.

Smith, Linda Tuhiwai. *Decolonizing Methodologies: Research and Indigenous Peoples*, 2nd ed. London: Zed Books, 2012.

Sotomayor, María Estrella. "Reproductive Rights in Puerto Rico: Sterilization, Contraception, and Reproductive Violence." PhD diss., University of Wisconsin-Milwaukee, 2020.

Taylor, Keeanga-Yamahtta. *How We Get Free: Black Feminism and the Combahee River Collective*. Chicago, IL: Haymarket Books, 2017.

Tuck, Eve, and K. Wayne Yang. "R-Words: Refusing Research." In *Humanizing Research: Decolonizing Qualitative Inquiry with Youth and Communities*, edited by Django Paris and Maisha T. Winn, 223–47. New York: SAGE Publications, 2013.

Vinson, Jenna, and Urmitapa Dutta. "Participatory Curation: Who has the Power to Exhibit in a Collaborative Community-based Project." *The Journal of Multimodal Rhetorics* 3, no. 1 (2019): 240–72.

Wilson, Shawn. *Research as Ceremony: Indigenous Research Methods*. Black Point, Nova Scotia: Fernwood Publishing, 2008.

PART III

Navigating Materiality, Memory, and Futurity

How can our research methods and methodologies adapt to the particular material and digital contexts that we simultaneously study and participate in? The third and final section of this collection, "Navigating Materiality, Memory, and Futurity," addresses the ways we make knowledge and negotiate different digital and physical spaces as scholars, researchers, and participants in specific communities. The ways we make knowledge are enmeshed in specific worlds, influenced by our dual roles as participants and researchers navigating power relations. Navigating digital worlds such as gaming means negotiating those power relations in ways that combat coded biases and also create space for marginalized Black women's bodies to participate in remaking those spaces so they can thrive (Jones). While seeking to transform digital spaces, we also have to consider how the digital tools with which we conduct our research can be understood and managed differently, especially when we are seeking to create histories inclusive of women of color (Graban and Healy). The material sites of historical remembrance also must be spaces for considering our methods for memorializing specific groups and individuals, factoring in questions of equity and inclusion (Enoch and Woods). Finally, listening to emerging scholars as they encounter a field and consider their approaches as researchers is a key way to think through what it means to take up the mantle of feminist rhetorical scholarship and think about probable futures while being mindful of precarity and possibilities (Jewell, Long, Turner, and Wilson). These chapters offer feminist rhetorical methods for remaking digital and physical spaces to help those who enter them thrive, now and in our shared futures.

NINE

Dangerous Moves

On Reclaiming Video Gaming through Black Feminist Rhetoric and Remix

Stephanie Jones

Modern video games typically start with cinematic quality backstories for the game's narrative. Usually, academics in the humanities do not have the budgets for that, so here is my backstory. I am a gamer. This was not always easy for me to say. There is a form of linguistic oppression embedded in video gaming culture that gatekeeps who can see themselves as part of digital narratives. When I think about the role video gaming has played in my life, my first thoughts are always of my grandmother. For as long as I can remember, she has loved technology. When I was in middle school, she bought me my first cell phone, and I would use it to call her and tell her about my day at school. She also really loves computer games. She has a frog statue on her computer desk she fights with as she plays her puzzle games. Her love of technology has always been inspiring to me. When I asked her why she still plays computer games in her nineties, she said she just enjoys it. She says that if it's something she "can touch onto and learn how to play," then she plays it. My mother is the same way. I have fond memories of her playing *Tetris* for hours while eating whole bags of sunflower seeds. Their tactile approach to video gaming made the experience so real to me that I did not know it was strange for Black girls to play computer or video games; the cruelty of schoolchildren taught me that. Time has taught me that the perception that someone like me—a plus sized Black girl who loved playing Pokémon Yellow Version on *Gameboy* more than being outside and who put in her own box braids—could not possibly be a "gamer" is not true. That's just racism. Having my mother and grandmother to look up to meant, for me, it was never weird that I played video games until the outside world told me it was strange.

As I got older, the games also started telling me I did not belong, since no one who really looked like me was part of the story. Although the last few years have brought more visual representations of Blackness into video game narratives, they are often choked allegories or metaphors of what we have come to believe as an African presence in video gaming.[1] To address those disparities, Black women have been providing the field with scholarship on the cognitive dissonance that occurs for Black people who love to play games but must negotiate the validity of our roles in the narrative. In this chapter, I offer you the Black Digital Rhetoric User Interface (UI), a methodology I have cultivated to identify gaps in current scholarship on what it means to do this work from a digital cultural matrix, help you select Afrofuturist feminist texts or artifacts,[2] and do rhetorical analysis with the Afrodigitized critical questioning tool, one that synthesizes methods of African American rhetoric with the ways Black people have had to write themselves into the digital world. This is the start to the Afrofuturist feminist world I want to build. I invite you to take the journey with me. Let's game!

The Black Digital Rhetoric User Interface

To do this work of the Black digital rhetoric of gaming we need new methodologies. We have to tell our own stories. Rather than providing a static definition of Black digital rhetoric, I have identified the four primary activities of a Black digital rhetoric of gaming, so we might embrace both intersectional practice and the ever changing nature of the digital world: (1) rhetorical analysis grounded in our own digital cultural matrix; (2) bringing wreck to media that continually marginalizes us; (3) formulating a Black identity in spaces or games when those features are excluded from the design; and (4) building safe communities. As a methodology deeply engaged with the definition of African American rhetoric, Black digital rhetoric allows us to explicate rhetorical theories that disrupt coded biases in digital texts and performances. Attention to these steps ensures more inclusive representation for Black women gamers who are contributing to this important need for change. Thinking of this methodology as an expression of Afrofuturist feminist praxis allows us to think of our place in the digital sphere as intersectional world building.

In many ways, this chapter is a tribute to the Black feminist gamers who took me under their wing—Kishonna L. Gray and Samantha Blackmon and all the women in the field whom I have talked to about gaming since I started this project. Most had stories about not feeling like they played video games in the right way, or of having negative experiences with other players. Kishonna L. Gray's article "Power in the Visual" argues that when mediated representations of Black bodies reach mainstream levels, they are often viewed through the dichotomy of positive and negative. Through this lens, Black characters are portrayed as individuals who are trying to survive in a (white man's) world with goals no different from those of their white counterparts. These narratives deploy the dangerous myth of assimilation for people of color without focusing on the racialized reality that people of color still reside within the myths associated with meritocracy.

Positive representations such as these are used to provide evidentiary claims that inequalities no longer exist.[3] However Gray dives further into how the dehumanization of Black people works against our engagement with video gaming media in her book *Intersectional Tech*, explaining that "[i]n society at large, black women are often reminded of their 'place'; the use of space and place to restrict the movement of Black women is common practice in both digital and physical spaces."[4] As such, "black women have used a variety of responses to continue existing and residing in these spaces, from self-segregating and isolating themselves to disrupting and invading the spaces anyway."[5] Thinking of my video gaming practices in this way directly informs how I think about writing studies, Afrofuturist feminisms, and Black digital rhetoric as intersectional practices.

The Afrofuturist Feminist Gamer Is Online

While video games, and in some respect novels too, may have fixed narratives, there is no one way to write yourself into a story. Informed by the Black feminist principle that our lived experiences are our knowledges bases, Afrofuturist feminist world building teaches us that our imaginations are liberatory spaces of invention. In the same way, Afrofuturist feminisms allows us to write ourselves into the future. How can you write in a world that does not see your story as important? In writing studies, we use invention to talk about a time of self-discovery in the writing process. To some it may be as simple as pre-writing, but I see it as an important place to inject liberatory writing practices in our classrooms. Introducing our students to culturally complex and self-reflective knowledge systems, like Afrofuturist feminisms, in the face of oppressive practices solidifies that the first step in the writing process is understanding that their stories matter.

This is an important intersection between rhetorical studies and game studies because video game narratives are becoming even more important to the ways our students understand world building and story structure. As video game technology simultaneously becomes both more user friendly and more complex, it should be more commonplace to see narrative-driven video games on our class reading lists. Video games are narratives that ask us to reside in the story.

A salient example of residing in these spaces appears in Samantha Blackmon's scholarship where she describes playing Mafia 3, an action-adventure game in which players game as Lincoln Clay, an African American Vietnam War veteran. She writes: "As I write this essay, I must also disclose that I have not yet finished the main campaign of the game because I find myself constantly exploring new areas and new experiences and just doing things like driving around and listening to radio personalities and callers talk about the racial, political, and social conditions in New Bordeaux. These are rich experiences that I don't want to let go of."[6] She goes on to say: "It is what drives me as a player. Seeing the connection between the news stories on the radio and gleaned from stories being shared between NPCs (Non-Playable Characters) on the street as I walk by and what is going on in the world around us at this moment drives me not only to play the game and pay attention to the stories, but to think about what it all means."[7] Blackmon thus brings wreck to normalized insistences of identity, self-knowledge, situated meaning, and cultural models about the world of gaming.

Blackmon's experiences with Mafia 3 stands in contrast to Gamergate, an online misogynistic harassment campaign, which Gray describes as a white supremacy movement tracing back to 1999 that, from "a feminist perspective . . . can be viewed as the response of the default gamer being forced to accept the inclusion of women and increased diversity in game narratives . . . [where] Toxic technoculture and geek masculinity centered themselves as victims in a social justice war."[8] These exclusionary narratives have made it so people who are not represented in the imagined center of a game narrative must rely on their own creativity to write themselves into these stories. This goes beyond world building. As women and people of color, we are used to superficial inclusion—a nameless faceless woman whose features are described with an embarrassing amount of food metaphors standing off to the right of the hero as he gives a grand speech. Sometimes, these characters are killed to substantiate the hero's quest, giving their lives stilted meaning, but we rarely know their overarching stories. But colorblind casting is not inclusion. It is merely the window dressing that covers up the fact that no one who represents change or diversity is in the room during the creation phase of a given game narrative.

In this chapter, I have given you an in-game map. First, the tool you need to get behind the waterfall is Afrodigitized critical questioning. I know it is like starting you off with the game Downloadable Content or DLC, but I want you to have the tools you need to uncover and understand the truths in the Black Digital Rhetoric UI. You will uncover the rest of the map as you read. I promise it will be worth it. After all, one of the most satisfying parts of an open world game is uncovering new areas.

Afrodigitized Critical Questioning

The year 2024 has shaped up to be a Black girl magical moment in video gaming. As I watch my favorite WNBA games, I see advertisements for PS5—in part, because Las Vegas Aces star A'ja Wilson appears on the cover of the WNBA edition of the popular video game series NBA 2K. An author, champion, and league MVP, Wilson is a Black girl with that Black girl magic atmosphere in her name. The method I advocate for in this chapter is the Afrodigitized critical questioning tool that can be used so we become part and parcel of the imagined center of digital narratives. The recognition of Wilson's career through her inclusion in an iconic video game is an excellent example of this. If nommo is the Afrocentric term for the power of the word to generate and create reality, then the "Afrodigital" is that power wielded and recoded in online or digital spaces.[9] Jacqueline Jones Royster's concept of "critical questioning" offers a tool of analysis that allows Black users to create "a speaking and a listening" self and a "responsive community" to write themselves into textual and digital spaces.

Royster contends that we can complicate the primary activities of digital rhetoric with Black ways of being and knowing in such a way that celebrates the Black people already doing this work in digital spaces.[10] Afrodigital critical questioning is imbued with the power of intersectional realities to demonstrate how Black women gamers use their realities to create speculative worlds that create and sustain a thriving Black future. When engaged with the primary activities of Black digital rhetoric Afrodigital critical questioning give us strategies of emergence from white supremacist dialectical symmetry in digital spaces and imagines how we are part of communities that honor Black lived experiences.

Black language exemplifies Black praxis in ways that are both lived in and familiar across Black history, but also dynamic because when faced with harmful constraints of white supremacy we have had to adapt and transform. Afrodigitized critical questioning is a method of equitably examining and questioning how *nommo,* the power of the word, makes meaning in Black through intersectional praxis the digital sphere.[11]

With Dangerous Moves, We Reclaim Video Gaming

We need to change how we think about digital rhetoric because of the pervasive nature of white supremacy, and Afrodigitized critical questioning helps us do that in four ways. First, it helps us with the identification of the coded biases that continually support "symbolic exclusion" in the "default programing" of video gaming culture. Starting with the engaging work Gray has done on social media with the hashtag #GrayTest, Gray has given us a way to think about "symbolic exclusion" and "default programming" as an integrated system of inclusion-centered evaluation. The frequencies "symbolic exclusion" and "default programing" tap into and cause needed disruptions of "dominant definitions" in game culture and liberate Black linguistic practices when engaged with video gaming discourses.

Secondly, Afrodigitized critical questioning allows us to identify areas of weaponized whiteness and other problematic rhetorics that sustain white supremacist dialectical symmetry in video gaming culture. Rhetorical analysis that engages this point must examine digital content and media that continually marginalizes Black people and that seeks to profit from caricatures of our identity. Third, the identification of digital performative blackface minstrelsy that perpetuates violence against Black gamers and Black culture because the overall game design does not draw on multidimensional Black identity as part of the design. Blackface minstrelsy has roots going back to the 1800s in America. Since people of African descent were barred from areas such as national theatre and, later, television, white actors would be cast and made up in black face paint with exaggerated lips and noses to depict harmful stereotypes of Black people for racist audiences. In games and gaming culture today, we see digital performances of blackface minstrelsy in memes, game play of racist gamers as they puppet Black characters and culture, as well as their racist regurgitation of harmful stereotypes.

Lastly, identification of rhetorical actions that build safe and responsive communities and dispel coded biases in digital spaces is crucial. Currently, the landscape of digital rhetoric does not account for Afrodigitized approaches to writing oneself into narratives in ways that recognize the danger women and people of color face in online spaces. James P. Zappen defines digital rhetoric in his article, "Digital Rhetoric," as the recognition that there is a marked transformation in the "rhetoric of persuasion" in discourse happening in digital spaces. As such, a framework for "digital rhetoric [helps] to explain how traditional rhetorical strategies of persuasion function and how they are being reconfigured in digital spaces."[12] He identifies the field

as lending itself to interdisciplinary exploration through four key components—the use of rhetorical strategies in production and analysis of digital
text/ identifying characteristics, affordances, and constraints of new media/
formation of digital identities/potential for building social communities."[13]
Additionally, Douglas Eyman suggests in his book, *Digital Rhetoric,* that
"digital rhetoric is not tied to a single discipline . . . [it] is strengthened by
drawing on theories and methods from multiple disciplines and fields while
remaining true to its foundation in rhetoric."[14] These definitions of digital
rhetoric do not account for what it means when the rules of engagement
for participating in a space are imagined to perpetuate your exclusion. As
Andrea A. Lunsford explains of the rhetorical tradition, "*Reclaiming Rhetorica* suggests that the realm of rhetoric has been almost exclusively male, not
because women were not practicing rhetoric—the arts of language are after
all at the source of human communication—but because the tradition has
never recognized the forms, strategies, and goals used by many women as
rhetorical."[15] Extending the "forms, strategies, and goals" concerning what
makes someone play a video game outside the realm of what is currently
considered video gaming culture takes us beyond the content provided by
AAA or top-tier video gaming studios.

Defining the Digital Cultural Matrix

Giving space to other forms of video gaming by drawing on a Black digital
rhetoric grounded in African American rhetorical traditions brings us closer
to an inclusive definition for the term "gamer" and gives us a way to reclaim
and write our own paths towards an inclusive gaming universe. Elaine Richardson and Ronald Jackson define African American Rhetoric in *African
American Rhetoric(s)* as "the study of culturally and discursively developed
knowledge-forms, communicative practices and persuasive strategies rooted
in freedom struggles by people of African ancestry in America."[16] I argue
that by putting these two definitions in conversation, we can synthesize a
better understanding of how Black ways of being and knowing are marginalized in digital spaces. I will do this by expanding upon Zappen's classifications of the primary activities for the field of digital rhetoric by utilizing
Royster's method to trace the Afrofuturist feminist frequency through each
of his classifications—"the use of rhetorical strategies in production and
analysis of digital text," the "identifying characteristics, affordances, and
constraints of new media," the "formation of digital identities," and the "potential for building social communities."[17] This "Afrodigitizes" Richardson

and Jackson's assertions and creates pathways for Black people to center their experiences of the digital sphere.

I was inspired to create an Afrodigitized framework of critical questioning because of the answer to a question about race, cyberspace, and inequality that Octavia Butler gave during a Black history month event at MIT in 1998. The question was: "What happens to race in cyberspace? Is it a good thing or a bad thing that people can choose to have a race or make their race disappear when they write in cyberspace? And what are some of the implications of that?"[18] Butler explains: "We've got this window where we can do that kind of thing and play that way and be whoever we choose to be in cyberspace. But soon, that window will close. With respect to showing people's pictures, at first it will be "Well, if you want to," and then it will be expected . . . I don't know how it'll work, but I'm wondering if by our pictures' being shown, or videos of us as we are speaking, that we lose the window."[19] Considering her answer now, when this window of opportunity to be Black and free online has closed, I have been thinking about the ways in which being both a Black woman and a Black gamer makes me hyper-visible in digital spaces. Because of the immersive nature of video gaming embodying a Black character and being a Black gamer today means that you are experiencing violence in two spaces that were thought to be locations of free expression by Butler: your imagination and your own home.

Bringing Wreck in the Digital Afrofuture

Much like Gwendolyn Pough says about hip-hop culture, we do not truly have a clear picture of the all the people who listen to hip-hop unless we count *all* the ways people participate in hip-hop culture.[20] Video gaming communities, often touted as made up of from a majority of young white straight males, are remarkably similar in this regard. It is inaccurate to credit one small group as defining what it means to be a gamer, who games are made for, and what games are popular in the United States without considering all the ways that people play games. This exclusionary approach erases the participation of people who play games primarily on their cellphones, games with puzzle-based mechanics, and romance storylines. To disrupt the narrative usually told about video gaming, I look to women's history of disruptions to the rhetorical tradition. Video gaming and the rhetorical tradition share similar problem in that tradition has excluded the multitude of ways women participate in the culture.

Exclusionary tactics are normalized forms of toxicity in video gaming culture, sustained through weaponized whiteness to retain power over the consumer base. Denoting video games as hypertexts and learning environ-ments, it is important to unpack the patterns of violence associated with the toxicity in video gaming culture if we are going to use games in our classrooms and profession. Kishonna L. Gray explains in *Intersectional Tech* that "[a]lthough women are present within these spaces, perhaps more so now than ever, they still are overlooked and rendered unimportant because of the presumed maleness of video gaming culture and spaces. . . . Verbal attacks, rooted in specific identities, often are instigated through linguis-tic profiling."[21] To disrupt these practices, Afrodigitized critical questioning gives us ways to create definitions rhetoricians might use when engaging with explorations into digital rhetoric when synthesized with African Amer-ican rhetorical practices. Women and Black gamers experience these attacks and instances of erasure already—we just need to reclaim the recognition of our shared experiences by taking ownership of the terms and conditions.

Women of all age groups and racial backgrounds are playing games—they are just not playing the games that get the most media coverage. As such, until we count those types of games, including narrative and puzzle games that explore different aspect of the romance genre, we do not have a clear picture of what it means to be a gamer. For example, the world record holder for the "largest collection of playable video gaming systems" is Linda Guillory, an African American woman from Garland, Texas.[22] Guillory be-lieves games are meant to be played, and she has many priceless games she plays instead of keeping them in the box. Her enthusiasm for all types of games is reflected in how she got started playing games. According to her video interview posted on the Guinness World Records YouTube account, Guillory credits her love of games to her mother who bought her and her siblings a broken video gaming system.[23] She was only eight years old and playing the hand-held basketball game changed her world. The game in-trigued her, so she took it apart and fixed it. The process inspired her to become an electrical engineer. Today, she hopes to donate her collection to a museum that encourages young people to play and enjoy games. Guillory's story is not unique in the video gaming world, but it is overlooked.

Black Identity and Gaming Black Feminist Remix

There are some rhetorical giants already publishing about digital topics to be sure, but explorations of race and gender can sometimes gloss over the complexity needed to see the video games community as diverse. James Paul Gee in his book *What Video Games Have to Teach Us* describes the learn-ing process in video games as a type of "situated cognition" that augments human learning in the "material, social, and cultural world."[24] He calls this "active learning," or the process by which video gamers are "experiencing the world in new ways, forming new affiliations, and preparation for future learning."[25] He goes on to imply that this type of learning is generally encouraged: "what determines this is your own experiences in interacting with other people who are members of various sorts of social groups, whether these are biblical scholars, radical lawyers, peace activists, family members, fellow ethnic group, or church members, or whatever. These groups work, through their various social practices, to encourage people to read and think in certain ways, and not others, about certain sorts of texts and things."[26] Thinking of Gee's words, written within the context of video game culture before 2003, we can see how white supremacist movements like Gamergate have changed the landscape of cross-cultural collaboration. This is particularly important when it comes to how agency is cultivated in games. Gray's analysis of Gamergate helps us understand that the "default programming" in games substantiate the white supremacist claims that narratives belong to only specific groups. This is underscored in Gee's analysis of what agency in video game learning should be. In 2005, Gee wrote an article called "Good Video Games and Good Learning" for National Forum's *Phi Kappa Phi Journal* where he stated that agency in game learning is "Thanks to all the preceding principles, [Identity, Interaction, Production, Risk Taking, Customized] players feel a real sense of agency and control and a real sense of ownership over what they are doing."[27] In his book of the same title, Gee flattens these principles, calling them "meta-game design concerns," and instead privileges a concept he calls "affinity spaces" to characterize forms of social organization within gaming narratives.[28] Neither of Gee's articulations of the principles of agency really attends to how violence based on gender and race might be accounted for within gaming communities.

To that point, scholar Elaine Richardson, in her book *Hiphop Literacies,* explores agency in a game called *Def Jam Vendetta.* Made in 2003 by AKI Corporation, a Japanese video game development studio and published by EA Sports, Richardson's playthrough of *Def Jam Vendetta* highlights what we can gain by following Blackmon's example of how to synthesize our lived experiences to cultivate joy and agency within gaming narratives. She explains, "Gee is interested in the model that video games provide for learning. My interest is slightly different. I am interested in what people already know, their worldly literacies and the ideological viewpoints manifested by interacting with video games that exploit Hip-hop content: symbology, music, language, and landscape."[29] Since Gee's model does not cover what

Richardson is exploring, the authorship of the video game narrative is not addressed. *Def Jam Vendetta* is a wrestling simulator designed by a gaming studio with no visible links to hip-hop communities. Instead, as Richardson describes, players engage in performative minstrelsy by superimposing what they know about hip-hop culture into their gaming experience. She writes, "Hip hop video-game players are drawing on their knowledge of how the real world works when they become engaged players of a game. Hip-hop video games, like other popular media, are sites of competing discourses, symbolizing ideologies, and worldviews."[30] Since Gamergate, we know that gamers who come from historically marginalized groups are subject to harassment because of the culture around games like *Def Jam Vendetta*. The responsibility of telling stories about historically marginalized groups falls on the storytellers. What gamers come to understand as a real hip-hop experience in-game is really another example of a choked representation of an Africanist presence. Blackmon critiques American cultural allegories and metaphors that dehumanize Black people written in as coded biases that the game narrative depends on to tell its story. Her glimpse into the fishbowl reminds us that "African American stereotypes that are prevalent elsewhere are simply being perpetuated in video games. . . . Video games are not the problem here; it is the way that the games are being written, drawn, and marketed that is the problem."[31] This is a strategy Blackmon has formulated to combat racism when streaming games for her Twitch channel *Not Your Mama's Gamer.*

A Safe Place for Black Gamer Dreams

Learning to game in worlds that do not recognize you as a "gamer" is similar. As such, Afrofuturist feminist gamers, aided by Afrodigitized critical questioning, must build our own maps and make our own meaning, engaging with narratives that would otherwise exclude us. Blackmon, with student Daniel J. Terrell, explains that "to some extent these characters become the player. As a gamer who is put into dicey situations, a player tends to make decisions that are very much affected by who the player is as a person as well as how the player is feeling emotionally and psychologically at that moment."[32] Octavia Butler explored and created new worlds in much the same way Blackmon ascribes to players, by making space for others to ask questions about the world around them. For those trying to game in spaces that marginalize us, the video gaming experience involves that same pain and rejection. Thinking of Blackmon in conversation with Octavia Butler crystalizes what it means for Black gamers to be included.

By reclaiming video gaming spaces and disrupting normalized narratives of exclusion, bringing video gaming into our classrooms and our work can be a liberatory experience for our students and for us. Blackmon explains that "video games give us the opportunity to look at different kinds of texts and to work with the notion that things that seem to be the most benign (at least in the mind of the student) are rhetorically charged and that it is important to pay close attention to both what [these games] are saying . . . and how they are saying it."[33] Blackmon's work is a call to begin to look at games as text. As such we, as Black rhetors, can find meaning making and linguistic practices through "texts that many students regularly interact with." Blackmon goes on to say that games are where our students live. In this way, "[v]ideo games give us an idea of what those who are not of the worlds represented in video games think of these worlds . . . [a place where] we can meet our students to talk about race, rhetoric, and representation."[34] A framework for Black digital rhetoric gives us the "critical questions" Blackmon is calling us to engage with to sustain a thriving Black future. To decode the oppression embedded in video gaming culture, we need to see what Blackmon is doing here as always already enacting Black digital rhetoric. Her understanding that a richer experience of a games' major storylines must be found in her own storytelling practices that creates a speaking and a listening self by Afrodigitizing the game environment which cultivates agency for marginalized gamers. Both Blackmon and Gray have been working within the games industry the same amount of time, if not longer, than other scholars who have yet to understand the point of our intersectional experiences. Their work is the code with which I wrote the framework for Black digital rhetoric uncovered through Afrodigitized critical questioning, and I hope marginalized voices can find themselves and thrive with its use.

For Black Future Girls When the Field Is Never Enuf

I believe we can take a fuller approach when considering how Black life is composed across media and the dangers of translation without the recognition of difference. In an interview she gave with Neal A. Lester in 1992, Ntozake Shange said the following: "I'm a firm believer that language and how we use language determines how we act, and how we act then determines our lives and other people's lives."[35] Black digital rhetoric is me breaking up with concepts and methods that limit linguistic difference. It is for the Black e-girlies, Black gamer girls, and Flyana Boss sing-a-Black-girl-song video girls who speak our digital futures into life. It is a doorway to the Afrofuture, so the roots will be there when you arrive.

One way I hope to expand the field of rhetoric and composition is complicating the word work used in the analysis of game narratives. Afrodigitized critical questioning helps me explore popular media with an Afrofuturist approach. Black culture is deeply rooted in hope and belief in a better future. Video games are one place where the future we imagine already exists. I have always had students who say they do not identify as readers, but as I engage with Game Studies in my work, I am realizing that as a field we are missing how and why our students read modern media. Every game has a narrative and a cast of characters that help tell its story. Seeing ourselves as central to the narrative in popular media means there is proof that we made it to the future; despite the violence and white supremacy of today. Video game developers write gamers into their games in a multisensory way that truly allows us to live in the worlds their game builds.

Now, more so than ever before, we are living our lives online. To be conscious consumers of gaming content, we must look to gaming studios who are rendering Black life with intentionality and purpose. Some video gaming studio leaders have taken up this task earnestly, such as CEO Mitu Khandaker and CXO Latoya Peterson of Glow Up Games Studios, whose mission is "centering innovative storytelling about Black and brown joy" by building "beautifully crafted mobile-first titles for the new gaming majority."[36] Their flagship game, *Insecure: The Come-Up Game,* follows the cast of the iconic HBO series *Insecure* while teaching players about gentrification in the county of Los Angeles and how to craft responsive rap lyrics.

The mobile game is a shining example of what it means to create inclusive narratives that are reflective of African American culture today. Glow Up Games Studio demonstrates that diversity and inclusion in video games makes a difference *if* the rhetorical actions of both the visuals and the narrative go beyond blackface performative minstrelsy. Since video game tie-ins to popular media are becoming more accessible through mobile games, a wider variety of publishing studios, and a greater availability of consoles, it is time to start building stronger bridges between visual rhetoric and game studies.

Something that is so unique about *Insecure* and the culture of Los Angeles Issa Rae explores across multiple seasons of the show is the layered, thoughtful, and intentional approach to the multitudinous nature of Black life. Spanning as many different neighborhoods, types of music, foods, and walks of life as there are freeways in LA, Rae's *Insecure* spoke to a moment in African American culture when people who were born and raised in the '80s and '90s were watching their neighborhoods, and the futures they imagined in them, disappear. I am one of those people. I grew up in an area called the Valley in LA. After getting into grad school near the apartments I grew up in, I took a drive around my old neighborhood and while some of the familiar places were still there, what was most prevalent was the overpriced sheen of gentrification. Glow Up Games Studios captures this experience in the mobile game version of *Insecure*. After moving into your gentrified apartment, players indulge in the escapism that frames Rae's performance in the show by looking into a bathroom mirror and learning to rap. As an expression of Afrodigitized critical questioning, these rap lessons help players ethically engage in self-discovery. Having the show as a type of intertext, Glow Up Games constructed their game narrative to allow players to use technology to question their own understandings of hip-hop culture.

If you study the roots of any major city, you will hear someone ignorantly say that there are good parts or some good gentrification, but the definition of the word never changes—we change our hearts towards the value of history. Gentrification will always be sorry meeting you at the door. Black digital rhetoric allows me to explore this show and mobile game using the same tools because my perspective is centered. These are Afrofuturist approaches—a blend of African American culture and technological remix that makes meaning and builds the future by centering African American experiences.

NOTES

1. Morrison, *Playing*.
2. The term *Afrodigitized* comes from the work of Carmen Kynard in working with how Black students claim agency as writers in digital spaces and Adam Banks works with how access to digital technologies creates a specifically Black schema for engaging with technology. Critical questioning, using the imagination as a space for doing research, comes from the work of Jacqueline Jones Royster. I synthesize their work together here to denote an African American rhetorical practice of shaping public discourse across time, disciplinary landscapes, and space.
3. Gray, "Power in the Visual."
4. Gray, *Intersectional Tech*, 162.
5. Gray, *Intersectional Tech*, 162.
6. Blackmon, "'Be Real Black,'" 102.
7. Blackmon, "'Be Real Black,'" 108.
8. Gray, *Intersectional Tech*, 98.
9. Banks, *Digital Griots*.
10. Royster, *Traces*, 237.
11. Gilyard and Banks, *On African-American Rhetoric*.
12. Zappen, "Digital Rhetoric," 319.
13. Zappen, "Digital Rhetoric," 319.
14. Eyman, *Digital Rhetoric*.

15. Lunsford, *Reclaiming Rhetorica*, 6.
16. Richardson and Jackson, *African American Rhetoric(s)*, xiii.
17. Zappen, "Digital Rhetoric," 319.
18. Octavia Butler, Samuel Delany, and Henry Jenkins, "Transcript: Octavia Butler and Samuel Delany, 1998," *MIT Black History Project*, https://www.blackhistory.mit.edu/archive/transcript-octavia-butler-and-samuel-delany-1998.
19. Butler, Delany, and Jenkins, "Transcript."
20. Pough, *Check It*.
21. Gray, *Intersectional Tech*, 98.
22. Guinness World Records, "Largest Collection of Gaming Consoles—Guinness World Records," *YouTube*, July 7, 2021, YouTube, 8:43, https://youtu.be/cCX7-jtj1cA.
23. Guiness World Records, "Largest Collection."
24. Gee, *What Video Games*, 164.
25. Gee, *What Video Games*, 451.
26. Gee, *What Video Games*, 43.
27. Gee, "Good Video Games and Good Learning."
28. Gee, "Good Video Games and Good Learning."
29. Richardson, *Hiphop Literacies*, 96.
30. Richardson, *Hiphop Literacies*, 97.
31. Blackmon and Terrell, "Racing," 211.
32. Blackmon and Terrell, "Racing," 208.
33. Blackmon and Terrell, "Racing," 214.
34. Blackmon and Terrell, "Racing," 214.
35. Lester, "Shange's Men," 725.
36. Glow Up Games, http://glowup.games/.

WORKS CITED

Banks, Adam J. *Digital Griots: African American Rhetoric in a Multimedia Age*. Carbondale, IL: Southern Illinois University Press, 2010.

Blackmon, Samantha. "'Be Real Black for Me': Lincoln Clay and Luke Cage as the Heroes we Need." *CEA Critic* 79, no. 1 (2017): 97–109.

Blackmon, Samantha, and Daniel J. Terrell. "Racing toward Representation: An Understanding of Racial Representation in Video Games." In *Gaming Lives in the Twenty-First Century: Literate Connections*, edited by Cynthia L Selfe and Gail E. Hawisher, 203–15. New York: Palgrave Macmillan, 2007.

Eyman, Douglas. *Digital Rhetoric: Theory, Method, Practice*. Ann Arbor, MI: University of Michigan Press, 2015.

Gee, James P. *Good Video Games + Good Learning: Collected Essays on Video Games, Learning, and Literacy*. New York: P. Lang, 2007.

Gee, James P. "Good Video Games and Good Learning." *Phi Kappa Phi Forum* 85, no. 2 (2005): 33.

Gee, James P. *What Video Games Have to Teach Us About Learning and Literacy*. New York: Palgrave Macmillan, 2003.

Gilyard, Keith, and Adam J. Banks. *On African-American Rhetoric*. New York: Routledge, 2018.

Gray, Kishonna L. *Intersectional Tech: Black Users in Digital Gaming*. Baton Rouge: LSU Press, 2020.

Gray, Kishonna L. "Power in the Visual: Examining Narratives of Controlling Black Bodies in Contemporary Gaming." *The Velvet Light Trap* 81, no. 81 (2018): 62–66.

Lester, Neal A. "At the Heart of Shange's Feminism: An Interview." *Black American Literature Forum* 24, no. 4 (1990): 717–30. https://doi.org/10.2307/3041798.

Lunsford, Andrea A. *Reclaiming Rhetorica: Women in The Rhetorical Tradition*. Pittsburgh, PA: University of Pittsburgh Press, 1995.

Morrison, Toni. *Playing in the Dark: Whiteness and the Literary Imagination*. Cambridge, MA: Harvard University Press, 1992.

Pough, Gwendolyn D. *Check It While I Wreck It: Black Womanhood, Hip-Hop Culture, and the Public Sphere*. Boston, MA: Northeastern University Press, 2015.

Richardson, Elaine B. *Hiphop Literacies*. New York: Routledge, 2007.

Richardson, Elaine B., and Ronald L. Jackson. *African American Rhetoric(s): Interdisciplinary Perspectives*. Carbondale: Southern Illinois University Press, 2004.

Royster, Jacqueline Jones. *Traces of a Stream: Literacy and Social Change Among African American Women*. Pittsburgh, PA: University of Pittsburgh Press, 2000.

Zappen, James P. "Digital Rhetoric: Toward an Integrated Theory." *Technical Communication Quarterly* 14, no. 3 (2005): 319–25.

TEN

The Promise(s) and Peril(s) of Big Data

Historiography, Data Feminism, and Tracing Women of Color

Tarez Samra Graban and Michael Healy

Preamble

On November 29, 1979, a student newspaper in Tallahassee, Florida reported that Geneva Smitherman, director of the Center of Black Studies at Wayne State University, had visited the campus of Florida A&M University (FAMU) one month prior, to speak about testifying in the 1979 "Martin Luther King Jr. Elementary v. Ann Arbor School District" case.[1] Smitherman's visit to FAMU, Florida's only public historically Black college or university, sparked a debate among professors in the English department on the question of whether there was a uniquely "Black English problem." The November 29th edition of FAMU's student newspaper, *The FAMUAN*, reported that "few English professors at FAMU accept Smitherman's viewpoint,"[2] citing FAMU faculty members Dr. Lowell Simmons, Dr. Henry Tolbert, and Ms. Bernice Reeves (Figure 10.1). Reeves, associate professor of English and co-founder of FAMU's first journalism degree, was quoted as saying that supplemental instruction would be beneficial "only if black children are constantly reminded that black English will not help them get jobs."[3] Instead, she advocated for educating the Ann Arbor students as if they were bilingual speakers.

The repercussions of Smitherman's visit to FAMU were likely marked and long. Smitherman's visit and its reporting at FAMU may well add nuance or complication to more commonly known histories of the Students' Right to Their Own Language (SRTOL) movement, yet we find no other evidence of this visit or of Bernice Reeves's response in rhetoric and composition journals, or in published discussions of the SRTOL movement, signaling a missed opportunity to account for the competing political and

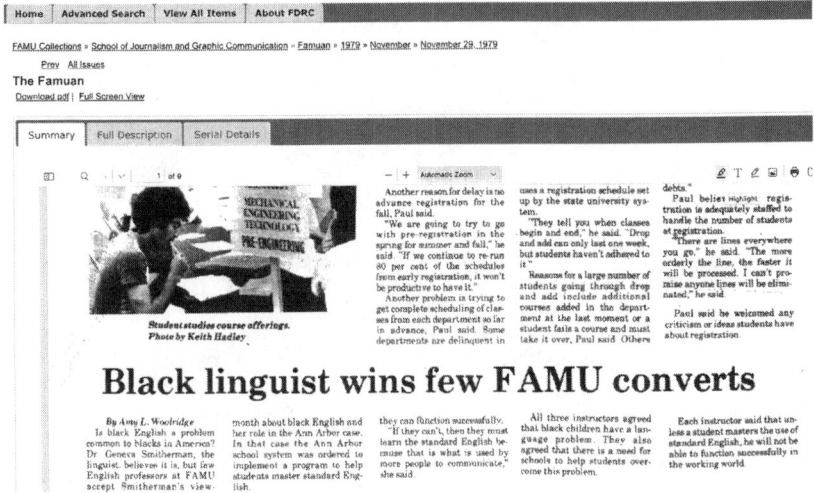

FIGURE 10.1. Partial screenshot of *The FAMUAN,* dated November 29, 1979.

economic pressures for Black academics, institutions, and students, and reinforcing the need to recover student voices from alternative or non-traditional spaces.[4] More importantly, how we discovered this article was inferential at best; we found it not by searching for Smitherman's or Reeves's names in a universal locating tool, but by reconstructing a data trail while searching for other figures in FAMU's institutional database.[5] Such inferential moments cause us to question the efficacy of recovering—systematically and digitally—the *institutional positioning* of women of color (WoC) owing to an overreliance on stable archival representation that puts HBCU libraries and archives at a material disadvantage if they cannot curate or steward whole collections; to a flattening of transient scholarly activity that renders faculty of color invisible in their institutional discourses; and thus to a history of minimizing or mis-classifying their intellectual labor. It demonstrates the unreliability of broad data sweeps to recall them, and the instability of the pathways by which we might find them again. To be clear, we do not argue that aspects of Smitherman's or Reeves's careers—and thus their influence on the discipline—are necessarily submerged into the digital dark spaces of field research. Rather, we argue for the importance of conveying overlooked intricacies of how digital histories get reconstructed using linked-data tools. Ultimately, we argue for *inferential* ways of tracing that privilege the archivally *un-*stable.

Three Principles for Privileging the Digital Archivally *Un*-stable

Institutional archival recovery of WoC is already a vexing problem for feminist rhetorical historiographers. Theirs is a legacy that is easily overlooked, either because their records are few and incomplete, or because their material presence occurs as a series of impressions in yearbooks, course catalogs, or curricular materials that are not systematically preserved. Often, the lack of stable archival collections or coherent database records for WoC raise vital questions about how they could have influenced their institutions and the profession, when their careers were mobile, contingent, or dictated by mostly invisible work.[6] Even the discovery of stable archives and rich primary materials in rhetorical recovery and historiographic work does not assuage if, by privileging stability within the institutions that sponsor archives, historians recreate the systematic erasure of WoC.

In response to this problem, our first tendency as two historiographers dedicated to digital recovery is to rely on the semantic operations of the Web and, if we have coding experience, on the scraping of Web content using workflows derived from data science, trusting that the prevalence of metadata from library archives, governmental records, and scanned back-copies of journals makes it possible to search for traces of pedagogical influence on post-secondary education. We might do these things because we erringly trust that looking at the data impressions of originating texts is enough to overcome erasure. Indeed, as feminist historiographers working in the digital humanities, we are torn between the impulse to employ computational methods to help the institutional legacies of WoC emerge more clearly, and the recognition that seductive tendencies of big-data applications promise outcomes that are antithetical to anti-racist and feminist goals.[7]

In the same moments that we enjoy the affordances of large and providential data sweeps, other inferential moments become difficult to record, and yet these inferential moments form the basis of our theorizing. What is needed is a mechanism for noticing the uptake that better reflects the migration of women's intellectual capital through these inferences, as well as an understanding of how this capital can shift or be moved through different stages of digital historical inquiry in order to better serve WoC. While Moravec raises important questions about how to revive data-driven visualization so that it becomes a limning rather than a stabilizing methodology for feminist historians,[8] we look more closely at the re/constructability of data sets—both partially structured and unstructured—that operate within, without, and around the academic institution. We are interested in the "complex historical question of who gets counted" among potentially reductive data hierarchies that are often reinforced by our expectation that they convey scientific truth because we believe that the figures whose legacies suffer the greatest neglect are WoC in our own field. Thus, we interrogate the ways in which our tools can and cannot bring such inferences together for feminist theorizing.

Our beginning realization is simple and stark—common-use scholarly data tools cannot reproduce the relational complexity that feminist historiographies require, and thus cannot adequately overcome the neglect experienced by WoC whose legacies remain invisible in the face of institutional and bibliographic privileging of big data. It isn't simply *that* WoC lack representation in stable archives or are difficult to locate through digital metadata—these omissions are historically obvious—it's the ways in which WoC continue to be excluded by the privileging qualities of institutional data (i.e., key terms, concepts, implied open-data relationships), even as they become the subjects of ramped-up searching. We have learned not to assume WoC career paths were anything alike, or that they suffered the same disparities. We have learned to expect mobility and dynamism in their careers and to look for the privileging of power—to recognize how deeply power structures are embedded in how disciplinary data works. In sum, our digital historiographic recovery signals a tension between big-data methods and critiques of big data—between the privileging of disempowered subjects and the privileging of powerful operations that make discoverability difficult—and presents complex ethical considerations for feminist researchers, leading us to suggest three framing principles that guide our discussion in this chapter.

First, we acknowledge the inherent difficulties with fitting WoC legacy data into existing workflows given the citational politics and differential power structures still at work in data recovery methods, which become visible when we look through broad-based data tools for their unstated organizational and hierarchical assumptions.[9] We wrestle with our reliance on powerful tools to recoup the legacies of WoC, knowing those tools are constructed from exclusionary logics that "foreground" rather than "middle" and are based on outmoded notions of power.[10] Over a decade ago, Rawson urged scholars to examine the legacy of "gendered analysis" (*qua* Susan Jarratt) whose patterns have formed the feminist rhetorical canon, by queering their methodologies in these ways—looking more closely at the complexities of identifying "woman" as a foundational construct; recognizing that "feminist rhetorical normativity is systemic," even in feminist historiography that aims to unseat normative categories; and re-imagining feminist recovery work as work that "publicly supports a spectrum of gender rights and a variety of gender expressions."[11] Similarly, drawing on Kirsch's feminist query a decade prior, McKee and Porter asked feminist researchers to contend with the ethical demands of a rapidly shifting networked environment, creating new demands for "handl[ing] the politics of location, interpretation, and publication," elaborating on six "key qualities" that would characterize this new ethos.[12] Two qualities suggest a different relationship between feminist researchers and their online data—being more self-reflexive and critically conscious of the heteronormative assumptions carried in and through these data; and approaching data sets with expectations of transparency and fallibility, rather than scientistic affirmation. While these methodological and ethical conundrums are not new for feminist historical work, today's digital feminist ethic requires a vision of reciprocity that accounts for nuanced distinctions between and among recovery methods, recognizing narratives and counter-narratives in the data streams themselves. What Cifor and Wood call an "archival impulse" to reconsider the politics of "neutrality" in a time of prolific preservation and curation becomes a challenge to digital historians to value archival data points as collective, generative, and unstable.[13]

Second, we recognize the practicality of abandoning "big-data" approaches for what Heidorn, Stolley, and Ball et al. call "boutique-data" approaches,[14] and the possibility of mining data not for "scientistic representations of what *is* [or is not] there," but for possible indicators of what could be there.[15] Kennedy and Long call for new methods of analyzing publication data so as to apply richer description to how historians trace "the evolution of discrete texts" within larger data ecologies, focusing on "manageably sized" data sets that invite rhetorical analysis of more "subjective elements" than can typically be recognized through big-data analytics.[16] We, too, recognize the importance of prioritizing intricate moments in the circulation of mundane text objects (i.e., curriculum, administrative files, etc.) and non-object inferences (i.e., mentions, dedications, appearances, etc.), viewing each inference as "its own complex body of interconnected and situated data that allows [them] to reconstruct authorial processes."[17] Tracing the intellectual legacies of WoC within and outside of institutional databases requires focusing on these complexities—toggling between micro and macro analyses—"tacking in," as Royster and Kirsch would say, to inferential mentions of their work and their teaching in course catalogs, faculty yearbooks, and other institutional ephemera and "tacking out" to the processes of digital archival curation that do/not (or can/not) make such information retrievable at all.[18] Graban and Sullivan argue that digital knowledge economies are best rendered by accounting for the "variety of shifting approaches" to historiographic searching, aligning those shifts with historical motives and archival decision-making, and looking for evidence of those motives and that decision-making in archival metadata or para-data.[19] We agree, yet we recognize not only the absence of a single tool that can capture such paradata, but also the potentially flattening momentum of such a tool if it fails to make information pathways more visible.

Third, we acknowledge the paradoxical nature of using digital material processes to get at the immaterial, where "immaterial" describes the inferential appearances and mentions of WoC, in the absence of circulating artifacts that might tell us more about their careers. How can researchers piece together the intellectual legacies of WoC in the absence of concrete text objects to trace? Since the 2010 publication of *Rhetorica in Motion,* critical interest in the immaterial, the disjointed, and the in-between—in the *betweenness* of metadata—has become more prevalent in feminist historical work.[20] At the same time, Schell's cautionary suggestion in *Rhetorica in Motion*'s introduction to not only follow "well-laid tracks of feminist inquiry" still applies.[21] Even with available digital humanities methods, and even with increased attention to the relationship between digital humanities histories and methods and intersectional feminist critique, feminist researchers must still account for the normalizing impulses or mechanisms by which the gender and race of their archived subjects become obfuscated—often without concrete objects to trace, and often through the very same metadata that should be rendering them more accessible. As Gitelman suggests, new media "bodies" are agential whether they consist of Web-based artifacts or data sets, and are no less historically volatile and no more liberated from protocol than physically cataloged objects.[22] And as Cheney-Lippold suggests, data are not useful on their own, not only because data get delivered through often unknown or unseen algorithmic interpretations, but because large bodies of data are at best constellations of socially constructed identity statements that need to be unpacked.[23]

Tracing Systemic Absences through Factors of Exclusion, or Tracing to "Fail"

Having admitted the tension between big- and boutique-data approaches for correcting the underrepresentation of WoC in rhetorical studies, we explore that tension further by reporting the results of a "digital trace"—an experiment in which we investigated the institutional and disciplinary legacies of three lesser-known participants in college literacy programs whose careers we had already been researching when we discovered inferences of Smitherman's visit to FAMU—Mary Edna Brown (Instructor of English and Mathematics, Howard University); Sarah Nevelle Meriwether (Instructor of English, Howard University); and Leonea Barbour Dudley (Instructor of Public Speaking, Howard University; later Assistant Professor of English, Howard University, and Coppin State Teachers College).

We selected Brown, Meriwether, and Barbour Dudley because none of them has a long publication record or is easily traceable according to one type of privileged intellectual currency. As a result, the most "accessible" and "reliable" digital retrieval tools proved absolutely unreliable for their systemic recovery. Also, their records in more than one repository were prone to fairly common typographical or cataloging errors. To conduct our trace, we used commonly accessible tools requiring minimal training, including Wikipedia, ArchiveGrid, WorldCat, the HathiTrust library, the Internet Archive, the JSTOR database, and the Virtual International Authority File (VIAF), tending to the various ways that each tool did (not) deliver expected results, and noting where metadata were recalled in one tool but omitted from another. We demonstrate not only the omissions themselves, but the ways in which historiographers might familiarize themselves with the hegemonizing nature and functions of those omissions. We also break our own reliance on searching in broad sweeps for marginalized subjects, which we now understand to be a kind of historical inaction.

Following our three framing principles above, we were keen to avoid two habits. First, we wanted to avoid assuming that the mere digitization of obscure archival materials could overcome the principles of cumulative advantage that reinforce historical neglect in our field, especially if historians continue to trace the digital presence of WoC bibliometrically (privileging citationality of published objects across information platforms) rather than altmetrically (privileging the real-time interactions of data circulation and recirculation, between and across information platforms or disciplines).[24] Second, and somewhat conversely, we wanted to avoid the kind of reverse-privileging that can occur when digital archival recovery is used to justify the careers of WoC, explain their presence or absence through digital archival serendipity, or otherwise support the model minority myth.[25] Stable archives, with their richness and stability, are also marked with the history of colonialism in their inclusions and exclusions, and here is where the legacy of WoC is absent.[26] As Prince and Messina argue, one of the core challenges for Black scholars working in the digital humanities is the anti-Black sentiment built into predominantly White systems, fields, and institutions.[27] This includes the ways in which Black bodies and subjects have not been at the center of most algorithmic queries nor have they helped dictate how data should be organized and queried.[28] We contend that the archival representation of WoC in rhetoric, composition, and literacy studies has been flattened by digital histories that privilege publication over pedagogical data, and favor bibliographic methods,[29] ultimately making the field's legacy of Whiteness and normativity difficult to disrupt.[30]

To avoid these two habits, we opted to do what historiographers typically do not—we conducted our data experiments not to succeed, *but to show failure.* We did so, first, to indicate where the failures occur if and when we approach these tools with deterministic expectations, and second, to become sensitized to how feminist scholars can better read the absences and gaps between data records, data expectations, and data reliances that these failures imply—how they can build from instability and imagine new linkages among inferential data points.[31] Our trace was guided by several core principles underlying D'Ignazio's and Klein's "data feminism," a term that accounts for an intersectional approach to studying power in data representation, including "how . . . differentials of power can be challenged and changed using data."[32] For D'Ignazio and Klein, data feminism brings into focus the disciplinary "matrix of domination" that privileges certain types of records over others—for example, published articles and books over course syllabi or administrative memos—and the long history of what records were kept and what labor was valued.[33] Furthermore, it offers scholars a way to elide the power structures embedded in the tools they use even to emancipate feminist data points. While not a new concept or even a singularity, "data feminism" helps ground our work in the very tensions that occur when this intoxication of data meets the realities of the discriminatory and exclusionary logics embedded within—"a way of thinking about data, both their uses and their limits, that is informed by direct experience, by a commitment to action, and by intersectional feminist thought."[34] In order to demonstrate these principles, we traced our subjects individually and prosopographically (see Appendix Table 10.3).[35]

Furthermore, to better assess the possible treatment that figures like these might receive, we traced a "control group" of two additional subjects whose searches yield more systematic results even as their records show factors we might contribute to digital historical amnesia (see Appendix Table 10.4): Hallie Quinn Brown (Professor of Elocution, Wilberforce University;

Dean, Allen University); and the late Marianna White Davis (Professor of English, Benedict College; NCTE's first African-American President). We consider these subjects "digitally stable" because their searches produce more consistent results in common metadata and linked open-data tools, usually a result of their publication records, municipal collaborations, or instruction, service, and administration at well-resourced (or traditional) academic institutions. At the same time, we recognize the practical ways in which the nature and kind of information that becomes digitally foregrounded as a result of what is or is not accessible, contributes to another kind of historical erasure.[36]

Finally, we traced for a series of factors that typically obscure historians' ability to determine the intellectual reach of each of our subjects through linked-open data (LOD) (see Appendix Table 10.5).[37] To enrich and enliven these "failures," we limn the characteristics of databases and digital archives that obscure and neglect, even as they claim to reveal. We provide snapshots of incremental searching methods in order to help readers envision the complex im/material entanglements that require care and curation when engaging with data-bound subjects.[38] Ultimately, we argue for the importance of careful, contextual incorporation of data feminism into digital recovery projects, while highlighting the potentials and the difficulties of recovering WoC in rhetorical studies.

Tracing Individually to Examine and Challenge Power

Brown and Meriwether have scant archival records, but we know that Brown graduated valedictorian with her AB from Howard before 1913, earned an MA from Oberlin College the following year, and joined the faculty from 1914 until her death in 1919, teaching as "Edna Brown Coleman," having recently married.[39] As a student at Howard, she helped found the Delta Sigma Theta sorority. In 1918, she served with the American Red Cross. She died in childbirth at the age of 24. Meriwether earned her AB in English and History from Howard University in 1910, earned an additional degree from Miner Normal School in 1912, then taught English and History at Dunbar High School in Washington, DC and taught at Howard University until marrying and moving away in 1920. Comparably more data records are available for Barbour Dudley, albeit under various spellings of her name, though the records offer little detail. After graduating from Howard, Barbour Dudley joined the faculty as an instructor of public speaking, later earning a PhD from Cornell and teaching at Coppin State Teachers College in Baltimore.

Two data feminist principles we find useful for this task are examining how power is embedded in our data and databases and challenging those power structures by investigating how the makers of data-gathering tools do (not) contribute to the systematic flattening of whole populations. Data tools carry assumptions that are homogeneous, derived from patriarchal perspectives, and capable of recreating hegemonic oppression.[40] Our three figures are difficult to trace because they are not always reflected in formal, searchable metadata records, therefore common Web-based tools cannot always bring them to light.

For example, in Table 10.1, Mary Edna Brown is digitally represented in 27 entries, including profiles in the Howard University alumni, faculty and staff, and student catalogs available through the HathiTrust repository. Her name appears alongside that of her husband, Lieutenant Frank Charles Coleman (formerly a professor of physics at Howard U), in a wedding announcement in the May 26, 1918, edition of the *Washington Post*. She appears in the Howard faculty yearbook once more in 1919, yet her university records end with her death in childbirth in September 1919, and thus her pedagogical and intellectual achievements are largely preserved in scattered (un-indexed) references within a handful of digitized catalogs available through the HathiTrust.

Sarah Nevelle Meriwether is digitally represented through scattered records at Howard University and Dunbar High School in Washington DC, which can be found through HathiTrust in course catalogs, alumni records, and faculty and staff lists. Her career is mentioned in Wikipedia, including her co-founding of the Alpha Kappa Alpha sorority, and following her movements from Washington, DC, to West Virginia, as well as her post-academic work in public advocacy and her nonprofit service with the NAACP and other local organizations.[41] While there are metadata records of archival materials at Penn State University, the artifacts themselves are not available digitally.

Leonea Barbour Dudley appears as a subject in 11 digitized faculty yearbooks locatable on HathiTrust and the Internet Archive, including Howard University, Columbia University, and Coppin State Teachers College, signaling a career that extended from at least 1920 to at least 1960. Aside from her dissertation's availability in three repositories, three items of her correspondence with W. E. B. Du Bois are in collections at the University of Massachusetts at Amherst, and she appears in course catalogs for Howard University, as an instructor in "Rhetoric and Oratory," and in Walter Dyson's 1941 publication of *Howard University, The Capstone of Negro Education, A History: 1867–1940*, as personnel in "Public Speaking" since 1929.[42] Yet, searching for her by name in any three tools at a time does not yield consistent results, or match that number of results.

The results we yielded in Table 10.1 are unsurprising but compelling when reported alongside the affordances of other WoC. These brief impressions suggest that their work is largely inferred by *what might have been* and *what might be indicated* within other materials that aren't digitized, or digitized but not linked to other centralized archival records. Just as we recognize where Hallie Q. Brown's textbooks are *not* referenced or historicized, we are interested in the factors determining where our three figures are *not* represented or are *mis*-represented. Digital researchers know well the random nature of semantic searching in tools such as HathiTrust, where the repository is limited by the holdings of its participating institutions—although, once digitized, all content becomes available as metadata—and the Internet Archive, whose digitized content is not synonymous with metadata. On HathiTrust, even searches that yield positive results can point toward documents that are unavailable in full-text, owing to their archival status, the quality of their digitization, or because a key term that is locatable within one scanned document yields inconsistent results when searching across documents within the broader corpus. On the other hand, the Internet Archive often makes full texts available, but lacks the rich, searchable metadata records that can facilitate the quick and efficient location of names. In short, these results reveal how our work with historical metadata occurs at the convergence of technological delivery and curatorial logics, or "techno-logics," and thus reminds us that our digital archival trusts are more tied to technological imaginaries dictated by existing disciplinary landscapes than to scientific realities—they are more dependent upon the narrative qualities of constructed data sets than on the assumption that there is such a thing as "race-blind" raw data.[43]

Two such techno-logics became clear after conducting individual searches. First, searching for Brown, Meriwether, and Barbour Dudley under their available nomenclatures did not yield accurate results if we had not already identified specific texts in which to perform our search, in part because digitized records are keyword-inefficient if they have not been prepared as readable documents or contextualized with detailed metadata. Second, scholarly publication is an academic currency that not only has real implications for lived experiences and represents particular power arrangements within the discipline, it also controls other layers of archived metadata.[44] These techno-logics can provide a way to challenge disciplinary expectations if we know where they reside. For example, Figure 10.2 visualizes a total

Table 10.1. Detailed set of findings after tracing our five subjects individually across six data tools

NAME	JSTOR	HATHITRUST	WIKIPEDIA	VIAF	INSTITUTIONAL ARCHIVES (ARCHIVES GRID, DPLA, WORLDCAT)	JSTOR DFR	TOTAL BY FIGURE
Leonea Barbour Dudley	0	6	0	0	3	3	12
Mary Edna Brown (Coleman)	0	27	0	0	1	2	30
Sarah Nevelle Meriwether (Nutter)	0	13	1	0	1	3	18
Hallie Q. Brown	313	1185	1	1	2	2887	4389
Marianna White Davis	143	341	0	1	7	160	652
Total by Source	456	1572	2	2	14	3055	5101

Note. This table displays the raw count of records found by observing the subjects' names and known variations such as Q. and Quinn, inclusions of married names, known abbreviations, and known misspellings. Our initial trace offers perspectives into the mutable roles or types of intellectual labor that WoC represent within the dataset and, moreover, how different data tools might mark (or value) their roles or that labor.

records count for each figure within three of our six source locations, and Figure 10.3 portrays the material problems with locating some women at all given the metadata limitations of the Google Books corpus. Such visualizations allow us to observe, at a glance, where Brown (Coleman), Meriwether, and Barbour Dudley do (not) occur as distinct data points in respect to their sisters in the discipline, and perhaps how they are represented in those tools/documents (i.e., as authors, pedagogues, coauthors, etc.).

Tracing Prosopographically to Rethink Binaries & Embrace Pluralism

The next phase of our trace—tracing prosopographically—required that we investigate linked open data (LOD) and cluster relationships between all five subjects. Two data feminist principles we found useful for this prosopographic trace are rethinking the tractable, administrative, performative, and paradoxical binaries and invisible hierarchies in a particular suite of tools; and embracing pluralism in one's data sets by synthesizing traditional with

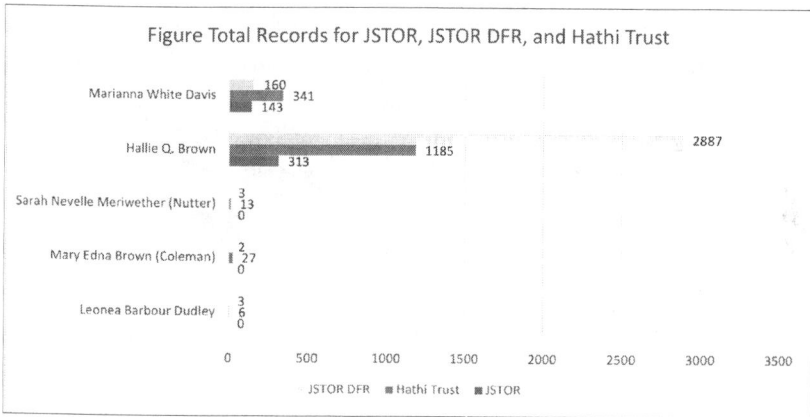

FIGURE 10.2. Total number of records found per figure in JSTOR's DfR, Hathi-Trust, and JSTOR. This figure stacks the total number of records found per figure in JSTOR's Data for Research (DfR), HathiTrust, and JSTOR. It offers a comparison of total metadata records found when searching for names and variations of names, including misspellings, abbreviations, and married names, providing an initial visual indication of what types of records can be found in our sweeps and the locations of those records.

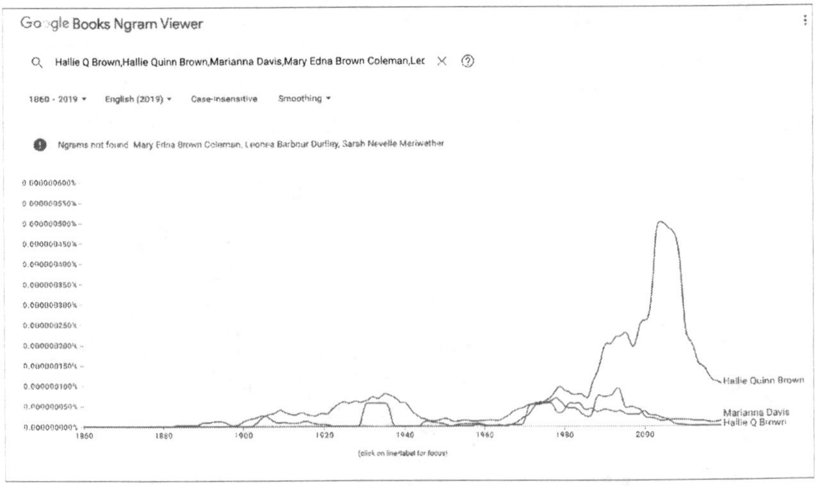

FIGURE 10.3. Google Books Ngram Viewer graph. This graph from Google Books Ngram Viewer demonstrates the limitations of how metadata functions. The orthostatic appearances and reappearances of Hallie Q. Brown after 1900 are unsurprising given her public works and their secondary representation in well-circulating anthologies and biographies, but a closer examination of each spike on the Ngram reveals how Google Books searches are prone to deliver irrelevancies.[45] Most of the references to Marianna Davis incorrectly point to a different person or are generated by an unrelated two-word phrase ("Jules Marianna, Davis Miles"). In addition, while Barbour Dudley, Meriwether, and Brown (Coleman) are represented in OCR texts that have been digitized as part of the Google Books corpus, that character recognition does not translate into searchability within the corpus, or visibility in the Ngram. In sum, the Ngram's part-of-speech tagging proved detrimental to our goal of locating accurate records.

non-traditional sources.[46] The following table and figures bring into deeper relief the lack of stable archival representation for Brown, Meriwether, and Barbour Dudley owing to their exclusion from traditional archives and privileged activities as we have outlined them above. Of note, and for our particular purposes, "embracing pluralism" involved looking for sites of *occlusion,* i.e., drawing attention to where some data points obscured other potentially important features.

Table 10.2 articulates the error types that occluded more often than they limned the women we sought. Matrimonial name changes, concatenated

Table 10.2. Seven different error types encountered across all our tools

NAME	ALT SPELLING OR SPELLING ERROR	MATRIMONIAL NAME CHANGE	ABBREV.	CODING ERROR	MISSING METADATA	OCR ERROR	FALSE POSITIVE
Hallie Q. Brown	Quinn; Quin	N/A	N/A	Has metadata; no text	Text coded; not in database	Concatenated entries	Hallie Q. Brown Memorial Library; Hallie Q. Brown Community Center
Marianna (White) Davis	N/A	Davis	N/A	Has metadata; no text	Text coded; not in database	N/A	Marianna v. Davis court case
Mary Edna (Brown) Coleman	N/A	Coleman; Mrs. Frank Coleman	E.B.	In scanned object; uncoded	Text coded; not in database	Concatenated entries	Common name

Table 10.2. Seven different error types encountered across all our tools *(continued)*

NAME	ALT SPELLING OR SPELLING ERROR	MATRIMONIAL NAME CHANGE	ABBREV.	CODING ERROR	MISSING METADATA	OCR ERROR	FALSE POSITIVE
Leonea Barbour Dudley	Barber; Barbor; Leona; Leone	N/A	B.	In scanned object; uncoded	Text coded; not in database	Concatenated entries; "dirty" OCR error	N/A
Sarah Nevelle (Meriwether) Nutter	Neville; Sarah Meriwether Nutter; Meriwhether; Meriweather	Nutter	N/A	In scanned object; uncoded	Text coded; not in database	Concatenated entries; "dirty" OCR error	Different person

Note. Uncoded = the woman's name is present in a scanned object but not searchable/readable as text, while "missing metadata" means the scanned object is searchable or text-readable, but the woman's name does not appear in a metadata record. N/A = insufficient metadata to determine.

entries, typesetting errors, and errors in optical-character recognition (OCR)—including misread scans—frustrated our searches the most. (See Appendix Table 10.5 for a finer representation of the presences and absences of error types.) Although we report the names separately, we conducted a "group sweep" of our five figures across the Google Books archive, yielding a weighted count of how many times each figure appears in different specific publications, and whether she appears as primary author or secondary subject.

From this initial trace we learned that the act of recovering individual "hidden figures" proved less insightful than tracing clusters of underrepresented women in groups. Individual tracing assumes a stable archival record, a problematic assumption for under-resourced institutions that cannot donate large sets of materials to digital repositories, or cannot themselves host processed collections or employ enough librarians or archivists to catalog the data. Furthermore, inconsistencies in the historical record often act as "errors" when records are read discretely, but when read together, those same inconsistencies enabled us to draw tentative assumptions about why some nomenclatures experienced greater circulation than others. Thus, as we traced, we treated variations in spellings, abbreviations, birth names and married names as if they referred to distinct identities before treating them together as a data stack.[47] The "stacks" principle reminds us that we can conceive of an "archive" as a nexus of activities and motives that highlight non-obvious relationships between even obscure metadata.[48] It also demonstrates the inadequacy of database tools to document women in relational networks, given the inherent necessity of first siloing women's data points in order to make them more searchable.

Orienting our trace towards stack relationships isn't driven by a need to determine with finality how and when WoC's paths overlapped, but to learn what WoC might have in common in terms of where universal search tools have failed them. For example, Figure 10.4 indicates one view of an ideal set of relationships, with each figure identified by a set of "triples," a principle underlying the syntactical organization of many digital tools, that should be discoverable through metadata searching, but ultimately isn't available without a mechanism for recognizing those relationships. Where Graban argues for viewing digital historiographic relationships as "networked data performances,"[49] and where proponents of historical altmetrics empower us to recognize data points as circulating, rather than fixed,[50] we consider how these perspectives could deepen our engagement with bodies of information beyond the bibliographic citation for measuring the intellectual impact of a WoC's work.

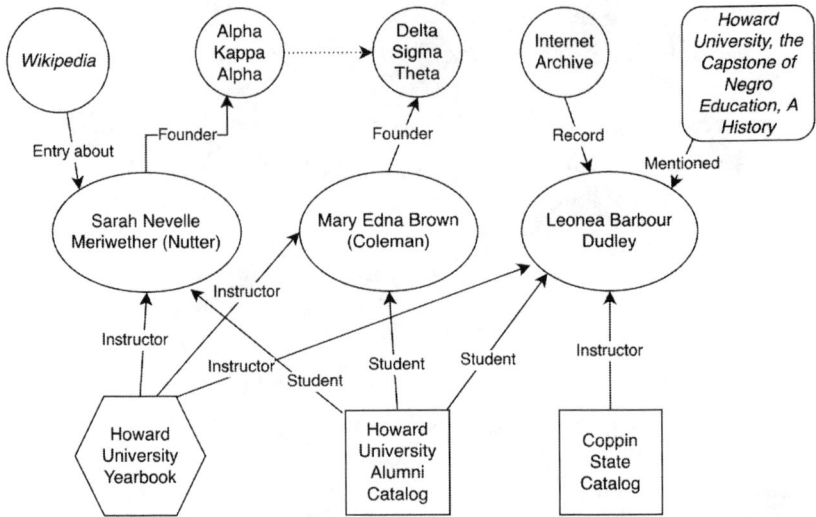

FIGURE 10.4. Linked Open Data relationships. This paradata assemblage visualizes how Linked Open Data (LOD) relationships could look for our three women under investigation. The information points displayed here *could* connect our three pedagogues across digital spaces, if easy-access digital tools were to operate according to less siloed principles. Of course, data representation is not a neutral act, even when it reveals a cross-pollination of occluding factors.

Both approaches to our trace revealed a triple conundrum. Tracing our three subjects individually across meta-search tools yielded fewer and less consistent results than if we traced them in individual publications or repositories, in spite of the vast reach of the universal search tools. Yet, to conduct a successful individual search, one would need prior knowledge of when and where they could be traced. While tracing our subjects prosopographically with a control group did yield more ways that they might be queried through metadata, five out of our six available tools still operate on the basis of bibliography or genealogy, i.e., privileging authorship and institutional reputation, even though they attempt to mark performances and inferences, and not just circulating text objects or material ephemera. Furthermore, while we yielded more accurate results with smaller, boutique, or more heavily curated networking tools whose LOD functions require human labor to remain current and expansive (e.g., social networks and archival context), we are aware that all liberatory contemporary technologies can be constrained by archival attitudes if those attitudes are rooted in positivist expectations.

These "failures" cause us to recommend alternative ways of tracing residual inheritance and knowledge economies that focus on the interstitial relationships suggested by or drawn between data and metadata to infer and visualize complex relationships and intellectual lives[51]—to rethink the spaces between figures, practices, and artifacts within the digital archive in order to better recognize the partial perspectives and marked occlusions offering impressions of figures that would otherwise be unavailable. By employing the "spaces between" metaphor to our "failed" traces for Brown, Meriwether and Barbour Dudley, we signal the importance of looking inferentially at the "not-figures, not-practices, and not-artifacts that are still located within the archival space though not identified as archived."[52]

Like Risam, we look to the so-called democratizing potential of open-access tools for lingering inequalities over how information is governed—factors that cause the digital cultural record to remain "shaped by tensions between freedom and restraint, openness and impenetrability, and noninterference and control."[53] Although our project does not trace postcolonized subjects whose identities fall along particular axes of class, nation, sexuality, and disability, we heed Risam's call to interrogate the expectations around historical scholarly genealogies that constitute digital work in any field. The politics of mis/representation driving our field's her-stories and re-stories can still be observed.

Making Historical Labors Visible

In the Preamble, we signaled our desire to help historiographers familiarize themselves with the hegemonizing nature of omissions in large-scale data sets by recommending alternative attitudes and approaches. A different kind of intellectual engagement is needed in order to problematize the cache of teachers, mentors, and administrators whose careers are reflected in interstitial metadata more reliably than in cataloged data. A different kind of intellectual engagement is needed to draw attention to the Bernice Reeveses of historic disciplinary conversations, or to measure the influence of out-of-print teaching texts composed by better known figures, such as Hallie Q. Brown's *Bits and Odds* and *First Lessons*—and moreover, to document and value these bits of information as equally meaningful landmarks in a moveable history of rhetorical traditions, figures, and methods, with or without the presence of stable artifacts. We offer one final recommendation, in concert with one final data feminist principle: making visible all the labors—digital, analog, affective, ideological—that contribute to the encoding of values in any data set.[54]

This visibility requires two actions in turn—imagining a role for digital curation that extends beyond the ethics of archival post-custodianship; and resisting digital closure.[55] Not even a commitment to post-custodial archival practices ensures fair representation of WoC. Much like Bordalejo exposes inequities in the gendered characteristics of dominant ideas in the digital humanities,[56] and much like Carbajal exposes inequities and hegemonic debts in the metadata produced by Indigenous stakeholders,[57] we suggest re-imagining LOD's potentialities and promises when guiding feminist digital historiography in our field. In spite of LOD's known affordances, relational networks are not devoid of hegemonizing functions. Our discussions above offer some evidence that LOD relationships can lead historiographers to make universalizing assumptions about social and intellectual movements, in turn creating a kind of historical in-action. Universalizing assumptions may be a necessary first step in network construction, but those assumptions should disrupt, rather than reinforce, relational typologies.

While data feminism offers a set of tenets to highlight the biases and inequities in researchers' use of data and data-seeking tools, there is still more work to be done to actively question the basic rhetorical and feminist tensions of working with intersectional data.[58] There is still much to trouble in the flattening moves that are necessary for abstracting human subjects into data for the purposes of storage and analysis. Like the paradata assemblage in Figure 10.4, we consider the locationality or locate-ability of a WoC, rather than her static positioning or placement, understanding "locations"—and, hence, influence and genealogy—as always already mobile constructs. Thus, we caution historians from relying too much on stable collections to determine representation of WoC subjects or relying too much on networks that are built around weighted centers, suggesting instead the utility of network relationships that operate on principles of dis-jointment.[59] We further caution historians from enabling relationships that mask institutional privilege based on the individualized nature of the academic genealogy, a mythos we think still needs to be troubled in order to more effectively recover WoC. Finally, while there is great potential in building and visualizing relational networks that draw from multiple sources of data, we suggest that historians' queries and visualizations should reach beyond not only the institutional structures that have historically been entrusted with their custodianship, but also the re/construction of simple relational networks that mimic the bibliometric factor-mapping used to measure the academic value of citations and citationality.[60] Beyond asking where artifacts were created, who created them, what repositories contain them, and what finding aids and indexes mark their metadata, we suggest asking an additional set of questions:

- Where else can they be found and under what circumstances or specific conditions?
- How do historians' own movements and queries influence those circumstances and conditions?
- What common motives guide those movements and queries?
- How does the mobility of WoC's careers align or not align with how historians currently conceptualize the field?

Rhetorical historiography invites opening up the past, and its formation of the present, to critical examination—specifically to direct attention towards the spaces in-between digital records and the materials left behind those formations. By examining how the pedagogical and metadata records of Brown, Meriwether, and Barbour Dudley disappear or reappear in the interstices, we encourage feminist historians who work digitally to look for ways to re-theorize. We hope they might decenter their publication-based epistemologies, critique core assumptions about what makes reliable archival "records," and recognize those LOD relationships that signal interruption and disruption in the preservation of legacies of WoC in the field. Ultimately, we encourage greater cognizance of patterns in the construction of archives and canons that systematically recreate normative structures of knowledge and access, shaping what and who counts through what is included in knowledge structures.[61] To echo Browdy, in calling for a dedicated subfield in Black Women's Rhetorics, we know that the contributions of all historical figures to Rhetoric and Composition are "undeniable, their works are unforgettable, what [we] learn from them is/was useful in [our] pursuit of understanding this field . . . , and yet, [we're] still left longing for more."[62]

APPENDIX

Starts on following page.

Table 10.3. Individual and prosopographic tracing

NAME	JSTOR SUBJECT	JSTOR AUTHOR	JSTOR DFR	HATHI TRUST	WIKIPEDIA	VIAF	INSTITUTIONAL ARCHIVES (VIA WORLDCAT AND ARCHIVEGRID)
Leonea Barbour Dudley	2	0	0	6	N/A	N/A	As "Leonea B. Dudley" (Howard University, R. Louise Burge Collection)
Leonea B. Dudley	3	0	3	27	N/A	N/A	Howard University (R. Louise Burge Collection); U Mass Amherst (W. E. B. DuBois Papers)
Mary Edna Brown	0	0	I	35	N/A	N/A	Founder, Alpha Kappa Alpha Sorority

Name						
Mary Edna Brown Coleman	o	o	o	2	N/A	N/A	Founder, Delta Sigma Theta Sorority
Sarah Nevelle Meriwether	3	o	o	13	As "Sarah Meriwether Nutter"	N/A	As "Sarah Meriwether Nutter" (Penn State University, Marian Anderson Papers)
Sarah Meriwether Nutter	o	o	o	11	"Sarah Meriwether Nutter"	N/A	Penn State University (Marian Anderson Papers)

10.4. Records, locations, and metadata types

NAME	JSTOR SUBJECT	JSTOR AUTHOR	JSTOR DFR	HATHI TRUST	WIKIPEDIA	VIAF	INSTITUTIONAL ARCHIVES
Hallie Q. Brown	202	1	3135	2971	"Hallie Quinn Brown"	Yes	Central State University; Hallie Q. Brown Community Center; Wilberforce University
Hallie Quinn Brown	126	0	252	509	Yes	Yes	Yes
Marianna White Davis	18	1	26	50	No	Yes	NCTE
Marianna W. Davis	139	10	149	297	No	Yes	South Carolina State U; University of South Carolina; Benedict College; Boston University; SC State Human Affairs Commission Bicentennial Project Editorial Board; College of Charleston (Septima P. Clark Papers; and William "Bill" Saunders Papers)

JSTOR ARTICLE	JSTOR CHAP-TER	JSTOR BOOK	JSTOR NEWS	JSTOR OTHER	HATHI SERIAL	HATHI BOOK	HATHI THESIS	HATHI JOURNAL	HATHI DIREC-TORY	HATHI OTHER
140	171	8	2813	3	1833	1138	N/A	932	472	474
113	108	1	27	3	130	379	N/A	109	3	190
17	9	N/A	N/A	N/A	29	21	N/A	19	N/A	14
137	10	1	N/A	N/A	190	107	N/A	169	17	51

10.4. Records, locations, and metadata types *(continued)*

NAME	JSTOR SUBJECT	JSTOR AUTHOR	JSTOR DFR	HATHI TRUST	WIKIPEDIA	VIAF	INSTITUTIONAL ARCHIVES
Leonea Barbour Dudley	2	o	o	6	No	No	No
Leonea B. Dudley	3	o	o	27	No	No	Howard University (R. Louise Burges Collection)
Mary Edna Brown	o	o	1	35	No	No	No
Mary Edna Brown Coleman	o	o	o	2	No	No	No
Sarah Nevelle Meriwether	3	o	o	13	"Sarah Meriwether Nutter"	No	Penn State University (Marian Anderson Papers)
Sarah Meriwether Nutter	o	o	o	11	Yes	No	No

JSTOR ARTICLE	JSTOR CHAPTER	JSTOR BOOK	JSTOR NEWS	JSTOR OTHER	HATHI SERIAL	HATHI BOOK	HATHI THESIS	HATHI JOURNAL	HATHI DIRECTORY	HATHI OTHER
N/A	N/A	N/A	N/A	N/A	4	2	2	2	2	0
N/A	N/A	N/A	3	N/A	25	2	N/A	24	6	0
N/A	N/A	N/A	1	N/A	30	5	N/A	22	2	2
N/A	N/A	N/A	N/A	N/A	2	N/A	N/A	2	N/A	0
N/A	N/A	N/A	N/A	N/A	13	N/A	N/A	9	N/A	0
N/A	N/A	N/A	N/A	N/A	4	7	N/A	4	N/A	2

Note. Table 10.4 illustrates records, locations, and metadata types, including alternative findings and errors. The "Hathi Other" category includes results with the following HathiTrust metadata tags: Biography, Encyclopedia, Dictionary, Conference, Statistics, Manuscript, Microform, Newspaper, CDRom, Video, Photographs and Pictorial Work. A numerical 0 indicates no records were returned in a JSTOR search. "N/A" indicates no marked metadata entries under that record type, and thus they weren't counted in our data sweep.

Table 10.5. Contributing factors to invisibility (or obscured visibility) of traced figures

NAME	HATHITRUST DOCUMENT (FULL TEXT)	HATHITRUST METADATA	JSTOR METADATA	JSTOR ARTICLE	JSTOR NEWS	GOOGLE BOOKS NGRAM	WIKIPEDIA	VIAF	INTERNET ARCHIVE	INSTITUTIONAL ARCHIVES	ORGANIZATION RECORDS
Visibility											
Hallie Q. Brown	Directory: alumni, faculty, organization; Biographies; Organizational records; Authorship; book	Volume	2838 total documents	Book review of work; Subject of history; Indexed in history	Indexed as subject	Appears as subject and author	Well documented page	Has entry	Records about; Index to periodicals; Book	Archival materials at Central State University	NAACP records; Hallie Q. Brown Community Center
Invisibility											
	Organizations: St. Paul city records; Hallie Q. Brown Community Center	N/A	References to Hallie Q. Brown named institutions — center, libraries, etc.	Primary authorship	Named community center	Subject and author mixed	Community center	Memorial library	Community center; references to	Archive at Hallie Q. Brown Community Center	N/A

Subject		Source 1	Source 2	Source 3	Source 4	Source 5	Source 6	Source 7	Source 8	Source 9	Source 10
Marianna (White) Davis	**Visibility**	Catalog; Directory; Editorship; Article	Author of article; subject of article	118 articles; 11 primary authorships; 10 chapters	11 authored articles	7 indexed appearances	Appears as subject	N/A	Has entry	Editorship	Archival materials at South Carolina State Univ., Boston Univ., Benedict College	NCTE Records as office holder; Black history tele-conference
	Invisibility	Different figure, same name; Placename; Court case	Same name, different figure; Citation in book; Possible inclusion in bibliography	Marked within proceedings	10 chapters marked without details	Difficult to parse text	N/A	No page; Same name, Different figure	N/A	Court case Marianna V. Davis	Reference indexed, no record	N/A
Mary Edna Brown Coleman	**Visibility**	Death notice	N/A	Marked name	N/A	1 newspaper mention	N/A	On Delta Sigma Theta founders page	N/A	Catalog	N/A	Mention in Delta Sigma Theta sorority
	Invisibility	Same name, different figure; Mrs. Frank Coleman	Same name, different figure	Different figure, same name	0 records	Different figure, same name	0 records	0 individual records	0 records	No metadata records; Similar name	0 records	N/A

Table 10.5. Contributing factors to invisibility (or obscured visibility) of traced figures *(continued)*

NAME	HATHITRUST DOCUMENT (FULL TEXT)	HATHITRUST METADATA	JSTOR METADATA	JSTOR ARTICLE	JSTOR NEWS	GOOGLE BOOKS NGRAM	WIKIPEDIA	VIAF	INTERNET ARCHIVE	INSTITUTIONAL ARCHIVES	ORGANIZATION RECORDS
Mary Edna Brown Coleman, as Mary Edna Brown	**Visibility**										
	Faculty and student catalog, directory	N/A	N/A	N/A	N/A	N/A	N/A	N/A	N/A	N/A	N/A
	Invisibility										
	N/A	N/A	N/A	N/A	N/A	N/A	N/A	N/A	N/A	N/A	N/A
Leonea Barbour Dudley	**Visibility**										
	Faculty catalog	Thesis record	3 records	N/A	3 records	N/A	N/A	N/A	Catalog	Archival materials at Howard University	National Association of Teachers Speech
	Invisibility										
	N/A	Same name, different figure; Archival record without detail	Difficult to parse newspaper	o records	N/A	o records	o record	o records	o metadata records	o publicly available archival materials	N/A

Figure										
Leonea Barbour Dudley as Leonea B. Dudley	**Visibility**	Faculty directory	Article author, catalog	N/A	N/A	N/A	N/A	N/A	N/A	N/A
	Invisibility	N/A	N/A	N/A	N/A	N/A	N/A	N/A	N/A	N/A
Sarah Nevelle Meriweather Nutter	**Visibility**	As Sarah Nevelle Meriweather in faculty catalog	N/A	N/A	N/A	N/A	N/A	Catalog	Archival materials at Penn State U	NAACP of West Virginia; Alpha Kappa Alpha sorority
	Invisibility	Sarah Nevelle Meriwether in OCR error	o records	o records	o records	o records	o records	o metadata records	Not digitally available	N/A

Note. Table 10.5 details some factors contributing to the invisibility (or obscured visibility) of our five traced figures, including our three principal subjects and two "controls," arranged by tool or source type (e.g., HathiTrust scanned objects, HathiTrust metadata records, JSTOR articles, JSTOR newspapers, etc.). N/A = indicates insufficient results to determine visibility or invisibility.

NOTES

1. Martin Luther King Jr., etc. v. Ann Arbor Sch. Dist., 473 F. Supp. 1371 (E.D. Mich. 1979).
2. Amy L. Woolridge, "Black Linguist Wins Few FAMU Converts," *The FAMUAN*, November 29, 1979, http://purl.flvc.org/famu/fd/AMDT367745.
3. Woolridge, "Black Linguist."
4. Sullivan, "Inspecting Shadows," 370.
5. Frustratingly, we could not reproduce our initial search to arrive at this record twice, a circumstance that speaks to the need for central metadata records to link together FAMU's disparate preservation efforts. This need is symptomatic of a greater problem caused by the devaluing or underfunding of HBCUs as sites for establishing substantial institutional and disciplinary archives.
6. Risam, "Beyond the Margins," http://www.digitalhumanities.org//dhq/vol/9/2/000208/000208.html; Moravec, "Feminist Research"; Losh and Wernimont, *Bodies of Information*.
7. Schell, Introduction; Ball, Graban, and Sidler, "The Boutique"; Kulak, "Ethics."
8. Michelle Moravec, "Beyond Citations: The Historian's Altmetrics," *The Politics of Women's Culture*, July 22, 2015, http://politicsofwomensculture.michellemoravec.com/uncategorized/beyond-citations-the-historians-altmetrics/.
9. Cifor and Wood, "Critical Feminism," *Journal of Critical Library and Information Studies* 1, no. 2 (2017), https://doi.org/10.24242/jclis.v1i2.27.
10. Graban and Sullivan, "New Rhetorics," 189–190. "Middling" refers to the practice of searching for underrepresented disciplinary activity in the spaces between static records (i.e., searching for evidence of women's intellectual contributions in circulation).
11. Rawson, "Queering," 40, 42, 47. Our trace may frustrate Rawson's argument, as it is not fully liberated from "cultural constructions and productions of gender" (Rawson, 46). At the same time, most bibliographic and archival data is marked for gender, in normative ways or by following normative assumptions, which, we argue, require disruption before (or alongside) other methods of canonization.
12. McKee and Porter, "Rhetorica Online," 153, 155.
13. Cifor and Wood, "Critical Feminism," 8, https://doi.org/10.24242/jclis.v1i2.27.
14. Here, "boutique" describes approaches to valuating and managing narrower, specialized, or niche data sets and queries.
15. Heidorn, "Shedding Light"; Stolley, "An API of Motives"; Ball, Graban, and Sidler, "The Boutique," 200, 202.
16. Kennedy and Long, "The Trees," 142, 148.
17. Kennedy and Long, "The Trees," 143.
18. Royster and Kirsch, *Feminist Rhetorical Practices*, 75.
19. Graban and Sullivan, "New Rhetorics."
20. Solberg, "Googling"; Graban, "From Location(s)"; Moravec, "Beyond Citations"; Graban and Sullivan, "New Rhetorics"; Rivard, "Turning Archives"; Van Haitsma, "Between Archival Absence."
21. Schell, Introduction, 16.
22. Gitelman, *Always*, 7.
23. Cheney-Lippold, *We Are Data*, 34, 46.
24. Bibliometrics privilege surname searches, official programs or bulletins, and published scholarship rather than exploring alternative genres or trying to assess the

genres' circulation or influence. By contrast, altmetric activity supports the understanding that a subject's importance (including the historian's) becomes assessed according to "how [it] is embedded in a network of social relationships." (See Priem et al., "altmetrics: a manifesto," October 26, 2010), https://digitalcommons.unl .edu/cgi/viewcontent.cgi?article=1187&context=scholcom; Bollen, Van de Sompel, and Rodriguez, "Towards Usage-Based Impact Metrics," 236.

25. Digital archival serendipity is often a byproduct of a particular institution's Special Collections mission and can be closely tied to an already implied academic genealogy.

26. Risam, *New Digital Worlds*, 48.

27. Prince and Messina, "Black Digital Humanities," par. 3, https://digitalhumanities .org/dhq/vol/16/3/000645/000645.html.

28. Cheney-Lippold, *We Are Data*, 46; Bordalejo, "Minority Report"; Noble, *Algorithms*.

29. Mueller, *Network Sense*; Moravec, "Beyond Citations"; Roemer and Borchardt, "From Bibliometrics."

30. Rawson, "Queering," 40.

31. Risam, "Beyond the Margins," par. 19, http://www.digitalhumanities.org//dhq/ vol/9/2/000208/000208.html.

32. D'Ignazio and Klein, "The Power Chapter," *Data Feminism*.

33. D'Ignazio and Klein, "Introduction," *Data Feminism*.

34. D'Ignazio and Klein, "Introduction," *Data Feminism*. The original seven principles have been adapted to a newer five-part intersectional approach, now guiding work carried out by the Data + Feminism Lab at MIT, which "uses data and computational methods to work toward gender and racial justice, particularly as they related to space and place." (See https://dataplusfeminism.mit.edu/.)

35. This approach is adapted from collective biography and extended toward digital historical methods that analyze corpora for the various commonalities that identify feminist subjects as individual persons linked by and through various social configurations. (See Stone, "Prosopography"; Flanders et al., "Feminist Literary History"; Hedley and Kooistra, "Prototyping.")

36. For example, while Hallie Q. Brown enjoys a comparably rich and stable archival record, some historical amnesia surrounds her legacy. Scrugg's 1893 and Delany's 1895 profiles make no mention of Brown's 1880 textbook, *Bits and Odds: A Choice Selection of Recitations for School, Lyceum, and Parlor Entertainments*, and later biographies fail to mention her 1920 *First Lessons in Public Speaking*. *Bits and Odds* appears in Brown's WorldCat record as held by only 11 member libraries worldwide but is not linked to Brown's publication record in the Virtual International Authority File (VIAF); *First Lessons* is out of print. Brown's textbooks may be mentioned in Dunlap's *Biographical Sketch of Hallie Quinn Brown* (1963), but Dunlap's book no longer circulates beyond the Ohio Historical Society.

37. The principle that data points have more value when they can be interlinked with other "open" data points, resulting in computer-readable connections regardless of their location or type. This principle underlies data discovery tools that build relationships by drawing connections between and among infrastructure stacks (Lynch, "Social Networks," http://www.digitalhumanities.org/dhq/ vol/8/3/000184.html). The same qualities allowing LOD to make rich relational representations of data points can also reinforce hegemonic values, as any relational

system still embeds assumptions about data (Risam, *New Digital Worlds*, 40), and many rely on the material conditions of well-resourced repositories.

38. Graban and Sullivan, "New Rhetorics," 193.

39. Pages from the 1918 Howard Academy Yearbook identify Mary Edna Brown and Sarah Nevelle Merriwether [*sic*], while pages from the 1919 Howard Academy Yearbook identify Meriwether again, and identify Mary Brown under her married name, Edna Brown Coleman (captioned "Mrs. M.E. Coleman"). The problem of patriarchal name change practices is not a new one for feminist historians of women or trans subjects, but such practices frustrate our ability to connect the disparate data points of our subjects' institutional memberships. These problems are further complicated by cataloging discrepancies, i.e., Brown's academic areas of emphasis are attributed to "History and Physiography" on p. 277 of the same 1913–1914/1915–1916 Howard University Yearbook in which she is later and more accurately mentioned among the faculty of English and Mathematics (p. 559).

40. D'Ignazio and Klein, *Data Feminism*. For example, Google's Ngram viewer reveals *a priori* assumptions—about how to organize, sort, and label data—that require deconstruction to enable more heterogeneous searching (Pechenick, Danforth, and Dodds, "Characterizing").

41. See, e.g., https://aka1908.com/about/founders/. Some of our most productive inferential searching occurred on the Web-accessible outskirts of extra-curricular organizations that need the university to operate and yet whose histories routinely operate outside of the university.

42. Leonea Barbour Dudley's single mention in Howard University's documentary history occurs in a personnel list on page 461 of Dyson's 1941 publication, which we accessed through HathiTrust in 2021, though we recognize that the HathiTrust data set continues to evolve. https://babel.hathitrust.org/cgi/pt?id=mdp.39015006964129&seq=7.

43. Carbajal, "Historical Metadebt"; Ramírez, "Being Assumed."

44. Osareh, "Bibliometrics"; Moravec, "Beyond Citations"; Johnson, "Modeling."

45. Pechenick, Danforth, and Dodds, "Characterizing."

46. D'Ignazio and Klein, "Unicorns, Janitors, Ninjas, Wizards, and Rock Stars," *Data Feminism.*

47. A "stack" refers to any collection of materials, programs, results, and/or documents that are joined together for a common purpose. Data stacks function hierarchically, and we invoke the principle here because it promotes uncertainty, reminding us that the construction of digital repositories is malleable and layered, not neutral and fixed. For example, a tool that traces the locations of contingent faculty within a particular chronology would use timeline data or geospatial coordinates as its principal entity, and all other relationships would be layered on top of that knowledge set, contingent upon that first set of relationships. In our study, we gathered data about each subject from multiple tools and divergent angles, before creating an informed assemblage. Once a stack is formulated, it becomes a framework for further searching through cyberinfrastructures (Lynch, "Social Networks"), http://www.digitalhumanities.org/dhq/vol/8/3/000184.html. Whether they are programmers or not, digital historians are unknowingly interested in metadata stacks because stacks power most of the tools they already use or observe.

48. Manoff, "Archive," 393.

49. Graban, "Ripple Effects," 110.

50. Moravec, "Feminist Research," 189.
51. Graban and Sullivan, "New Rhetorics," 202.
52. Dobrin, "The Spaces," 319.
53. Risam, *New Digital Worlds*, 23.
54. D'Ignazio and Klein, "Show Your Work," *Data Feminism*.
55. Coined by F. Gerald Ham as a response to the growing preservation of electronic records, "post-custodial" theory describes a paradigmatic shift in archival handling—from the idea of curators and archivists as stewards of their collections to the empowerment of collection creators in retaining agency over their work.
56. Bordalejo, "Minority Report."
57. Carbajal, "Historical Metadata," 95.
58. D'Ignazio and Klein, *Data Feminism*.
59. For a longer discussion of how disjointment principles might influence the production of data visualizations for digital feminist historiography, see https://lwp project.org/wp/encounter-3/.
60. Johnson, "Modeling"; Osareh, "Bibliometrics."
61. Rawson, "Queering," 44.
62. Browdy, "Black Women's Rhetoric(s)," par. 10, https://cfshrc.org/article/black -womens-rhetorics-a-conversation-starter-for-naming-and-claiming-a-field-of-study/.

WORKS CITED

Ball, Cheryl, Tarez Samra Graban, and Michelle Sidler. "The Boutique is Open: Data for Writing Studies." *Composition and Big Data*, edited by Amanda Licastro and Ben Miller, 196–211. Pittsburgh, PA: University of Pittsburgh Press, 2021.
Bollen, Johan, Herbert Van de Sompel, and Marko A. Rodriguez. "Towards Usage-Based Impact Metrics: First Results from the MESUR Project." In *Proceedings of the 8th ACM/IEEE-CS Joint Conference on Digital Libraries*, 231–40. New York: Association for Computing Machinery, 2008.
Bordalejo, Barbara. "Minority Report: The Myth of Equality in the Digital Humanities." In *Bodies of Information: Intersectional Feminism and the Digital Humanities*, edited by Elizabeth Losh and Jacqueline Wernimont, 231–40. Minneapolis, MN: University of Minnesota Press, 2018.
Browdy, Ronisha. "Black Women's Rhetoric(s): A Conversation Starter for Naming and Claiming a Field of Study." *Peitho* 23, no. 4 (Summer 2021). https://cfshrc.org/ article/black-womens-rhetorics-a-conversation-starter-for-naming-and-claiming -a-field-of-study/.
Carbajal, Itza A. "Historical Metadata Debt: Confronting Colonial and Racist Legacies Through a Post-Custodial Metadata Praxis." *Across the Disciplines: A Journal of Language, Learning, and Academic Writing* 18, no. 1 (2021): 91–205.
Cheney-Lippold, John. *We Are Data: Algorithms and the Making of Our Digital Selves.* New York: New York University Press, 2017.
Cifor, Marika, and Stacy Wood. "Critical Feminism in the Archives." *Journal of Critical Library and Information Studies* 1, no. 2 (2017). https://doi.org/10.24242/jclis .v1i2.27.
D'Ignazio, Catherine, and Lauren F. Klein. *Data Feminism.* Cambridge, MA: MIT Press, 2020.
Dobrin, Sidney I. "The Spaces Between." In *Circulation, Writing, and Rhetoric*, edited by Laurie Gries and Collin G. Brooke, 315–22. Logan, UT: Utah State University Press, 2018.

Dyson, Walter. *Howard University, The Capstone of Negro Education, A History: 1867–1940*. Washington, DC: Howard University Graduate School, 1941.

Flanders, Julia, Susan Brown, Jacqueline Wernimont, and Martha Nell Smith. "Feminist Literary History." Panel at the annual meeting for the Digital Diversity Conference, Edmonton, Alberta, Canada, May 7–9, 2015.

Gitelman, Lisa. *Always Already New: Media, History, and the Data of Culture*. Cambridge, MA: MIT Press, 2006.

Graban, Tarez Samra. "From Location(s) to Locatability: Mapping Feminist Recovery and Archival Activity through Metadata." *College English* 76, no. 2 (2013): 171–93.

Graban, Tarez Samra. "Ripple Effects: Toward a *Topos* of Deployment for Feminist Historiography." In *Networked Humanities: Within and Without the University*, edited by Jeff Rice and Brian McNely, 106–27. Anderson, SC: Parlor Press, 2018.

Graban, Tarez Samra, and Patricia Sullivan. "New Rhetorics of Scholarship: Leveraging Betweenness and Circulation for Feminist Historical Work in Composition Studies." In *Circulation, Writing, and Rhetoric*, edited by Laurie Gries and Collin G. Brooke, 189–207. Logan, UT: Utah State University Press, 2018.

Hedley, Alison, and Lorraine Janzen Kooistra. "Prototyping Personography for *The Yellow Nineties Online*: Queering and Querying History in the Digital Age." In *Bodies of Information: Intersectional Feminism and Digital Humanities*, edited by Elizabeth Losh and Jacqueline Wernimont, 157–72. Minneapolis, MN: University of Minnesota Press, 2018.

Heidorn, P. Bryan. "Shedding Light on the Dark Data in the Long Tail of Science." *Library Trends* 57, no. 2 (2008): 280–99.

Hook, J.N. *A Long Way Together: A Personal View of NCTE's First Sixty-Seven Years*. Champaign, IL: National Council of Teachers of English, 1979.

Johnson, Nathan. "Modeling Rhetorical Disciplinarity: Mapping the Digital Network." In *Rhetoric and the Digital Humanities*, edited by Jim Ridolfo and William Hart-Davidson, 96–110. Chicago, IL: University of Chicago Press, 2015.

Kennedy, Krista, and Seth Long. "The Trees within the Forest: Extracting, Coding, and Visualizing Subjective Data in Authorship Studies." In *Rhetoric and the Digital Humanities*, edited by Jim Ridolfo and William Hart-Davidson, 140–51. Chicago, IL: University of Chicago Press, 2015.

Kulak, Andrew. "Ethics in Big Data Composition Research: Cybersecurity and Algorithmic Accountability." In *Composition and Big Data*, edited by Amanda Licastro and Ben Miller, 230–44. Pittsburgh, PA: University of Pittsburgh Press, 2021.

Losh, Elizabeth M., and Jacqueline Wernimont, eds. *Bodies of Information*. Minneapolis, MN: University of Minnesota Press, 2018.

Lynch, Tom J. "Social Networks and Archival Context Project: A Case Study of Emerging Cyberinfrastructure." *Digital Humanities Quarterly* 8, no. 3 (2014). http://www.digitalhumanities.org/dhq/vol/8/3/000184.html.

Manoff, Marlene. "Archive and Database as Metaphor: Theorizing the Historical Record." *Libraries and the Academy* 10, no. 4 (2010): 385–98. https://doi.org/10.1353/pla.2010.0005.

McKee, Heidi A., and James E. Porter. "Rhetorica Online: Feminist Research Practices in Cyberspace." In *Rhetorica in Motion: Feminist Rhetorical Methods and Methodologies*, edited by Eileen E. Schell and K.J. Rawson, 152–70. Pittsburgh, PA: University of Pittsburgh Press, 2010.

Moravec, Michelle. "Beyond Citations: The Historian's Altmetrics," *Politics of Women's Culture*, July 22, 2015, http://politicsofwomensculture.michellemoravec.com/uncategorized/beyond-citations-the-historians-altmetrics/.

Moravec, Michelle. "Feminist Research Practices and Digital Archives." *Australian Feminist Studies* 32, no. 91–92 (2017): 186–201. https://doi.org/10.1080/08164649.2017.1357006.

Mueller, Derek. *Network Sense: Methods for Visualizing a Discipline*. Louisville, CO: University Press of Colorado, 2017.

Noble, Safiya Umoju. *Algorithms of Oppression: How Search Engines Reinforce Racism*. New York: New York University Press, 2018.

Osareh, Farideh. "Bibliometrics, Citation Analysis, and Co-Citation Analysis: A Review of Literature I." *Libri* 46, no. 3 (2011): 149–58.

Pechenick, Eitan Adam, Christopher M. Danforth, and Peter Sheridan Dodds. "Characterizing the Google Books Corpus: Strong Limits to Inferences of Socio-Cultural and Linguistic Evolution." *PLOSOne* 10, no. 10 (2015). https://doi.org/10.1371/journal.pone.0137041.

Prince, Alanna, and Cara Marta Messina. "Black Digital Humanities for the Rising Generation." *Digital Humanities Quarterly* 16, no. 3 (2022), https://www.digitalhumanities.org/dhq/vol/16/3/000645/000645.html.

Ramírez, Mario H. "Being Assumed Not to Be: A Critique of Whiteness as an Archival Imperative." *The American Archivist* 78, no. 2 (2015): 339–56.

Rawson, K.J. "Queering Feminist Rhetorical Canonization." In *Rhetorica in Motion: Feminist Rhetorical Methods and Methodologies*, edited by Eileen E. Schell and K.J. Rawson, 39–52. Pittsburgh, PA: University of Pittsburgh Press, 2010.

Risam, Roopika. "Beyond the Margins: Intersectionality and the Digital Humanities." *Digital Humanities Quarterly* 9, no. 2 (2015). http://www.digitalhumanities.org/dhq/vol/9/2/000208/000208.html.

Risam, Roopika. *New Digital Worlds: Postcolonial Digital Humanities in Theory, Praxis, and Pedagogy*. Chicago, IL: Northwestern University Press, 2019.

Rivard, Courtney. "Turning Archives into Data: Archival Rhetorics and Digital Literacy in the Composition Classroom." *College Composition and Communication* 70, no. 4 (2019): 527–59.

Roemer, Robin Chin, and Rachel Borchardt. "From Bibliometrics to Altmetrics: A Changing Scholarly Landscape." *College & Research Libraries News* 73, no. 10 (2012): 596–600. https://crln.acrl.org/index.php/crlnews/article/view/8846/9480

Royster, Jacqueline Jones, and Gesa E. Kirsch, eds. *Feminist Rhetorical Practices: New Horizons for Rhetoric, Composition, and Literacy Studies*. Carbondale, IL: Southern Illinois University Press, 2012.

Schell, Eileen E. Introduction to *Rhetorica in Motion: Feminist Rhetorical Methods and Methodologies*, edited by Eileen E. Schell and K.J. Rawson, 1–20. Pittsburgh, PA: University of Pittsburgh Press, 2010.

Solberg, Janine. "Googling the Archive: Digital Tools and the Practice of History." *Advances in the History of Rhetoric* 15, no. 1 (2012): 53–76.

Stolley, Karl. "An API of Motives." Panel at Networked Humanities: From Within and Without the University: A Digital Humanities Symposium, Lexington, KY, February 15–16, 2013.

Stone, Lawrence. "Prosopography." *Daedalus* 100, no. 1 (1971): 46–79.

Sullivan, Patricia. "Inspecting Shadows of Past Classroom Practices: A Search for Students' Voices." *College Composition and Communication* 63, no. 3 (2012): 365–86.

Van Haitsma, Pamela. "Between Archival Absence and Information Abundance: Reconstructing Sallie Holley's Abolitionist Rhetoric through Digital Surrogates and Metadata." *Quarterly Journal of Speech* 106, no. 1 (2020): 24–47.

ELEVEN

What Should We Ask?

Feminist Methodological Inquiries into Commemoration

Jessica Enoch and Carly S. Woods

In 2017, sculptor Sharon Hayes created *If They Should Ask* (*ITSA*) as part of a commemorative initiative called Monument Lab–a "nonprofit public art and history studio [. . . that] cultivate[s] conversations about the past, present, and future of monuments as a means to animate democracy and foster generational change."[1] Hayes, an award-winning Philadelphia-based artist who has created a range of art performances and pieces that engage themes of gender, sexuality, memory, race, politics, and space, joined twenty other artists to respond to the prompt, "what is an appropriate monument for the current city of Philadelphia?" Hayes installed *ITSA* with the goal of centering questions of women's (lack of) representation on the public landscape.[2] She articulates this issue in her artist's statement, explaining, "[a]lthough the city of Philadelphia is home to over 1,500 public sculptures, there are only two that celebrate the life of a real, historic woman—Joan of Arc and Mary Dyer, neither of whom were Philadelphia residents."[3] To inspire audiences to wrestle with such a commemorative absence (and to consider what it would mean to fill it), Hayes crafted a temporary monument composed of nine pedestals grouped together in the highly regarded and trafficked area of Philadelphia's Rittenhouse Square.

In this work, Hayes challenges statuary expectations that often "exude a stereotypically masculine quality" in which a larger-than-life replica of a heroic, individual figure cast in enduring materials (stone, marble, or bronze) stands (or sits on horseback) atop a tall pedestal.[4] Hayes creates this challenge not only by grouping nine pedestals together but also by refusing to place figures on top—the pedestals within the assemblage are empty. The absence of women's presence upon these pedestals is complimented by acrylic-lettering inscriptions around the bottom of the pedestals. Inscribed

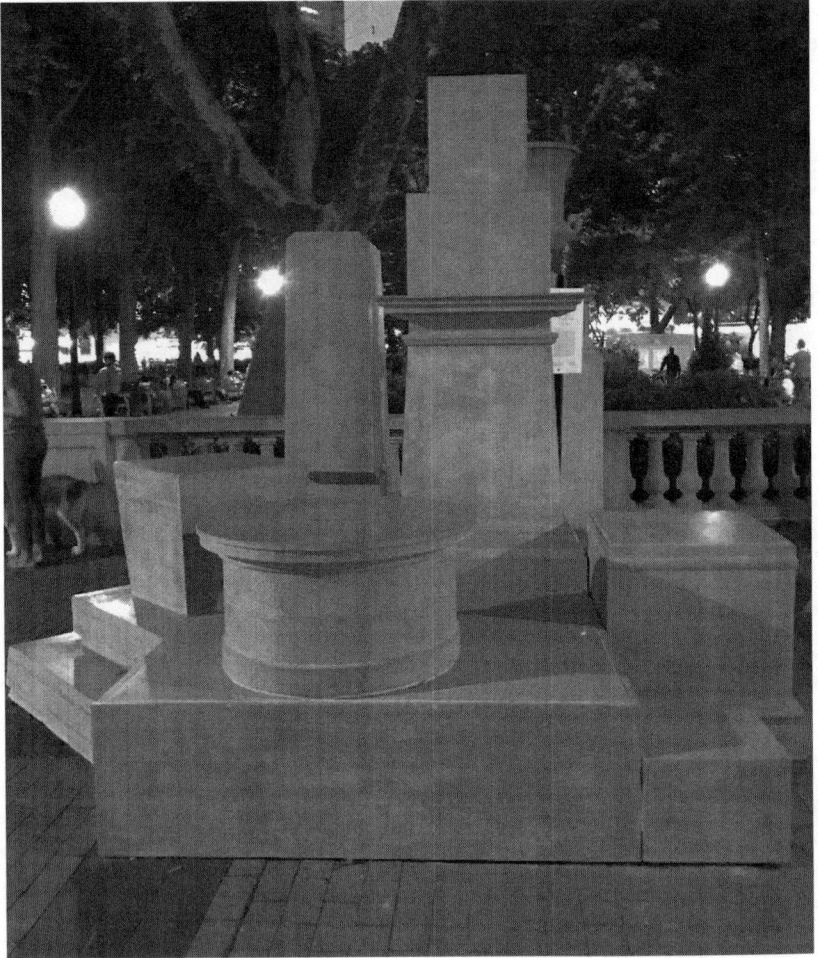

FIGURE 11.1. *If They Should Ask.* Photograph by Jessica Enoch.

there is a racially diverse and trans-inclusive list of women's names who contributed to Philadelphia's civic life—women who could potentially be figured atop the pedestals but are not.

Indeed, the title of Hayes's piece prompts audiences to take on a specific kind of feminist inquiry—*if they* (public audiences, city stakeholders, members organizations dedicated to the erection of monuments) *should ask* about potential figures who might stand atop these pedestals, what should be the response? Who, among the names inscribed around the bottom of

FIGURE 11.2. Detail of *If They Should Ask*. The text on the statue is "On this site there could be a statue of" and then it lists numbers of figures. The names in the photo are Alice Paul, Crystal Bird Faucet, the transwomen at the 1965 sit-in at Dewey's cafe, Happy Fernandez, Jaci Adams. Photograph by Jessica Enoch.

the pedestals (or other nominations), should be chosen for statuary selection? In this chapter, we extend the questions *ITSA* puts forth and elaborate on the feminist inquiry it encourages. Here we use *ITSA* as a springboard to explore and explicate feminist rhetorical methods for studying commemoration, identifying specific questions feminist scholars might ask as they conduct studies of women's commemoration and gendered public memory. As feminist public memory scholars, we (the authors) include ourselves in this number and revise Hayes's titular query using this overarching question to drive our work: *What should we ask* as we conduct our research and contribute to conversations relating to feminist memory studies? As our chapter details, this overarching question elicits and generates still more specific inquiries that we hope will direct and invigorate work in this new and burgeoning field.

Public memory studies is a robust and significant area within rhetorical scholarship, one that intersects with historiography, space and place, rhetorics of display, and visual rhetoric.[5] Yet, *feminist* rhetorical approaches to memory studies would benefit from further definition and refinement. To be sure, a non-exhaustive list of scholars who have made valuable methodological contributions by identifying ways to work at the nexus of rhetoric, gender, memory, and history might include Carole Blair, Katie Bramlett, Jessica Enoch, Thomas R. Dunn, Tasha Dubriwny, Letizia Guglielmo, Amy J. Leuck, Roseann M. Mandziuk, Kristan Poirot, Karrieann M. Soto Vega, and Patricia A. Wilde.[6] Moreover, scholars have analyzed particular memory projects using a feminist analytic, such as Carol Mattingly's study of the erasure of Women's Christian Temperance Union temples and fountains and Catherine R. Squires and Aisha Upton's analysis of Harriet Tubman on the recently redesigned $20 bill.[7] Yet by and large, the methods through which feminist scholars can and should conduct this work have yet to be fully detailed. Our aim in this chapter is to deepen this methodological conversation, and we use Hayes's *ITSA* as a springboard to do so.

Feminist memory studies encompasses a broad range of scholarly engagements that center remembrance, power, privilege, and (in)justice and explore gender's intertwined relationship with race, sexuality, class, culture, ability, and nation. While there are a multitude of commemorative genres for feminist scholars to study, for the purposes of this essay and because of our tie to Hayes's innovative work, we narrow our focus here to the memorial genre of the statue to consider how feminist rhetorical sensibilities should guide us to analyze this prominent and esteemed commemorative form. As a structure for this essay, we engage *ITSA* to identify six methodological inquiries and then we explore them as a way to clarify how feminist scholars might conduct public memory research. The lines of inquiry we set out encompass method and methodology as they invite conversations around both "technique[s] for (or a way of proceeding in) gathering evidence" (method) and a "theory and analysis of how research does or should proceed" (methodology).[8] Ultimately, we hope to offer heuristic strategies that feminist memory scholars can work from, add to, and revise. Before we initiate this discussion of method, however, we first step back to contextualize the memorial moment Hayes engaged when she produced *ITSA* and the larger, national conversation around women's commemoration that feminist scholars must consider.

Contextualizing Commemorative Culture

Since the 1980s, US commemorative culture has manifested what Erika Doss terms "memorial mania" in which the "pace of commemoration has quickened, and the numbers of memorials have escalated because numbers of Americans view public art as a particularly powerful vehicle of visibility and authority."[9] As Doss describes, "memorial mania is shaped by individual impulses and factional grievances, by special interest claims for esteem and recognition, and by efforts to symbolize and enshrine the particular issues and aspirations of diverse and often stratified publics."[10] These conversations gained depth and focus as commemorative symbols honoring white supremacy were increasingly challenged in the years following the 2015 murder of nine Black congregants at Emanuel AME Church in Charleston, South Carolina by white supremacist Dylan Roof. The murderer's overt allegiance to the Confederate flag catalyzed an activist movement that called for the removal of the over 2,000 Confederate symbols that honored white supremacy across the United States.[11] This movement directed the nation's attention to questions relating to rightful commemoration throughout the 2010s (and extending to the present). By contributing to Philadelphia's Monument-Lab discussions in 2017, Hayes joined this conversation about rightful commemoration, and through *ITSA,* she accentuated questions of gender.

Hayes was by no means alone in drawing attention to the ways gender animates public memory. Many interlocutors initially focused on the gender disparity within large-scale, public memory projects, and with good reason. In audits of public statuary and commemoration, groups such as the Smithsonian found that of the "5,575 outdoor sculpture portraits of historical figures in the United States, 559 portray women, a mere 10% of all statues."[12] In response, organizations like New York City's Monumental Women formed to "challeng[e] municipalities across the country and across the world to rethink the past and reshape the future by including tributes in their public spaces to the diverse women who helped create and inspire those cities."[13] Articles such as "It's Way Too Hard to Find Statues of Notable Women in the U.S.," "The Gender Gap in Public Sculpture," "Inside the Push for More Public Statues of Notable Women," and "Why We Should Put Women on Pedestals" documented and critiqued women's underrepresentation on the public landscape and called for a greater memorial balance in terms of gender.[14] This is especially true for representations of women of color. For example, activist Michelle Duster points to the fact that in Chicago, where in 2022 thirty percent of the population is Black, there are only two Black women represented on the public landscape—a bust of Gwendolyn Brooks and an image at Ida B. Wells's monument.[15]

Given the country's "memorial mania," the deep investment in rightful commemoration, and especially the push for women's representation on the commemorative landscape, the time is ripe for feminist scholars invested in public memory studies not only to conduct feminist analysis but to think capaciously about the questions that can and should propel this work forward. Using *ITSA* as a heuristic, the sections below move forward on the latter prerogative, hoping this methodological discussion generates more and diverse feminist memory research.

Commemorative Absence and Presence

As Figure 11.1 indicates, Hayes's temporary monument challenges commemorative expectations by displaying a collective of nine empty pedestals rather than a singular populated pedestal that exalts a specific individual. Herein, Hayes creates a commemorative moment in which visitors must contemplate and deliberate about commemorative absence or silence(ing). A starting point for feminist scholars of public memory could thus be to mine questions of both absence and presence, working from the knowledge that "male bodies" are the primary "kinds of bodies [that] have been deemed 'appropriate' or acceptable markers of national history and identity."[16] Feminist scholars thus should ask, where do we find commemorations dedicated to women's and gendered experiences? How do we understand the mechanisms that enable commemorative absence and presence?

One significant consideration should be an acknowledgment of the type of absences feminist scholars, artists, and citizens are observing, and the changes that they are calling for. For indeed, some women's *bodies* are already present—even ubiquitous—in the public memorial landscape when we consider how they manifest as symbols of public ideals—as Lady Liberty or Lady Justice—or as fictional characters like the statue of Alice in Wonderland in New York City's Central Park.[17] To wit, the number of mermaid monuments far outnumber monuments to congresswomen in the United States.[18] As Megan O'Grady observes, "We've no lack of statues of women, really; it's just that too many of the ones we have are devoid of personhood."[19] Hayes's work nods to this point with the listing of real historical figures around *ITSA*'s pedestals, and she invites audiences within and beyond the *ITSA* context to consider these questions: Why haven't these figures been memorialized? What are the assumptions around and practices of commemoration that led the public to ignore these figures' contributions to Philadelphia?

Here too, we're led to think with complexity when it comes to commemorative absence. In focusing on public statuary as we do here, our attention is drawn to sites of "commemorative privilege" at prestigious memory places such as the National Statuary Hall of the Capitol Building in Washington, DC, or prominent parks such as Philadelphia's Rittenhouse Square.[20] Scholars, however, should trouble such priorities to consider alternative, innovative commemorative practices that honor actual women, remember gendered experience, and produce gendered memory. In so doing, feminist scholars might inspect a variety of commemorative genres including the temporary, ephemeral, and the handcrafted through which women may be remembered and, too, how women may be remembering. For example, several scholars have explored the commemorative power of cookbooks, scrapbooks, albums, and quilts to understand how women have remembered and been remembered.[21] These alternate projects draw attention to the ways gendered and women's commemorative practices are not only conditioned by access to the public sphere and funding but also inflected by the positionalities of race, class, culture, ability, sexuality, and citizenship status of the commemorator as well as those they aim to remember. Scholars should thus know about gender disparity in public statuary but also understand that this absence within public and prominent sites of memory is not the end of the story. How *else* can people and experiences be remembered beyond the statue on the pedestal? Exploring questions of access and modality prompt us to be creative in thinking about how memories about women and gender may have been composed and consumed, and how they may have circulated.

Commemorative Criteria

For the purposes of this chapter, we keep focus on prominent statuary in large part because of the vociferous clamoring for women's memorial presence in highly visible and prestigious public spaces. Within this conversation, we contend that feminist scholars must also be attuned to commemorative criteria, which we define as the argument or assertion of significance that acts as the rationale for commemorative presence. Through the inscriptions at the bottom of *ITSA*'s pedestals, Hayes asserts that there are plenty of women to add to the pedestal, and her statuary move prompts viewers to ask, what is the reason and rationale for placing *this* woman atop the pedestal?

Feminist scholars must therefore inspect existing memorializations that highlight women and gendered experience by attending to the criteria used to bring them onto the memorial landscape. We should especially consider how these criteria send messages about gender, access to power, intersectional realities, as well as dominant, white, heteronormative culture. As Sierra Rooney states, when scholars think about "attributes of commemoration," we must aim to learn more about the ways "gendered norms regulate public art practices and, conversely, how [. . .] public art practices regulate notions of gender."[22] To be sure, criteria for women's commemorative presence often relies on reinscribing reductive and binaristic ideals of masculine and feminine ideals of excellence. In many instances, women qualify for public recognition if they can demonstrate that they met (or exceeded) masculine forms of heroism—Philadelphia's gilded Joan of Arc statue is a good case in point. That is, placement on the pedestal has required "success in very particular kinds of public acts, namely waging war, winning political power, making peace, harnessing science, leading the faithful, and exploring the world."[23] One important consideration here is the valuation of *individual* achievement—traditional statuary often reveres the singular exemplary individual. Hayes's nine pedestals draw attention to this problematic, but she also deepens this point by naming on the bottom of the pedestal a collective of trans women who protested through a 1965 sit-in at the city's Dewey café, effectively nominating them for statuary elevation. Through these statuary moves, Hayes invites visitors to meditate on how collective struggle, collaboration, and gendered experience could (and should) earn a place on the pedestal (and why it often has not).

Taking up Hayes's invitation, if there is a statuary trend focused on collective gendered experience, it would be monuments dedicated to maternity, evidenced, for example, in the Whistler's Mother Statue, the Pioneer Mother's Memorial, the Madonna of the Trail monuments, and the Confederate Mother's Monument. Here of course, the commemorative project is to revere a particular type of gendered experience (and to teach others to follow their lead of maternal dedication and sacrifice). In examining statutory (or any commemorative form), feminist scholars should thus consider the relationship between commemorative criteria and the reinstatement, revision, or remaking of gendered practice and gendered norms, asking, how are ideas about gender conveyed or complicated through commemorative criteria? What gendered practices did these figures (or collectives) have to take on to make their way to the pedestal? And how are these ideas about gender animated by realities of race, culture, class, ability and citizenship status?

A final important point regarding criteria—of course, trauma and violence are prevalent rationales for public remembrance. Yet, as Christine Bold, Ric Knowles, and Belinda Leach explain, since *gendered* violence is often coded as private and personal, it is often deemed unworthy of public commemoration. These authors call scholars to consider the "active forgetting" that corresponds with gendered violence—a forgetting that codes this form of violence as "normal" and therefore an unremarkable part of gendered experience.[24] To resist such forgetting, the authors imagine how memorials might remember the "systematic nature of gendered violence":

instead of seeing "each violent act [. . .] treated in isolation as the patho-
logical behavior or a deranged individual," memorials might mark how
gendered violence is a "behavior into which such individuals have been so-
cialized."[25] Such claims inspire still more questions about commemorative
criteria and statuary composition: How might commemorations mark not
gendered victory but gendered harm and how might such memorialization
resist silences around gendered violence?[26]

Commemorative Representation

These questions about statuary criteria lead directly to concerns regarding
commemorative representation. *ITSA*'s empty pedestals with the inscribed
possibilities on the bottom prompt visitors to imagine not only which
women (or groups of women) would take their place on the pedestal (and
why) but what these women would look like once they make their way
up there. Feminist scholars should thus ask, how does statuary represent
women in public spaces? How are gendered bodies put on commemorative
display? What does it mean to render these bodies in particular ways, especially when it comes to visual depictions of gender, race, class, age, sexuality,
nationality, and/or ability?

Responding to these questions requires engaging with issues of representation, so scholars should be attuned to decisions about depiction and
the ways each statuary choice is a rhetorical (and a Burkean) matter of selection (as well as reflection or deflection).[27] Thinking about decisions regarding likeness (what the figures look like) and statuary action (what they are
doing) often surface unarticulated claims about what it means to configure
gender in general and "womanhood" more particularly and to etch these
physical characteristics into marble, granite, or bronze. Building on our
point above regarding remembering gendered violence and trauma, scholars
such as Dongho Chun have analyzed representational debates over monuments dedicated to Korean survivors of sexual slavery (known euphemis-
tically as "comfort women"). Here, interlocutors deliberate about whether
statuary should represent these survivors as teenagers or girls, as they had
been during the war, or as elderly women activists who demonstrate in front
of the Japanese embassy every week.[28]

As scholars think through such representational questions, we might
also consider how decisions about statuary likeness not only contribute to
the audience's understanding of historical figures and groups themselves
but also send messages about how, through representational decisions, the
statues intervene in contemporary debates and discussions. As a case in

point, Mandzuik's exploration of the ways Sojourner Truth is represented through statuary in Battle Creek, Michigan and Northampton, Massachusetts, adeptly reveals how commemorative decisions regarding "embodiment" were "suited to the needs and values of the community from which it emerged."[29] Such examinations of representation make clear that it is possible for feminist scholars to appreciate and applaud attempts to increase the presence of women in public statuary (and other forms of commemoration) while simultaneously being attentive to (and even skeptical of) how they are represented and the consequentiality of those representations.[30]

Commemorative Process

The absence of figures atop the pedestals in Hayes's monument suggests it is unfinished; that the work is still in process. Viewers are thus prompted to imagine the path to the project's completion, asking, how does the artist and community move from pedestal to figure? What stages do communities and stakeholders move through? What discussions and debates take place at each stage? We assert here that questions like these prompt investigations into commemorative process—investigations that guide feminist memory scholars to inspect the full cycle of statuary creation from exigency, idea generation, and proposal to composition, completion, and visitor response. Feminist scholars might also consider constraints, opportunities, and the necessary labor that affects commemorative processes, keeping a close eye on how power inflects the process at each stage.

Delving into *ITSA,* not only would we consider how Hayes's monument fits into the larger project of Monument Lab, but we would also study Hayes's own investment in process. To create the list of women cited at the bottom of the pedestals, Hayes "convened a group of intergenerational, intersectional, and civically engaged women" to collect "names of Philadelphia-area women who have contributed to the social, cultural, political, and economic life of the city" but who have been excluded from public memorialization.[31] Thus, Hayes's process was collaborative and community-sourced, as she invited a diverse group of Philadelphians into her work and to ask questions about commemorative presence.

To explore commemorative process, feminist scholars might consult planning documents and drawings, meeting minutes, proposals, artist's statements, archival artifacts, and media accounts, as well as calls for and entries to monument competitions. Scholars should research not only the artist who crafted the commemoration but also the groups who argued for and funded these projects. Concerning this latter point, feminist memory scholars should know that while women lack *representation* in public commemorations, they have played major roles in the *production* of them. After the Civil War for example, women's preservationist groups like the Daughters of the American Revolution and the Daughters of the Confederacy led the way in the national obsession to commemorate an American past that exalted nationalism, patriotism, and colonialism (along with white, male, and masculine heroism) and that positively remembered (and mourned) the Confederacy.[32]

Hayes in fact engages this processual concern in her artist statement for *ITSA*. Here she reminds readers that white women have traditionally served as critical sponsors for public memory production in Philadelphia, and through their sponsorship, they emboldened the white dominant patriarchal culture that both privileged and disempowered them. Hayes writes, "many white women were involved, individually and collectively, in organizing, advocating, fundraising, and commissioning large sculptures." Through this process, these women "asserted their public power by constructing a material reality that consistently excluded them, and certainly excluded any women of color."[33] Hayes's artist statement orients scholars to a pressing and persistent concern that infuses commemorative process: Who wields power within contexts of and stages that lead to memorial creation?

Commemorative Feeling

Curator Jodi Throckmorton explores the affective response Hayes's work elicits by focusing on *ITSA*'s pedestal absences, writing, "This emptiness feels palpable and perceivable—a nothingness that occupies space and feels distinctly physical. In *If They Should Ask,* Sharon Hayes used empty sculptural platforms to invoke the memory of important, yet forgotten, women and to create a place for social activism, engagement, and a reflection on the discriminatory structure that monumentalizes a white, male version of history."[34] Throckmorton thus attempts to assess the feeling *ITSA* evokes—there's a "palpable" sense of nothingness, but in that feeling of lack there is expectation and anticipation. For Throckmorton (and for us), *ITSA* cultivates a sense of discomfort, expectation, and even hope. There's a felt sense that something should be there, but what? Examining what the statuary experience feels like is yet another important arena for feminist inquiry, for as Erin J. Rand observes, feminist and queer scholars explore questions of affect and feeling because this work "often highlights gendered, raced, sexualized embodiment, is attentive to the ways that the capacity to act is embedded within relations of power, and aims for the horizon of potentiality in unsettling the status quo."[35]

Of course, scholars cannot know with certainty how all visitors will interact with a commemorative project, but we can ascertain how it is crafted to engage visitors, cultivated with an eye toward creating a particular kind of embodied experience and eliciting a particular kind of feeling. Consider traditional statues—those that stand on a tall pedestal and cast figures in bronze larger-than-life images. Visitors must look up; they are made to feel physically smaller; they are kept at a distance from the exalted person on display. These configurations *do something* for the visitor and, in this doing, there is the cultivation of feeling. Feminist scholars should thus consider affective elicitations to monumentality by starting with the physical construction of the monument—what is the size, relationship to the viewer, possibilities for viewer interaction and relationship? We might consider how visitors are expected to engage and interact with the monument, how they are guided to approach, take in, and exit the commemorative experience, accounting especially for the information that contextualizes the statue and the ways visitors are expected to comport themselves (sit, stand, continue moving, stop in one's tracks) as they interact with it. Feminist scholars should be especially attuned to how emotions may change given one's positionality, intersectional experience, history, and (dis)connection to the commemorative subject. They should inspect such important and varied responses to monumentality with care, respect, and deep critical consideration.

As yet another consideration, it is important to note that monuments change in meaning over time. As Barbie Zelizer explains, memory "is a process that is constantly unfolding, changing, and transforming."[36] These changes in monumental meaning will affect and be affected by public opinion and emotion. As we know with recent responses to Confederate monuments, feelings can shift to disdain and antipathy given new information, contexts, and circumstances. These shifts in feeling will change what the monument is and becomes for audiences and the value it holds. Feminist scholars should thus assess and investigate the ways public emotion shapes and punctuates commemorative creation, process, and response.

Commemorative Power

Hayes was intentional in inscribing the range of Philadelphians who could be featured in the city's commemorative monuments—she lists, for instance, Cuban American LGBTQ activist Ada Bello, Black jazz singer Billie

Holiday, Black abolitionist Frances Harper, and the trans women who protested through a 1965 sit-in at the city's Dewey café. In doing so, Hayes defies the expectation that only white, cisgender, straight women would find their way onto the pedestal and instead asserts a diverse array of commemorative possibilities. But diverse representation is not Hayes's only concern (nor should it be for feminist memory scholars). As she writes in her artist's statement, the "common understanding that [commemorative] exclusion is a consequence of a patriarchal system that did not value women's contributions to public life tells only part of the story."[37] Instead, the commemorative point that Hayes wants to make is about power—her goal is to highlight how "monuments were utilized as part of a larger racial and gendered project in which whiteness and maleness are produced as identities of civic and political power."[38]

Hayes is explicit in identifying her motivation for this attention to power, explaining that the reason why "political, social, and cultural labor done by women often did not move into or onto the historical record" is a result of not only of patriarchy but also the "intersecting conditions of racism, settler colonialism, homophobia, and transphobia."[39] She highlights here a key issue for feminist memory scholars—women's intersectional experiences, or the idea that structures of power inflect women's lives differently contingent on their gendered, raced, classed, sexual, civic, and ability status. Power too shapes the connections we implicitly make to gender, as commemorations overtly or subtly (re)tell dominant stories about what it means to be a woman or man, how to enact femininity, masculinity, and heteronormativity and the ways these positionalities are informed by race, culture, ability, and citizenship. Thus, we want to emphasize that a critical feminist methodological strategy within memory studies should move beyond a narrow concern for diverse representation and instead focus attention on intersectional operations of power that explore the multiple and often overlapping ways power animates decisions about who is commemorated and how.

As Brittney Cooper explains, intersectionality demonstrates "what it mean[s] for systems of power to be interactive, [. . .] explicitly tying the political aims of an inclusive democracy to a theory and account of power."[40] Within feminist memory studies, scholars could explore the intersecting power dynamics that accompany recent efforts to commemorate trans women of color. In 2019, a New York City initiative called She Built NYC announced plans to erect statues honoring the co-founders of Street Transvestite Action Revolutionaries (STAR)—Latine transgender activist Sylvia

Rivera and Black transgender activist Marsha P. Johnson. When in 2021, the statues had still not been erected due to COVID-19 delays, activists decided to take matters into their own hands on the occasion of Johnson's 76th birthday, installing their own bust of Marsha P. Johnson in New York's Christopher Park.[41] While this was not a permanent intervention on the commemorative landscape, it is a fascinating example of how activists can use public art to intervene in commemorative power dynamics.

What Should We Ask

This chapter sets out lines of inquiry for feminist rhetorical examination, thinking specifically about what we should ask as scholars invested in intersectional approaches to commemoration. We are indebted to Sharon Hayes's innovative work on *ITSA*, Monument Lab's prompt, and the exemplary scholarship that we have highlighted to both model possibilities and spark new directions for feminist rhetorical methods. Our six named heuristics—commemorative absence and presence, criteria, representation, process, feeling, and power—should help to set out critical approaches to feminist memory work, but they are certainly not exhaustive of the methodological possibilities in this area of interdisciplinary inquiry. Indeed, there is always more work to do, and we invite feminist scholars to name and describe more. For if anyone should ask, the conversation about feminist memory studies is just beginning.

NOTES

1. Monument Lab, "About," https://monumentlab.com/about.
2. Like Hayes's work, our use of the term "women" throughout this chapter is trans-inclusive.
3. Monument Lab, "Sharon Hayes, If They Should Ask," https://monumentlab.com/projects/sharon-hayes-if-they-should-ask.
4. Griffin, "The Intimate Monument," 105.
5. See Dickinson, Blair, and Ott, *Places*; Prelli, *Rhetorics of Display*; Olson, "Intellectual."
6. Blair, "Reflections"; Bramlett, "Genres"; Enoch, "Suffrage"; Enoch, "Releasing Hold"; Dunn, "Whence the Lesbian"; Dubriwny, and Poirot, "Gender and Public Memory"; Guglielmo, "Re-Collection"; Lueck, "Haunting"; Mandziuk, "Commemorating," Soto Vega, "Afterlives"; Wilde, "(Re)telling."
7. Mattingly, "Woman's Temple"; Squires and Upton, "The Color."
8. Harding, introduction, 2–3.
9. Doss, *Memorial Mania*, 37.
10. Doss, *Memorial Mania*, 37.
11. See Southern Poverty Law Center, *Whose Heritage? Public Symbols of the Confederacy*, 2022, https://www.splcenter.org/sites/default/files/whose-heritage-report-third-edition.pdf.

12. Shachar Peled, "'Where Are the Women?' New Efforts to Give Them Just Due on Monuments, Street Names," *CNN*, March 8, 2017, https://www.cnn.com/.

13. Monument Lab, "About." https://monumentlab.com/about.

14. Danny Lewis, "It's Way Too Hard to Find Statues of Notable Women in the U.S.," *Smithsonian Magazine*, February 29, 2016, https://www.smithsonianmag .com/; Kriston Capps, "The Gender Gap in Public Sculpture," *Bloomberg*, February 24, 2016, https://www.bloomberg.com/; Maya Rhodan, "Inside the Push for More Public Statues of Notable Women," *Time*, August 17, 2017, https://time .com/; Julia Baird, "Why We Should Put Women on Pedestals," *New York Times*, September 4, 2017, https://www.nytimes.com/.

15. Michelle Duster, "So Few Images of African American Women, So Much Resistance to Adding More," *NCPH History @Work*, February 1, 2022, https://ncph .org/.

16. Blair, "Reflections," 275.

17. See Warner, *Monuments and Maidens*. For a consideration of the meanings and possibilities of Lady Rhetoric (Rhetorica) and Peitho, see Kennerly and Woods, "Moving Rhetorica."

18. Monument Lab, *National Monument Audit*, 2022, https://monumentlab.com/ monumentlab-nationalmonumentaudit.pdf, 18.

19. Megan O'Grady, "Why are There So Few Monuments that Successfully Depict Women?" *New York Times Magazine*, February 18, 2021, https://www.nytimes .com/2021/02/18/t-magazine/female-monuments-women.html.

20. Fitzmaurice, "Commemorative Privilege."

21. See, for example, Collings Eves, "A Recipe"; Fleckenstein, "Remembering Women"; Arellano, "Sexual Violences."

22. Rooney, "Guest Editor's Statement," 2.

23. Dunn, "Whence the Lesbian," 206.

24. Bold, Knowles, and Leach, "Feminist Memorializing," 127.

25. Bold, Knowles, and Leach, "Feminist Memorializing," 128.

26. One powerful example of this is the Memorial to Survivors of Sexual Violence at Boom Island Park, created by Black and Indigenous artist Lori Greene, the first permanent memorial to rape survivors in the United States. On three concrete columns beside the Mississippi River, five colorful mosaic panels reference the experiences of non-White, LGBTQ+, and disabled victims.

27. Burke, *Language*, 45.

28. Chun, "The Battle," 363.

29. Mandziuk, "Commemorating," 272.

30. Dunn, "Whence the Lesbian," 205.

31. Monument Lab, "Sharon Hayes."

32. See Cox, *Dixie's Daughters*; Des Jardins, *Women*; Enoch, "Embroidering History."

33. Monument Lab, "Sharon Hayes."

34. Throckmorton, "The Meaning of Absence," 98.

35. Rand, "Bad Feelings," 161–62.

36. Zelizer, "Reading the Past," 218.

37. Monument Lab, "Sharon Hayes."

38. Monument Lab, "Sharon Hayes."

39. Monument Lab, "Sharon Hayes."

40. See Cooper, "Intersectionality," https://doi.org/10.1093/oxfordhb/9780199328581 .013.20.

41. Jen Carlson, "Activists Install Marsha P. Johnson Monument in Christopher Park," *Gothamist*, August 25, 2021, https://gothamist.com/arts-entertainment/marsha -p-johnson-statue-bust-christopher-park.

WORKS CITED

Arellano, Sonia C. "Sexual Violences Traveling to El Norte: An Example of Quilting as Method." *College Composition and Communication* 72, no. 4 (2021): 500–15.

Blair, Carole. "Reflections on Criticism and Bodies: Parables from Public Places." *Western Journal of Communication* 65, no. 3 (2001): 271–91.

Bold, Christine, Ric Knowles, and Belinda Leach. "Feminist Memorializing and Cultural Countermemory: The Case of Marianne's Park." *Signs: Journal of Women in Culture and Society* 28, no. 1 (2002): 125–48.

Bramlett, Katie. "Genres of Memory and Asian/American Women's Activism." PhD diss., University of Maryland, 2022.

Burke, Kenneth. *Language as Symbolic Action: Essays on Life, Literature, and Method.* Berkeley, CA: University of California, 1966.

Chun, Dongho. "The Battle of Representations: Gazing at the Peace Monument or Comfort Women Statue." *positions asia critique* 28, no. 2 (2020): 363–87.

Collings Eves, Rosalyn. "A Recipe for Remembrance: Memory and Identity in African-American Women's Cookbooks." *Rhetoric Review* 24, no. 3 (2005): 280–97.

Cooper, Brittney. "Intersectionality." In *The Oxford Handbook of Feminist Theory*, edited by Lisa Disch and Mary Hawkesworth. Oxford Handbooks Online, 2016. https://doi.org/10.1093/oxfordhb/9780199328581.013.20.

Cox, Karen. *Dixie's Daughters: The United Daughters of the Confederacy and the Preservation of Confederate Culture.* Gainesville: University of Florida Press, 2003.

Des Jardins, Julie. *Women and the Historical Enterprise in America: Gender, Race, and the Politics of Memory, 1880–1945.* Chapel Hill, NC: University of North Carolina Press, 2003.

Dickinson, Greg, Carole Blair, and Brian Ott, eds. *Places of Public Memory: The Rhetoric of Museums and Memorials.* Tuscaloosa: University of Alabama Press, 2010.

Doss, Erika. *Memorial Mania: Public Feeling in America.* Chicago, IL: University of Chicago Press, 2010.

Dubriwny, Tasha N., and Kristan Poirot. "Gender and Public Memory." *Southern Communication Journal* 82, no. 4 (2017): 199–202.

Dunn, Thomas R. "Whence the Lesbian in Queer monumentality? Intersections of Gender and Sexuality in Public Memory." *Southern Communication Journal* 82, no. 4 (2017): 203–15.

Enoch, Jessica. "Embroidering History: The Gendered Memorial Activism of the Daughters of the American Revolution." In *Nineteenth-Century American Activist Rhetorics*, edited by Lisa Zimmerelli and Patricia Bizzell, 207–20. New York: Modern Language Association Press, 2021.

Enoch, Jessica. "Releasing Hold: Feminist Historiography Without the Tradition." In *Theorizing Histories of Rhetoric*, edited by Michelle Ballif, 58–73. Carbondale, IL: Southern Illinois University Press, 2013.

Enoch, Jessica. "Suffrage Statuary and Commemorative Accountability: An Intersectional Analysis of the 2020 Women's Rights Pioneers Monument in Central Park, New York." *Rhetoric Society Quarterly* 53, no. 2 (2023): 104–20.

Fitzmaurice, Megan Irene. "Commemorative Privilege in National Statuary Hall: Spatial Constructions of Racial Citizenship." *Southern Communication Journal* 81, no. 4 (2016): 252–62.

Fleckenstein, Kristen. "Remembering Women: Florence Small Babbitt and the Victorian Family Photograph Album." In *Remembering Women Differently: Refiguring Rhetorical Work*, edited by Lynée Lewis Gaillet and Helen Gaillet Bailey, 137–54. Columbia, SC: University of South Carolina Press, 2019.

Griffin, Sylvia. "The Intimate Monument: Memorialising from a Feminist Perspective." In *Feminist Perspectives on Art: Contemporary Outtakes*, edited by Jacqueline Millner and Catriona Moore, 105–16. New York: Routledge, 2018.

Guglielmo, Letizia. "Re-Collection as Feminist Rhetorical Practice." In *Remembering Women Differently: Refiguring Rhetorical Work*, edited by Lynée Lewis Gaillet and Helen Gaillet Bailey, 1–17. Columbia, SC: University of South Carolina Press, 2019.

Harding, Sandra. Introduction to *Feminism and Methodology*, edited by Sandra Harding, 1–14. Bloomington, IN: Indiana University Press, 1987.

Kennerly, Michele, and Carly S. Woods. "Moving Rhetorica." *Rhetoric Society Quarterly* 48, no. 1 (2018): 3–27.

Lueck, Amy J. "Haunting Women's Public Memory: Ethos, Space, and Gender in the Winchester Mystery House." *Rhetoric Review* 40, no. 2 (2021): 107–22.

Mandziuk, Roseann M. "Commemorating Sojourner Truth: Negotiating the Politics of Race and Gender in the Spaces of Public Memory." *Western Journal of Communication* 67, no. 3 (2003): 271–91.

Mattingly, Carol. "Woman's Temple, Women's Fountains: The Erasure of Public Memory." *American Studies* 49, no. 3/4 (2008): 133–56.

Olson, Lester C. "Intellectual and Conceptual Resources for Visual Rhetoric: A Re-Examination of Scholarship since 1950." *The Review of Communication* 7, no. 1 (2007): 1–20.

Prelli, Lawrence, ed. *Rhetorics of Display*. Columbia, SC: University of South Carolina Press, 2006.

Rand, Erin J. "Bad Feelings in Public: Rhetoric, Affect, Emotion." *Rhetoric and Public Affairs* 18, no. 1 (2015): 161–76.

Rooney, Sierra. "Guest Editor's Statement." *Public Art Dialogue* 11, no. 1 (2021): 1–11.

Soto Vega, Karieann M. "Afterlives of Anticolonial Dissent: Performances of Public Memory Within and Against the United States of América." *Journal for the History of Rhetoric* 24, no. 1 (2021): 69–86.

Squires, Catherine R., and Aisha Upton. "The Color of Money or How to Redesign a "Monument in Your Pocket." *Humanity & Society* 44, no. 1 (2020): 12–36.

Throckmorton, Jodi. "The Meaning of Absence: Sharon Hayes's *If They Should Ask*." In *Monument Lab: Creative Speculations for Philadelphia*, edited by Paul M. Farber and Ken Lum, 98–99. Philadelphia, PA: Temple University Press, 2019.

Warner, Marina. *Monuments and Maidens: The Allegory of the Female Form*. Berkeley, CA: University of California Press, 1985.

Wilde, Patricia A. "(Re)telling the Times: The Tangled Memories of Confederate Spies Rose O'Neal Greenhow and Belle Boyd." *Rhetoric Review* 38, no. 3 (2019): 297–310.

Zelizer, Barbie. "Reading the Past Against the Grain: The Shape of Memory Studies." *Critical Studies in Mass Communication* 12, no. 2 (1995): 214–39.

Conclusion

Moving Forward with a Feminist Method of Response

Curtis J. Jewell, Abigail H. Long, Sidney Turner,
and Gabriella Wilson

Rhetorica Rising serves as a space where developing and emerging feminist rhetorical approaches are in conversation with established feminist methods and methodologies, with the shared goal of pushing scholarship and the field forward. Our contributing authors explicate varied ways feminist rhetorical methods and methodologies may impact rhetorical work through trauma-informed methodologies, digital rhetorics, and intersectional feminist methodologies, to name a few. We imagine *Rhetorica Rising* being employed within graduate seminars, with those fresh to the field encountering this text similarly to how the four of us learned from *Rhetorica in Motion*. With this in mind, we intentionally write this concluding chapter for graduate students and emerging scholars, for those encountering *Rhetorica Rising* as one of their first feminist methodological texts, and for those contemplating their position within ongoing conversations as the next generation of rhetorical scholars.

As graduate coeditors, focusing on graduate student experiences allows us to draw on our collective embodied knowledges. Acknowledging that we all hold unique perspectives and experiences, we foreground our positionalities and research ethics in ways that overlap, intertwine, and diverge. To conclude the collection, we reflect on how our perspectives as scholars entering the field who are thinking critically about collaboration, social action research, editorial logistics, navigating collective decision-making amongst colleagues and mentors, and remaining true to our respective feminist ethics has developed through our collaboration and discussions around feminist rhetorical methods and methodologies. Inspired by what this volume has taught us about feminist rhetorical methods and methodologies, we also share a series of prompting questions that guide our research endeavors as an offering to other emerging scholars beginning to consider how feminist methods and methodologies influence their scholarly orientation.

Reflecting on our experiences of coediting this volume, we notice a through line that unifies our approach—we aspire to enact a *feminist method of response,* which we understand as an orientation towards research, scholarly formation, collaboration, and editing that centers reflexivity, responsivity, reciprocity, and embodied experiences. Informed by feminist work on standpoint epistemology, situated knowledges,[1] and a theory of the flesh,[2] a *feminist method of response* foregrounds situated inquiry and embodied knowledge, urging us to ask questions of our work and our place in rhetorical studies.

As we've navigated collaborating with each other, each of us had to ask ourselves—How do we create space for those we collaborate with? How do we remain responsive to the ways scholarship can uphold, complicate, and challenge collective histories and the values we each carry? Our approach holds space for us to understand how our feminist ethics inform our orientations as both individuals and a collective. This process prompts us to iteratively raise questions and practice trust among collaborators, curating space for each collaborator's positionality, lived experiences, and ways of making knowledge. While we write this conclusion together, we include individual reflections to allow each of us (Abby, Curtis, Gabby, and Sidney) to speak to our scholarly commitments, research ethics, and the questions that inform our commitments to social action. We reflect on our research orientations and positionalities to demonstrate how we enact a *feminist method of response* that asks questions about our research and research process. It is a crucial task for graduate students and emerging scholars to define their positionality and work collaboratively with other colleagues and communities. Together, we apply a *feminist method of response* within this conclusion because it is valuable within collaborative projects to interrogate relations of power, representation, and reciprocity.

In this conclusion, we (1) flesh out our understanding of a *feminist method of response,* (2) consider the ways it has shaped our approaches to research, (3) reflect on its role in our collective research practices, (4) share how mentorship and collaboration can incorporate this *feminist method of response,* and (5) close with questions as a resource for approaching future research collaborations with care.

Our positionalities inherently shape our research ethics and approaches, and thoughtful engagement of our positionalities enables us to transform our scholarly practices from situational attunement to an intentional ethic of care that "forg[es] informed, self-reflexive solidarities" across identities and borders.[3] Focusing on responsivity encourages researchers to interrogate how feminist practices and positionality influence, for instance, the material conditions of person-to-person interactions, consideration of ethical responsibility, and labor concerns. Importantly, a *feminist method of response* fosters space for recursive inquiry, informed by one's positionality and entanglements, as situations and contexts continually change around us.

Our conceptualization of a *feminist method of response* builds on our understanding of feminism as not a self-contained field of study but instead a collection of developing relations, methods, and methodologies that shape research and daily life. The construction and enactment of a *feminist method of response* is personal, requiring us to be attentive to our lived experiences, areas of inquiry, scholarly trajectories, and research ethics. Enacting this approach requires us to acknowledge larger contexts that shape how we develop our ethics throughout the process. Many of the chapters in *Rhetorica Rising* carefully attend to these concerns. For instance, part one, "Reclaiming Space and Centering the Body," foregrounds embodied relations and experiences across various spaces. Specifically, Christina V. Cedillo's chapter in part one interrogates Eurowestern concepts such as ethos and exigence and dissects how individualist approaches to these concepts "other" Indigenous communal modes of communication. Cedillo instead embraces how social, cultural, and political contexts shape physicality, identity, and embodiment, paralleling the importance of positionality in research.

Positionality and the Impassioned Directions of Feminist Rhetorical Action

As emerging scholars constructing their scholarly and professional identities, we see the interdisciplinary deployment of feminist methods as one way to begin encouraging the self-reflexive research practices integral to ethical feminist research. In all three parts of this edited collection, authors grapple with the ways their positionality and identities impact or influence their research projects and agendas. For example, in part three, in "Navigating Materiality, Memory, and Futurity," the authors consider how embodiment shapes ways of knowing and being, especially in research. In that part, Stephanie Jones draws on embodied experience to situate her theoretical work, grounding her exploration of Afrodigitized critical questioning in gamer spaces through her experiences as a scholar and gamer, becoming hyper-attuned to the ways that Black women's bodies are narrativized. Like Jones, in what follows, we each reflect on connections between our positionality and research projects, sharing the situated concerns we each bring to the collaboration, which shape our collective understanding of a *feminist method of response* and its influence on our research methods and methodologies.

As I (Sidney) reflect on the writing of this collection and that of this concluding chapter, I return to the question that was asked in our call for proposals—"How can feminist rhetorical methods and methodologies foster productive engagement with our social and material worlds?" This question asks us to consider our own positionalities and the ways in which we take up space and enact our own "fight" amidst a turbulent social reality. My own attention is torn as I navigate my graduate journey in New York state while witnessing my home state of Florida experience an education back-slide. With the passing of House Bills 1467, 1557 (referred to as the Don't Say Gay or Don't Say Period bill), and 7 (referred to as the Stop WOKE Act), Florida has banned teaching critical race theory, enforces surveillance of student bodies regarding sexual orientation, gender identity, and sexual health, and is censoring information accessible to students by removing books and other media from library shelves. These policies have far-reaching material implications as other states and institutions pass similar policies and restructure education systems.[4] Informed by a feminist ethic and attuned to the institutional embodiment[5] experienced by my students and myself, I intentionally reflect on the ways my personal life and identity direct my energy and focus as an instructor and researcher. By embracing a *feminist method of response,* I ask—What are the possible impacts my work has on my own life and the communities I belong to? How have events (e.g. the passing of the Florida Stop WOKE Act, the COVID-19 pandemic) hindered the learning experiences of students? How will the narratives of this time shape public memory?[6] Considering the material implications of the present that shape the narrativizing of history, we can turn to an adaptation of feminist recovery and unsettling[7] methods that seek to understand the processes and power that preservation has on the rewriting of public memory. This line of feminist memory inquiry is nuanced by Carly S. Woods and Jessica Enoch in this volume, whose proposed heuristics and questioning help us better understand how local and transnational social movements may be remembered through public memory places.

As a neurodivergent CHamoru (the Indigenous people of Guåhan) rhetorical scholar, I (Curtis) regularly find myself negotiating knowledge-making norms and the practices of the communities to which I belong. Enacting a *feminist method of response* within my research entails considering how power fluctuates as I navigate between and make space for different communities. My experience as white-passing CHamoru has exemplified how outing myself via non-dominant rhetorical strategies in academic spaces engenders anxiety stemming from explicitly stated and perceived risks. While digital spaces aid communication and accessibility between differently placed peoples, transnational feminist rhetorical scholarship is complicated via temporal boundaries and a continual re-attunement to how one's positionality influences what can be known, the spaces we may operate in as well as how, and what knowledge we have a right to share as a "middle-ground." Navigating disparate rhetorics is not a simple task when serving Indigenous and differently placed bodies. As researchers, editors, and community members, we must take care to consider questions such as these—How do we make space for and honor various knowledge making practices? Where can we establish relationships of solidarity across differences without villainizing its existence?[8] When can we adjust our projects to account for peoples elsewhere and otherwise?[9] While answers to these questions may vary, we cannot pursue social change without complicating established academic practices, their histories, and interrogating our respective roles within them. For myself, answers to these questions have materialized in my research practices, in which I chose to not disclose study findings or withdraw from conferences; I prioritize explicit consent of participants at each stage and iteration of publication to ensure participants retain sovereignty over their interviews, stories, and knowledges; this limits the amount of work I make public as the communities I serve do not always operate along the timelines of academia.

As someone who both writes about and experiences disability, I (Abby) am attuned to ways embodiment and disability shape the editorial process, feeling out the spaces where a *feminist method of response* could intervene. In this collective editorial, writing, and publication process, as well as in my own research on graduate teaching assistants, I pay attention to the complications of access that accompany encultured "norms" about time, process, and seamlessness in academic spaces. In particular, while coediting this collection, I felt the pinch of publication process deadlines and the long spaces between our communications with contributors, all of whom are operating under different configurations of temporal, academic, and embodied pressures. How might awareness of the differential crunch publishing places on disabled writers translate into more inclusive practices? Accessibility is inherently tied up in methodology, including our developing approaches to editorial work, and "tending to disability . . . should transform our scholarship and ways of knowing and center the work of those most impacted."[10] I wonder how attending to the ethics of pace and the contours of crip writing time might inflect both composing and editorial processes in a way that opens space for the unpredictability of disability without demanding additional access labor from writers and editors, especially those in the precarious position of graduate students.[11] Who was excluded from our published collection due to the conflict between the demands of academic timelines and the emotional, physical, mental, social, and material needs of a precarious body, further exacerbated during the ongoing mass-disabling event of the COVID-19 pandemic? As a graduate editor at the start of my career, I acknowledge and mourn these absences and the possibilities they hold, committing to approach upcoming publishing and collaboration opportunities with trauma-informed crip methodologies as my guide. Learning from Megan Schoettler's exploration of trauma-informed feminist methodologies and sarah madoka currie and Ada Hubrig's insights into the complex intersections of feminist methods and m/Mad studies, I invite our readers to attend to the experiences, refusals, and insights of traumatized, m/Mad, and disabled bodyminds.

Feminist rhetorical methods and methodologies make clear that collaboration is a key component of feminist work and research, but collaboration can only work when all members of the collective are accounted for; this means considering how participation and the distribution of labor across the collective impacts different bodyminds. My (Gabby) experiences as a first-generation, disabled graduate student of color leave me concerned with the dynamics of collaboration and different forms of precarity as they manifest in the academy and impact labor distribution and temporal flows. Moya Bailey argues that "efficiency and productivity drive the pace of" academic life, mainly benefiting the institution. This is because capitalist logics drive the pace of academic life, affirming academic timelines and maintaining specific benchmarks that measure productivity.[12] While varying levels of contingency and precarity impact all faculty and staff at university institutions, as a graduate student, my experiences and observations during my graduate education have left me especially concerned with how graduate education in rhetoric and composition does not tend to account for different bodyminds.

High attrition rates and general feelings of frustration across PhD programs suggest that the associated precarity and liminality of these roles contribute to general feelings of unwellness among graduate students, who experience this unwellness to different degrees depending on other structures and social identities they may embody.[13] Graduate students are expected to navigate the responsibilities of their liminal roles while lacking institutional support. Tessa Brown aptly depicts "the great irony of graduate study: it teaches us to understand the world . . . through the impoverishment of our living and working conditions."[14] Recognizing the struggles we share based on our working conditions can unite graduate students to organize for better working conditions, as evidenced by growing graduate unionization. However, it's equally important to recognize the differences among graduate students and how those differences contribute to inequitable experiences and untenable working conditions. Given the context of our conclusion, I wonder what is necessary to encourage open interrogation of difference and valuing all bodies beyond the ability to produce as quickly and as much as possible.

Though our individual embodied experiences and research inquiry areas differ, we take up a *feminist method of response* together in this editorial collective as a shared orientation towards knowledge-making. Our own lived experiences, identities, and orientations move us to action—be it physically moving our bodies, interrogating culturally ingrained harm, or starting with a question that closes the distance between the local and transnational through feminist rhetorical research. The questions we raise individually echo a shared concern for people, specifically, a desire to acknowledge, make known, and improve the material circumstances experienced by marginalized communities and individuals we care about and possibly relate to. Our orientations to feminist rhetorical scholarship inform our research agendas, reflecting our current material realities.

Developing Mentorship and Collaborative Practices within the Editorial Process

In this section, we share some ways a *feminist method of response* can inform mentorship and collaborative practices, drawing on our own experiences as coeditors. The opportunity for us as graduate students to participate in this editorial collective is itself the fruit of a *feminist method of response*. In the context of a graduate feminist rhetorics seminar, Eileen E. Schell shared her plans to collaborate with K.J. Rawson and interested graduate students to develop a second installment of *Rhetorica in Motion*,[15] providing information about the projected timeline, steps, and uncertainties that the process would entail. By extending this invitation to collaborate within the context of a graduate course, Schell ensured participating graduate students would come to the process equipped with a shared background in feminist rhetorics; further, this open invitation dissolved some of the barriers graduate students face when entering academic publishing. Recognizing the kairotic moment that had been curated, we each opted in to participate, joining the collective and, ultimately, developing this volume.

As we've moved through the editorial process, Eileen and K.J. grappled with the uncertainties inherent in collaborating with newcomers to rhetorical studies. Graduate students often come to projects like this with limited experience with professional collaboration, the publishing process, and/or editorial work. However, in choosing to invite us in as collaborators, Eileen and K.J. demonstrated that they value our potential to learn from the opportunity. Collaborating in a group introduces more variables for potential miscommunications, misunderstandings, and conflicting schedules. Bringing on four graduate students to form a collective of six editors has the potential to slow down the collaborative editorial process even more, considering the necessity of explaining the process and the often-unstated rules and expectations that accompany academic publishing. Teaching graduate students how to craft a call for papers and compose feedback letters involves a steep learning curve. Yet, guided by their shared feminist ethic, Eileen and K.J. took the risk of collaborating with us—they chose to mentor us in real-time throughout the editorial process by showing up to meetings, giving feedback on drafts, and guiding us through our developing understandings of the genres, negotiations, and decisions that structure a published edited collection.

In listening to and learning from us, Eileen and K.J. have demonstrated their commitment to intergenerational mentoring, joining us to grapple with "concretized ways in which collaborating across rank and age can facilitate reinterpreting and recalibrating existing scholarly conversations."[16] Their decision to deprioritize the convenience of working with known collaborators in favor of mentoring newcomers initiates the cycle of a *feminist method of response* in mentorship. Specifically, Eileen and K.J. model how feminist mentorship relationships benefit from reflection, reciprocity, open communication, and a drawing on embodied knowledge. After moving through this experience, we graduate students are now more equipped to engage in future collaborations and mentor others in due time. While we believe all graduate students should have access to mentorship and collaborative opportunities to learn professional skills beyond academic writing and teaching,[17] we understand that the kairotic moment that led to our editorial collaboration may not be presented to all graduate students; therefore, in an effort to make these hidden knowledges more accessible, we are compelled to share four takeaways from what we have learned.

First, we've learned that taking graduate student concerns seriously is a critical component of intergenerational mentoring and, for that matter, intergenerational collaboration. Given the precarious positions graduate students hold within academic institutions, we bring perspectives that can illuminate gaps and explore new directions in feminist rhetorical research. We are positioned to question existing methods, methodologies, and academic publishing traditions not out of critique but inquiry. Mentoring and collaborating with graduate students is necessary for the field's development. We most appreciate feminist mentoring practices that function through horizontal (rather than hierarchical) mentoring models, remaining attentive to power dynamics and ensuring that graduate students feel valued and heard within the collaboration.[18] In this edited collection, we played a pivotal role in shaping the collection and the ways that feminist rhetorical methods were employed throughout the publishing process. While it's important for graduate students to learn from the experiences of those who came before us, it's equally as important that intergenerational collaborations consistently engage in reflective thinking and remain receptive to new approaches to knowledge making that may not align with traditional academic practices or commonplace ideas in feminist rhetorics.

Second, we underscore the fact that mentors shouldn't assume graduate students come into the academy with a working knowledge of the publishing process. Mentoring and facilitating collaboration with graduate students by offering them opportunities to advance their careers and exposing the hidden curriculum creates space to diversify the field and engage new perspectives. Further, mentoring minimizes barriers to entry for scholars unfamiliar with or historically excluded from academic institutions. In our experience, the most influential feminist mentoring happens in collaborative relationships that prioritize transparent procedures, recursively attend to the equitable distribution of labor among collaborators, and attempt to account for the power dynamics inherent in intergenerational collaboration. As coeditors, we learned to appreciate the importance of frequent, open reflection about the power dynamics that exist when collaborating together across identities and embodiments. In line with a *feminist method of response,* our mentors, Eileen and K.J., have helped us contend with some of the unknowns of collaboration and given us valuable insights into the publishing process.

Third, in our experiences working together, we discovered the importance of taking into account the experiences of collaborators and balancing the needs and expectations of partnerships (e.g., contributing authors, publisher, editors). The collaborative editorial process is a difficult one, involving the labor of not only editorial work but also collaboration, consensus, and negotiation with other participants of the edited collection. Collaborators' capacities fluctuate depending on their shifting roles within the institution, dynamic personal lives, affective labor demands, and experiences of disability. Throughout our editorial process, we prioritized engaging with all chapter contributors as colleagues, offering patience and generosity regardless of contributors' "status" within the field; we provided extensions and adjusted our feedback in an attempt to accommodate our contributors. We encourage all collaborators, regardless of role, to embrace a *feminist method of response* as a practice of cyclical reflection as requirements and responsibilities fluctuate over time. We promote flexibility as the collaborative dynamics change and recognize that these changes require shifts in understanding. Due especially to ableist expectations around productivity, it is necessary for collaborators to interrogate any internalized stigma against expressing a need for more time or asking to redistribute labor to ensure readjustments to time frames are welcomed and supported throughout the process.

Finally, we also learned that reflecting on labor distribution within a collaboration requires each member of the collective to do an honest self-audit and identify what we really need. As graduate students, we found ourselves navigating the demands of our precarious positioning, questioning, "How can I navigate the complexities of competing degree timelines, coursework demands, exam deadlines, teaching responsibilities, and my personal life while remaining responsive to contributors and following an external publishing schedule?" The answer to this question has varied from person to person and has changed as the demands within our personal and professional lives have shifted. This is especially true when collaborating with graduate students as their responsibilities and commitments shift dramatically as they move through graduate programs. To collaborate effectively as a group, we needed to become familiar with our own needs and boundaries as individuals. As part of our *feminist method of response,* we had to evaluate our own priorities in relation to the needs of the developing edited collection and grant ourselves permission to adhere to the boundaries we set for ourselves. As we reflected on our own roles in the collaboration, we considered the following questions.

1. What is my investment in the ongoing project?
2. In what ways am I able and willing to collaborate with others?
3. Am I communicating my own expectations (i.e., communication, labor, performance, time) to the collaborating group?
4. Am I able to fulfill my stated commitments, and if not, am I communicating this to my collaborators?
5. How can I create the space needed for collaborating and the processes of negotiation, communication, and challenges that come with effective collaboration?
6. How can I move from thinking individually to thinking collectively about the overall project?

A practice of consistent questioning and reflection, while demanding, opened up space for us to consider how the collaboration could move forward responsively in more equitable ways while acknowledging the inherent complexity of long-term collaborations with each other.

Feminist Care in Research and Collaboration

A central thread woven throughout this collection is the care of communities and research participants. Contributors across this volume demonstrate ethical ways to interrogate the history of our field, inquire into the methodologies that guide us, and consider the methods we employ as feminist rhetoricians to avoid perpetuating acts of violence and harm on communities and participants. They also address the epistemological assumptions embedded within their scholarship and take responsibility for how feminist research practices respond to and create the spaces we inhabit.

Given feminist rhetorical commitments to centering marginalized and liminal identities, feminist rhetoricians are equipped to be attentive to rising social movements and precarious identities while reflecting on and assessing their capacity to show up. Acknowledging how precarity varies from person-to-person, enacting a *feminist method of response* becomes a shared responsibility to eschew performative allyship and note that social change is often accompanied by risk that is felt in different ways by different bodies. For these intersections and connections to materialize across and outside of the academy, it is necessary to attune our methods and methodologies to current social and political crises. This calls for dedicating additional time to reflecting on what our research does and analyzing our processes and relations as we also consider burgeoning conversations about theory, social movements, and the ongoing expansion of the networked relations within which our work lives. It also requires an assessment of the kinds of crises and social movements important to each researcher as they construct their scholarly orientation and research agenda. Researchers should consider their relationship to the research and social movements with which they work.

A desire for social change can inspire and guide the material work of mentorship and collaboration, leading to scholarship that contributes to the work of social justice movements. Throughout the edited collection, contributors rely on embodied knowledge and lived experiences of people actively advocating in these spaces to bridge the gap between academic scholarship, structural action, and responding to current crises. This method requires scholars to evaluate how their own positionalities and lived experiences influence how they "show up" in traditional and non-traditional research spaces, relationships, and contexts.

Recognizing the complexity of establishing our own rhetorical praxis and the inequities that exist across mentorship in graduate education, we share a series of questions intended to prompt thought on how we might integrate feminist rhetorical methods and methodologies into our scholarship. While not exhaustive, we intend these questions to serve as gentle guides throughout the research process for feminist rhetorical researchers (e.g., during data collection, analysis, composing findings, and circulating your work). We invite you, our readers, and particularly those among us who are emerging scholars, to engage with these questions and consider which apply to your work.

1. What is my investment in this project? Why am I pursuing this work?
2. What are my boundaries in regard to my (1) topic expertise, (2) identity within the research space(s), (3) how I interact with and portray participants, and (4) how I want my work to be circulated?
3. What do I need to learn and ask questions about before engaging in this work?
4. Who benefits from the research? How does my positionality and identity impact how I engage with my participants and fellow collaborators? My research ethic? In what ways do I need to evaluate my ethics, considering my work's larger contexts and power structures?
5. Does my research engage in work outside of my communities? How does my work reference communities that I don't specifically serve/research/represent? How is my work valuable to those communities? How are community voices and perspectives represented in my data collection and findings?

6. Does my work engage with global and/or transnational perspectives? Have I considered how my research sites, methods, and methodologies move beyond a western lens?

In considering these questions, we give ourselves permission to ask questions, to not know, to sit and wonder, to rethink, go back, revise, to not publish right away. As academics, creating space and time to reflect and develop our ethics is crucial to conducting meaningful research that contributes to transformative social change. In the process of taking up a feminist method of response in our collective, we have been transformed, learning from the contributors and from the process of editing, collaborating, and publishing. These questions and the insights accompanying them travel with us from this project into our future research endeavors.

NOTES

1. Collins, *Black Feminist Thought*; Haraway, "Situated Knowledges"; Kirsch, *Ethical Dilemmas*; Rich. "Notes toward a Politics of Location."
2. Moraga and Anzaldúa, *This Bridge*. 23.
3. Mohanty, *Feminism,* 251.
4. Friedman et al., "Educational Censorship Continues; The 2023 Legislative Sessions So Far," *Pen America*, February 16, 2023, https://pen.org/.
5. Nicolas and Sicari, *Our Body of Work*, 6.
6. Blair, Dickinson, and Ott, "Introduction: Memory/Rhetoric/Place," 6.
7. Kirsch et al., *Unsettling.*
8. Tambe and Thayer, *Transnational Feminist Itineraries.*
9. García and Baca, *Rhetorics Elsewhere.*
10. Hubrig, "Access," https://compstudiesjournal.com/2021/04/19/access-from-as-the -start-on-writing-studies-and-accessibility/.
11. Bailey, "The Ethics"; Chen, "Chronic Illness"; Price, "The Precarity."
12. Bailey, "The Ethics," 287; Erevelles, *Disability, 62*; Puar, "Spatial Debilities," 396.
13. Young et al., "Factors," 34; Driscoll et. al. "Self-Care," 454.
14. Brown, *Graduate Students*, 16.
15. Schell and Rawson, *Rhetorica.*
16. Gaillet, "Growing Pains." https://cfshrc.org/article/growing-pains-intergenerational -mentoring-and-sustainability-of-the-coalitions-mission/.
17. Lutkewitte, Kitchens, and Scanlon, *Stories*, 122.
18. Van Haitsma and Ceraso, "'Making It,'" 211.

WORKS CITED

Bailey, Moya. "The Ethics of Pace." *The South Atlantic Quarterly* 120, no. 2 (April 2021): 285–99.

Blair, Carole, Greg Dickinson, and Brian L. Ott. "Introduction: Rhetoric/Memory/ Place." *Places of Public Memory: The Rhetoric of Museums and Memorials*, edited by Greg Dickinson, Carole Blair, and Brian L. Ott, 1–54. Tuscaloosa, AL: University of Alabama, 2010.

Brown, Tessa, ed. *Graduate Students at Work: Exploited Scholars of Neoliberal Higher Ed*. Lawrence, KS: University Press of Kansas, 2023.

Chen, Mel Y. "Chronic Illness, Slowness, and the Time of Writing." *In Crip Author-ship: Disability as Method*, edited by Mara Mills and Rebecca Sanchez, 33–37. New York: New York University Press, 2003.

Collins, Patricia Hill. *Black Feminist Thought*. New York: Routledge, 2009.

Driscoll, Dana Lynn, S. Rebecca Leigh, and Nadia Francine Zamin. "Self-care as Pro-fessionalization: A Case for Ethical Doctoral Education in Composition Studies." *College Composition & Communication* 71, no. 3 (2020): 453–80.

Erevelles, Nirmala. *Disability and Differences in Global Contexts*. New York: Palgrave Macmillan, 2011.

Gaillet, Lynée Lewis. "Growing Pains: Intergenerational Mentoring and Sustainability of the Coalition's Mission." *Peitho* 24, no. 4 (2022). https://cfshrc.org/article/growing -pains-intergenerational-mentoring-and-sustainability-of-the-coalitions-mission/

García, Romeo, and Damián Baca. *Rhetorics Elsewhere and Otherwise*. Champaign, IL: National Council of Teachers of English, 2019.

Haraway, Donna. "Situated Knowledges: The Science Question in Feminism and the Privilege of Partial Perspective." *Feminist Studies* 14, no. 3 (1988): 575–99.

Hubrig, Ada. "Access from/as the Start: On Writing Studies and 'Accessibility.'" *Com-position Studies* (2021). https://compstudiesjournal.com/2021/04/19/access-from-as -the-start-on-writing-studies-and-accessibility/.

Kirsch, Gesa. *Ethical Dilemmas in Feminist Research: The Politics of Location, Interpre-tation, and Publication*. New York: SUNY Press, 1999.

Kirsch, Gesa E., Romeo García, Caitlin Burns Allen, and Walker P. Smith, eds. *Unset-tling Archival Research: Engaging Critical, Communal, and Digital Archives*. Carbon-dale, IL: Southern Illinois University Press, 2023.

Lutkewitte, Claire, Juliette C. Kitchens, and Molly J. Scanlon, eds. *Stories of Becoming: Demystifying the Professoriate for Graduate Students in Composition and Rhetoric*. Denver, CO: University Press of Colorado, 2022.

Mohanty, Chandra Talpade. *Feminism Without Borders: Decolonizing Theory, Practicing Solidarity*. New Delhi, India: Zubaan, 2006.

Moraga, Cherríe, and Gloria Anzaldúa, eds. *This Bridge Called My Back: Writings by Radical Women of Color*. 4th ed. Albany, NY: SUNY Press, 2015.

Nicolas, Melissa, and Anna Sicari, eds. *Our Body of Work: Embodied Administration and Teaching*. Logan, UT: Utah State University Press, 2022.

Price, Margaret. "The Precarity of Disability/Studies in Academe." In *Precarious Rhet-orics*, edited by Wendy S. Hesford, Adela C. Licona, and Christa Teston, 191–211. Columbus, OH: Ohio State University Press, 2018.

Puar, Jasbir K. "Spatial Debilities: Slow life and Carceral Capitalism in Palestine." *South Atlantic Quarterly* 120, no. 2 (2021): 393–414.

Rich, Adrienne. "Notes toward a Politics of Location." In *Blood, Bread, and Poetry: Selected Prose 1979–1985*, 210–31. New York: W.W. Norton & Company, 1986.

Schell, Eileen E., and K.J. Rawson, eds. *Rhetorica in Motion: Feminist Rhetorical Meth-ods and Methodologies*. Pittsburgh, PA: University of Pittsburgh Press, 2010.

Tambe, Ashwini, and Millie Thayer. *Transnational Feminist Itineraries: Situating Theory and Activist Practice*. Durham, NC: Duke University Press, 2021.

Van Haitsma, Pamela, and Steph Ceraso. "'Making It' in the Academy through Hori-zontal Mentoring." *Peitho* 19, no. 2 (2017): 210–33.

Young, Sonia N., William R. Vanwye, Mark A. Schafer, Troy A. Robertson, and Ashley Vincent Poore. "Factors Affecting PhD Student Success." *International Journal of Exercise Science* 12, no. 1 (2019): 34–45.

ACKNOWLEDGMENTS

This volume first took shape through conversations in Eileen E. Schell's Fall 2021 graduate seminar Feminist Rhetorics in the midst of an ongoing global pandemic. The class was held in one of the residence hall classrooms on the Syracuse University campus where we had to present our IDs to enter the building and pass by masked students strolling the halls in pajamas and slippers. We wore masks inside the classroom and building, but halfway through the class, we often went outside in the dorm's courtyard and sat in Adirondack-style chairs around an unlit fire pit so we could be unmasked and enjoy what was uncharacteristically good fall weather. Around the fire-pit, students discussed and debated feminist theory.

Over the next several months, class members completed promising projects on varied aspects of feminist rhetorics, some of which has shaped ongoing dissertation projects and publications. Toward the end of the semester, Eileen discussed the possibility of creating a new volume on feminist rhetorical methods and methodologies that would complement the work of *Rhetorica in Motion,* the first volume that Eileen E. Schell and K.J. Rawson completed in 2010. Four students stepped up to take on the project with Eileen E. Schell and K.J. Rawson. This volume would not have been possible without the collaborative work of the *Rhetorica Rising* editorial collective: Curtis J. Jewell, Abigail H. Long, Sidney Turner, and Gabriella Wilson with K.J. Rawson and Eileen E. Schell as returning coeditors.

Eileen would like to thank the graduate students in the Feminist Rhetorics seminar who stepped up as coeditors to work on *Rhetorica Rising*: Abby, Curtis, Sidney, and Gabby for your ideas, leadership, and insights as coeditors of this volume. You took on the responsibility of coediting on top of your coursework, doctoral exams, dissertations and other aspects of your lives. Your energy, vision, and hard work is appreciated. Eileen would also like to thank K.J. Rawson for stepping up once again to serve as one of the lead editors of the volume amidst many responsibilities at work and home. K.J.'s ability to multitask, stay organized, solve problems, and not tarry on revision tasks was much appreciated and made this volume possible. It was a lot of fun to work together again, and our talks and check-ins made the collaboration doubly rewarding. Finally, Eileen would like to thank her husband Tom Kerr and Siberian husky named Xena for making sure she got out on hikes, runs, and walks instead of always being inside hunched over a desk. Facetime calls from her college-attending daughter Autumn Kerr were a welcome diversion and invariably fun. Workouts with teammates in Syracuse Fleet Feet's Triathlon program have provided exercise, fun, and adventure to round out academic life. Endurance sports can be good training for coediting a volume!

K.J. is grateful to the coeditors of this volume—Eileen, Abby, Curtis, Sidney, and Gabby—who each stepped up at key moments to push this project forward and shape it with their own vision. In the midst of their PhD programs, a notoriously challenging time when countless things compete for your attention, the graduate students on this editorial collective worked particularly hard to contribute to this project. K.J. was also delighted to have an excuse to collaborate with Eileen again, who for decades has offered him inspiring leadership, feminist mentorship, and supportive friendship, all of which were threaded through every stage of this project. Last, but always first, K.J. extends his deepest love and gratitude to his family—Steph, Morgana, Finley, and Elliot—who are always his biggest supporters and the center of his world.

Sidney is grateful to her coeditors, Eileen, K.J., Gabby, Abby, and Curtis, for their teachings, generous teamwork, and moments of laughter. She would like to thank K.J. for his openness to model intercollegiate collaboration and his mentorship. Sidney is especially thankful to Eileen for her encouragement and mentorship that remains invaluable as she navigates the many facets of academic life. Sidney is also grateful to her family and friends for their continued love and support. A special thank you to Emily Pifer and Gabi Diaz for their friendships, Zoom calls, and sharing their joy of the field. Finally, Sidney would like to thank Chris Young, her greatest admirer who never ceases to amaze.

Gabby appreciates the time and energy each of her coeditors—Eileen, K.J., Sidney, Abby, and Curtis—contributed to the project. She would like to thank them for their shared laughs, generous collaboration, and supportive mentorship. Gabby would especially like to thank K.J. and Eileen for their encouragement, feedback, guidance, and commitment to feminist intergenerational mentorship and collaboration. Gabby would also like to thank her husband, Bryan, and their dog, Buzz, for their love and support. Finally, Gabby expresses gratitude for the variety of seasons and trails she walked throughout Syracuse with her family, providing insight, inspiration, and clarity as she collaborated on the volume.

Abby holds deep gratitude for the many collaborators who shaped this volume, including her coeditors—Curtis, Eileen, Gabby, K.J., and Sidney—and the contributing authors, research participants, and knowledge-makers whose lived experience, praxis, and theories animate this volume. In particular, she appreciates each collaborator's individual willingness to risk investing in the possibilities that can emerge from collective conversations, to engage the revision cycle with patience, courage, and an enduring commitment to the value of their contributions. Furthermore, the mentorship that Eileen and K.J. have provided throughout the editorial process has been an invaluable gift, extending beyond the scope of this project to expand Abby's understanding of the accordioned genres within the editorial process and the dynamic contours of feminist collaboration. Abby would also like to thank her parents, Phil and Lori, and her friends, including Karisa Bridgelal, Urmi Parekh, and Zakery Muñoz, for their support, encouragement, and periodic reminders to rest through the duration of this project.

Curtis extends both thanks and respect for his coeditors—Abby, Eileen, Gabby, K.J., and Sidney—as well as the contributing authors and participants invaluable to this volume. He is honored to have worked and learned alongside such caring, patient, and insightful scholars. He thanks Jeff, Mary, Matthew, and Nicole Jewell who continually offer advice, solace, and laughter throughout his academic journey. Curtis would like to offer a final thanks to his fianceé Genesis Yamilex Ayala Sanchez, who unfailingly offers unending love, support, and encouragement which makes his work possible.

We would like to thank our contributors for their willingness to share their knowledge and insights and belief in this volume as it took shape. Your insightful chapters will help shape the future of feminist rhetorics research and activism for years to come. It has been an honor to work with you!

We also thank Aurora Bell and Vicki Gallagher for their championing of this volume. We are honored to be part of the Movement Rhetoric/Rhetoric's Movement series at the University of South Carolina Press. We also would like to thank the two anonymous external reviewers for their thoughtful reviews and revision suggestions for the volume.

Cailin Roles deserves a hearty thanks, too, for their expert formatting skills and attention to detail. Jennifer Jeffery of SUNY Potsdam has been a wonderful indexer—thank you for your efforts.

Finally, thanks to our readers of our first volume *Rhetorica in Motion* and all who urged us to complete a second volume!

CONTRIBUTORS

RACHEL BLOOM-POJAR is a bilingual (English-Spanish) researcher, educator, and consultant whose work focuses on Latine community health, storytelling, trust, reproductive justice, and language access. She is the director and co-founder of Cuentos de Confianza, a bilingual community writing project that features stories written by promotores de salud (health promoters) who work with reproductive and sexual health education and advocacy. Her published work can be found in NCTE's Studies in Writing & Rhetoric Series, *Community Literacy Journal, College Composition and Communication, Reflections, Present Tense,* the *Journal of Applied Communication Research,* and the Routledge edited collection, *Methodologies for the Rhetoric of Health and Medicine.*

CHRISTINA V. CEDILLO (she/they) is an associate professor of writing and rhetoric at the University of Houston-Clear Lake. Christina's research draws from cultural rhetorics, critical race theory, disability studies, and decolonial theory to focus on embodied rhetorics and rhetorics of embodiment at the intersections of race, gender, and disability. Their work has appeared in *College Composition & Communication, Rhetoric Society Quarterly,* the *Journal for the History of Rhetoric, Composition Forum,* and other journals and edited collections. Christina's current project examines spatiotemporal tropes that affect how marginalized rhetors and their messages are perceived and received based on modernity's colonial/modern epistemics. Christina is also the lead editor of the *Journal of Multimodal Rhetorics.*

SARAH MADOKA CURRIE (@kawaiilovesarah) earned her PhD in 2023 with a manifesto on higher education's violent relationship with mentally ill students. She has given over 40 workshops; invited talks and keynotes on mad-positive pedagogy; universal design for learning (UDL) strategy; classroom facilitation training; disability rhetoric; and applying equity, diversity, and inclusion (EDI) practices.

JESSICA ENOCH is professor of English and director of the Academic Writing Program at the University of Maryland. Her recent publications include *Domestic Occupations: Spatial Rhetorics and Women's Work*; *Mestiza Rhetorics: An Anthology of Mexicana Activism in the Spanish-Language Press, 1887–1922* (coedited with Cristina Ramírez), *Women at Work: Rhetorics of Gender and Labor* (coedited with David Gold), and *Retellings: Opportunities for Feminist Research in Rhetoric and Composition Studies* (coedited with Jordynn Jack). *Domestic Occupations* won the Winifred Bryan Horner Outstanding Book Award in 2020. Her work has appeared in such outlets as *Rhetoric Society Quarterly*, *Rhetoric Review*, *Quarterly Journal of Speech*, *College English*, and *College Composition and Communication*. She has served on the Executive Boards for the Conference on College Composition and Communication, the Rhetoric Society of America, and the Coalition of Feminist Scholars in the History of Rhetoric and Composition.

TAREZ SAMRA GRABAN is associate professor of English, director of Rhetoric and Composition, and Honors Teaching Scholar at Florida State University. From 2018–2021 she codirected the Demos Project for Studies in Data Humanities at FSU (https://demos.fsu.edu), and from 2023–2025, she led the *Linked Women Pedagogues* project team in migrating their data discovery tool to a new platform (https://lwpproject.create.fsu.edu). She is author of *Women's Irony: Rewriting Feminist Rhetorical Histories;* co-author (with Charlton et al.) of *GenAdmin: Theorizing WPA Identities in the Twenty-First Century;* coeditor (with Hui Wu) of *Global Rhetorical Traditions;* and co-editor (with Wendy Hayden) of *Teaching through the Archives.* Her work on feminist historiography appears in *African Journal of Rhetoric, Rhetorica, Gender and Language, Peitho,* and *College English* and in several anthologies and edited collections.

MICHAEL HEALY is currently an instructor of English at Western Kentucky University where he teaches in the Professional Writing Program. His research uses digital humanities methods and data feminism for historiographic inquiry into disciplinary publication and formation. He has also collaborated on using design thinking in the teaching of technical and professional writing courses and approaching AI in college composition. He and his partner spend their free time watching Star Trek, listening to The Mountain Goats, and being supervised by their two dogs, Janeway and Tendi. He also likes to run long distances.

ADA HUBRIG (they/them; X @AdaHubrig) is an autistic, genderqueer, disabled caretaker of cats. They live in Huntsville, Texas, where they labor as assistant professor and director of Composition at Sam Houston State University as their day job. Their scholarship centers disabled and queer/trans communities, and is featured in *College Composition and Communication, Community Literacy Journal*, and *Journal of Multimodal Rhetorics* among others, and their words have also found homes in *Brevity* and *Disability Visibility*.

CURTIS J. JEWELL is a PhD student and instructor at Syracuse University who explores the intersections of rhetoric and the cultural practices of Guåhan (Guam). His work examines the power of language and action in shaping perceptions, identities, and social dynamics within the CHamoru community. Engaged in ongoing projects that explore rhetoric's role in cultural preservation, community empowerment, and the evolving narratives of Guam, he is committed to shedding light on the voices and stories that often go unheard.

STEPHANIE JONES is assistant professor of English in Digital Rhetoric at the University of Oregon. Her dissertation, "Afrofuturist Feminism as Theory & Praxis: Rhetorical Root Working in the Black Speculative Arts Movement" explores Black women's speculative writing practices. She was awarded the 2021 Geneva Smitherman Award for Research in Black Language, Literacies, Cultures, and Rhetorics from NCTE/CCCC Black Caucus, the 2023 Rhetoric Society of America Dissertation Award, and the 2023 NWSA/Routledge Book Series Prize on "Subversive Histories, Feminist Futures." Her research interests include Afrofuturist Feminisms, Black Feminist Rhetorical Studies, Digital Humanities, and Video Game Studies. She was born and raised in Southern California.

DANIELLE KOEPKE is a teaching assistant professor at Marquette University where she teaches classes such as Business Writing, Health Science Writing, and Writing for Social Change. Her research areas include cultural rhetorics, reproductive justice, and digital design; these areas influence her practices of care as a teacher and as a community-engaged researcher. In her current book project, she is studying the strategies for and impacts of sharing stories of reproductive [in]justice on social media since the *Dobbs* decision. Her work can be found in publications such as *Composition Studies* and in edited book collections including *Digital Literacies for Human Connection* (NCTE), *Practicing Digital Activisms: On Rhetoric, Writing, and Technical*

Communication's Social Justice Obligations, and *Designing for social justice: Community-engaged approaches in technical and professional communication* (ATTW).

RACHEL LEWIS organizes and teaches in prisons, jails, and universities in Boston, MA. Their work has appeared in *Reflections, Peitho,* and *The SAGE Handbook of Feminist Research.*

ABIGAIL H. LONG is a PhD candidate in Composition and Cultural Rhetoric at Syracuse University. Her research interests include disability rhetorics, pandemic rhetorics, material methods, accessible writing pedagogy, feminist research practices, and teacher preparation. In her roles as a writing instructor and an assistant director of TA Education, Abby is passionate about teaching undergraduate writing courses, mentoring graduate teaching assistants, and advocating for access to pandemic mitigation measures in service of disability justice and community care. She is currently working on her dissertation, which explores how friction operates in the composing process, focusing on the implications for inclusive writing pedagogy and emerging disabled scholars.

ANDREA RILEY MUKAVETZ is a mother, writer, community-based researcher, and an enrolled citizen of the Chippewa of Thames First Nation. Growing up in Metro Detroit, Andrea comes from Chaldean and Lebanese heritage as well as Anishinaabeg. Andrea has a PhD from Michigan State University in Rhetoric and Writing. Her research and writing focuses on Michigan Anishinaabeg histories and lifeways, Indigenous approaches to research and writing, and centering story in how we form relationships with each other. Currently, Andrea is the Community Engagement Manager for the City of Grand Rapids. In her spare time, Andrea enjoys foraging and harvesting, sewing, reading romance novels, coaching youth softball, and lifting heavy weights.

TIMOTHY OLEKSIAK (he/they) is associate professor of English and the Professional and New Media Writing Program director at the University of Massachusetts Boston. His works have appeared in *College English, Pedagogy, Peitho, College Composition and Communication, Pre/Text, QED: A Journal in LGBTQ Worldmaking,* and in several edited collections including *The Routledge Handbook of Queer Rhetoric, The Cultural Impact of RuPaul's Drag Race,* and *Reinventing (with) Theory in Rhetoric and Writing Studies.* With

Joshua Barczewski he is coediting a forthcoming collection *Adequate: Re-writing the Logics of Success in Rhetoric and Composition*. If he had a theme song, it would be "Everything is Awesome" by Tegan and Sarah. He loves his given and chosen families and Philip Glass.

K.J. RAWSON is professor of English and Women's, Gender, and Sexuality Studies at Northeastern University where he also serves as director of the Humanities Center. He is the founder and Director of the Digital Transgender Archive, an award-winning online repository of trans-related historical materials, and he is the chair of the editorial board of the Homosaurus, an international LGBTQ+ linked data vocabulary. His work is at the intersections of the Digital Humanities and Rhetoric, LGBTQ+, and Feminist Studies. Focusing on archives as key sites of cultural power, Rawson studies the rhetorical work of queer and transgender archival collections in both brick-and-mortar and digital spaces. Rawson's scholarship has appeared in *The American Archivist, Archivaria, Enculturation, Peitho, Present Tense, QED, RSQ, TSQ*, and several edited collections.

JESSICA RESTAINO is professor and chair of Writing Studies at Montclair State University. Her interests include feminist rhetorics and research methods, rhetoric of health and medicine, queer theory, and activist and community-engaged writing and teaching. She is co-founder, with Jacqueline Regan, of Text Power Telling, a nonprofit that offers writing workshops and a digital creative arts magazine to sexual trauma survivors. She also spent a proud nine years as a board trustee for Planned Parenthood of Metropolitan New Jersey. She is the author of *Surrender: Feminist Rhetoric and Ethics in Love and Illness; First Semester: Graduate Students, Teaching Writing, and the Challenge of Middle Ground;* and coeditor, with Laurie Cella, of *Unsustainable: Re-Imagining Community Literacy, Public Writing, Service-Learning, and the University.* Her essays and book chapters appear in a range of venues.

NELESI RODRIGUES (she/her) is assistant professor at the Institute for the Study of University Pedagogy and the Ontario Institute for Studies in Education. Nelesi's experiences as a Luso Venezuelan migrant living in Turtle Island, an English writing teacher, and a lifelong dance practitioner inform her scholarly research. One question serves as a through line in her work: How can attention to movement—creative, geographical, political—help develop more just and accessible pedagogies? In her work, she brings together critical composition pedagogies, feminist rhetorics, mobility studies, and dance and performance sensibilities. Nelesi's research has been recognized through several competitive fellowships, including the Fulbright Foreign Student Program Fellowship and the Mellon/ACLS Dissertation Completion Fellowship. Her writing has been published in the journals *Spectator*, *Inmaterial*, and *Peitho*.

EILEEN E. SCHELL (she/her) is professor of Writing and Rhetoric and the Laura J. and L. Douglas Meredith Professor of Teaching Excellence in the Department of Writing Studies, Rhetoric, and Composition at Syracuse University. She is also a faculty affiliate in Women's and Gender Studies and Gerontology Studies. Schell has published seven books and edited collections and over 50 articles and book chapters addressing contingent labor, writing program administration, feminist rhetorics, composition studies, veterans' writing, and rural literacies and agricultural rhetorics. Schell leads two long-standing community writing groups for senior citizens and military veterans as well as coordinating the Moral Injury Project for Veterans at Syracuse University and Le Moyne College.

MEGAN SCHOETTLER is assistant professor of Professional and Technical Writing at West Chester University of Pennsylvania. She studies feminist rhetorics and literacy practices, with an emphasis on serving sexual trauma survivors and their advocates. Her publications appear in peer reviewed journals and books, including *Communication Design Quarterly*, *Computers and Composition*, *Capacious: Journal for Emerging Affect Inquiry*, the *Naylor Report on Undergraduate Research in Writing Studies*, and *Standing at the Threshold: Working Through Liminality in the Composition and Rhetoric TAship*. In addition to practicing a feminist trauma-informed methodology, she teaches (and grows) this approach in courses on professional and technical writing, research methods, and writing pedagogy.

SIDNEY TURNER is a lecturer at the University of Central Florida. Previously, while pursuing her PhD in Composition and Cultural Rhetoric at Syracuse University, she held positions as assistant director of Writing Across the Curriculum and assistant director of TA Education. Turner's research bridges feminist rhetorics, pedagogy, memory studies, and digital humanities. Recovering feminist microhistories of composition history, her dissertation contributes to the reception of women-serving institutions and deepens the field's understanding of how women of the past shape higher education and disciplinary values.

GABRIELLA WILSON is a PhD candidate in the Composition and Cultural Rhetoric program at Syracuse University. Gabby has worked as a graduate assistant for the RSA2024 Conference and as a coeditor of *Project Mend*, a publication composed and produced by persons impacted by incarceration. She is also the cochair of the CCCC Disability Studies Standing Group. Her writing spans a range of diverse topics, including disability rhetorics, feminist rhetorics, and anti-racist pedagogies, and appears in *Peitho*; *Rhetoric, Politics, Culture*; *The Journal of Rhetoric, Professional Communication and Globalization*; and *The Journal of Multimodal Rhetoric*. Her dissertation explores the professional identity construction of disabled graduate students in rhetoric and composition to consider material recommendations for creating accessible departmental structures and fostering a culture of access.

CARLY S. WOODS is associate professor in the Department of Communication at the University of Maryland, where she is also an affiliate faculty member in the Harriet Tubman Department of Women, Gender, and Sexuality Studies. Her research is published in several academic journals, including the *Quarterly Journal of Speech*, *Rhetoric Review*, *Rhetoric Society Quarterly*, and *Women's Studies in Communication*. Woods is author of *Debating Women: Gender, Education, and Spaces for Argument, 1835–1945* (Michigan State University Press), which received the National Communication Association's James A. Winans-Herbert A. Wichelns Memorial Award for Distinguished Scholarship in Rhetoric and Public Address and the American Forensic Association's Daniel Rohrer Memorial Outstanding Research Award.

INDEX